# Study Guide

## for use with

# Adolescence

### Eleventh Edition

John W. Santrock
*University of Texas at Dallas*

Prepared by

Daniel D. Houlihan
*Minnesota State University*

Boston   Burr Ridge, IL   Dubuque, IA   Madison, WI   New York   San Francisco   St. Louis
Bangkok   Bogotá   Caracas   Kuala Lumpur   Lisbon   London   Madrid   Mexico City
Milan   Montreal   New Delhi   Santiago   Seoul   Singapore   Sydney   Taipei   Toronto

The McGraw·Hill Companies

## McGraw-Hill Higher Education

Study Guide for use with
ADOLESCENCE
John W. Santrock

1 2 3 4 5 6 7 8 9 0 QPD/QPD 0 9 8 7 6 5

ISBN-13: 978-0-07-325276-6
ISBN-10:     0-07-325276-X

www.mhhe.com

# CONTENTS

# PREFACE

# HOW TO USE THE STUDY GUIDE

You are about to undertake the challenging and exciting task of learning about biological, cognitive, and sociocultural influences on adolescents. This *Study Guide* will assist you as you read *Adolescence* by John W. Santrock by testing your understanding of key terms and persons and the facts and theories covered in the text. Its use should **supplement** your text, not **substitute for** a careful and thorough reading of the text.

Each chapter of the *Study Guide* includes features designed to help you master the content of the corresponding chapter in *Adolescence:*

- Learning Goals with Key Terms in Boldface

- Key Terms

- Key People

- "Dr. Detail's" Mastery Exercises

- Adolescent Myth vs. Fact

- Section Reviews

- Cognitive Challenge

- Adolescence in Research

- Comprehensive Review

- Adolescence in Books

- Adolescence in Movies and Videos

- Answer Key

The *Study Guide* presents detailed learning goals with key terms and key people in boldface. You will find the objectives organized by major chapter headings and subheadings with the learning goals numbered accordingly. For example, the objectives for the first section after "Preview and Images of Adolescents" in each chapter starts with 1.0 and the associated goals appear as 1.1, 1.2, and so on. These goals cover the bulk of the material in the chapter. The learning goals indicate, as specifically as possible, what you should understand after you have read and mastered the material in a chapter.

You should make extensive use of these learning goals. Reviewing learning goals as you work through each section will help you learn and remember the material. In addition, review the key terms before and after reading each section or subsection of a chapter. These simple steps will help you do your best on the examinations.

## Key Terms

The exercise has you devise definitions for these key terms based on your understanding of the text's definitions and on how you use the key terms by completing a sentence. Students do not understand a term until they can define it and use it in their own way.

## Key People

These exercises ask you to match the key adolescent researchers (related to the chapter's content) to the idea or concept they examined. The text discusses some of these people in the margins of the book along with quotations about their theories and research, and the text explores others in the narrative. In all cases, the chapter provides a discussion of the individual's research.

## Dr. Detail's Mastery Exercises

Most chapters include a "Dr. Detail's" section that can cover almost anything relevant to the chapter. Some focus on percentages, others present "not so key" people in the chapter, and still others offer crossword puzzles or theory mastery exercises. The section reviews material that the textbook does cover in detail, and it could appear on a test.

## Adolescent Myth vs. Fact

Each chapter includes true or false questions that focus on matters that are frequently misinterpreted along with research that tends to prove or dispel longstanding beliefs.

## Section Review

The Section Review provides a variety of exercises designed to help you review and study important concepts and material in the section. The activities include matching, classifying, completing tables, defining terms, and providing short-answers to many questions.

## Cognitive Challenge

Each chapter features one or more exercises that will allow you to apply specific concepts and principles to your own life. Generally, the exercises do not include answers because the answers will vary for each student. Nonetheless, these responses help you understand how well you can work with the information you are learning in class and from your text.

## Adolescence in Research

For chapters with articles on research, the *Study Guide* asks you to analyze the research hypothesis, methods, and conclusions. In addition, it prompts you to suggest the relevance of the findings for adolescent development for one or more of those articles.

## Comprehensive Review

Each chapter contains a selection of multiple-choice questions that covers the main content of the chapter. These questions are factual and conceptual in nature; they assist in the review the chapters' content, and they are a good tool for preparing for multiple-choice exams.

## Adolescence in Books and Movies

The Study Guide also suggests books and movies that explore or depict some facet of the chapter material.

## Answer Key

Each Study Guide chapter ends with an Answer Key. Answers for short-answer questions are merely a guide, and individual responses should vary. If you have questions about whether your answer is accurate, refer to the text for confirmation and clarification.

# Some Final Thoughts ...

This *Study Guide* offers activities that will enhance your ability to learn information, retrieve it, and remember knowledge and facts about *Adolescence*. However, effective studying involves more than learning the specific things in the textbook. Effective studying requires good general study habits, time management, and strategies that lead to active learning. The learning activities in the *Study Guide* will encourage you to be an active learner. Research has shown that study activities do not really help you unless you use them in a very active way (e.g., working through the section review, studying on your own, and checking the material you could not remember). Likewise, practice makes perfect. Therefore, the Study Guide addresses material more than once to make it easier to master difficult materials. I encourage you to view the *Study Guide*'s exercises as ready-made suggestions for study and as models for activities that you invent on your own to achieve your course goals. I also want to take a second to thank my daughter, Meghan, for her help in developing several of the problem solving and puzzle sections of this guide over the past three issues.

Lastly, the publishers include a brief section on "Being an Excellent Student" in this guide. Read this section, written by Anita Rosenfield of DeVry Institute of Technology, Southern California, for in-depth tips and suggestions on how to succeed in this and other courses.

Enjoy the class!

*Dan Houlihan*

# Being an Excellent Student

*by Anita Rosenfield*

*DeVry Institute of Technology, Southern California*

When you chose your college or university, and, perhaps, identified your major interest or concentration, you had certain goals in mind, which likely included doing well in school, earning good grades, and graduating. Unfortunately, many students do not do as well in college as they had hoped and expected. Let's examine some of the reasons for this disappointing outcome to see how to avoid them and to learn, instead, how to be a good student and guide your behavior to improve your chances of achieving your goals.

A common definition of education is that it is "how people learn stuff." For most of our history, educators focused on the "stuff." Teachers were required to be masters of their respective academic fields. Even today, some states only require that teachers be qualified in the subject matter they teach, not in the teaching methods themselves.

In the 1960s, we became more interested in the "people" part of the definition, which was evidenced by moving to strategies like open classrooms and free universities. The idea was that, given the opportunity to do so, people will naturally learn. Although these experiments were dismal failures, they taught us something.

The key to the definition of education is the word *how*. Today, thanks to a wealth of research on the principles that guide the phenomenon of learning, and on the nature of learning and memory, we know much more about how learning occurs and how we can make it better. By using these principles, we can become better students.

## Formulating the Plan

Anything worth having is worth planning for. Whether you hope to learn to teach, to fly, to write for profit, or to change diapers correctly, you have a goal. An everyday question from the first days in elementary school is, "What do you want to be when you grow up?" The answer to this question is one way of formulating a goal. Now that you are a college student, many people will expect you to know what you want to do for a profession or career. Yet you may not have the foggiest notion, or you might have an idea that is still slightly foggy. That is OK. What is clear, however, is that you want to succeed in your college courses. This is a relatively long-range goal, and as such can help keep you on track.

But our day-to-day behavior is often hard to connect to our long-range goals. We need short-term goals to keep us organized and to be sure that the flow of our activities is in the direction we want to be going. To accomplish our long-range goals, we need to focus on three types of short-term goals. First, we need goals for the day; second, we need goals for the week; and third, we need goals for the semester or term. Let's look at each of these separately.

## Goals for Today

It is helpful to keep a daily checklist, diary, or schedule as a reminder of what must be done each day. Check off the things as you accomplish them. A pocket calendar is particularly helpful for this task.

## Goals for the Week

Successful college students schedule their time weekly. Sometime during the course of registration, you made up a schedule showing your classes for the whole week. If you have a job, you must allow time for that, too. Also, many college or university students have family obligations that must be considered. Finally, everyone needs some time for relaxing, eating, sleeping, and playing (even in graduate school we were advised that we needed to find some time to have fun in order to keep our balance). With all these things in mind, it is no wonder many students find little time to study.

Good students do all these things, too, yet they study. Do they have more time? No, we all have the same amount of time, but successful students schedule their time carefully. So, make up a weekly schedule and block off time for all these necessary events: classes, work, relaxation, eating, sleeping, playing, family, and studying. Students who actually schedule their time and keep to their schedules are amazed at how much time they find they have! Tape this schedule above your desk.

As you make up your weekly schedule, you may find your study time is in a large block. If this is true, please remember to take a short break every twenty to thirty minutes. This is called distributed practice and is far more efficient than studying for hours on end. After the first twenty or thirty minutes, most of us become much less efficient. When you take that break, reward yourself somehow; then get back to your studying. Something I always tell my students is never to try to read a whole chapter in one sitting. In fact, when I am preparing for a new class or have changed texts in a class I have been teaching, I take that advice myself!

## Goals for the Semester

At the beginning of each semester, students find themselves immersed in many new courses. Often, you have several new professors with whom you have never worked before, and it is difficult to sort out the expectations and demands of these courses. This makes it important to organize the information that you will need to complete all the course requirements to be successful in the courses.

If you can, obtain a large wall calendar and mark it with all the dates of tests, exams, and term paper due dates, being sure to write on the calendar the course for which each date applies. Now, estimate how long it will take you to make final preparations for those exams, and mark those dates as warning or alert dates. Look over the dates on which papers are due, and see if they are bunched together. If your college is typical, they will probably be close. You can help avoid the last-minute all-nighters if you simply determine a spread of due dates for yourself, and mark those on the calendar too. As you do this step, be sure to avoid any days that have personal significance for you, such as birthdays, anniversaries, and so on. This calendar then provides an overview of major dates in your semester.

If you have followed this carefully, you now have a large semester calendar plastered on your wall, a weekly schedule of major life events, classes, and study times taped over your desk, and a daily checklist of must-do items in your pocket or purse. **Your scheduling is on its way. Now, let's look at other important strategies.**

# Attending Classes

Many students believe that, since they are in college, they can decide whether to go to class at all. This is true. Some students also believe that attendance in class is not important to their grade. This is not true! Some colleges or universities have attendance requirements, so that if students miss a given number of classes it will either lower their grade a full letter grade, or the instructor may drop the student from the course; some instructors have in-class activities that count toward students' grades, so if students are not in class, they do not get credit for participating. Even without such strategies, students who do not attend class sessions generally do more poorly on the tests and exams. Perhaps they were absent when a crucial item was discussed or when the instructor lectured over the material the examination covered. Remember, that more often than not, instructors will include information in their lectures that is not in your textbook, and that information (whether from class lecture, videos shown in class, guest lectures, and so on) can appear on tests. Moreover, if you are not in class, the instructor cannot get to know you, and therefore cannot give you the benefit of the doubt on your answers. It should come as no surprise that in study after research study, the data clearly show that those students who attend class regularly receive the highest grades and actually learn more, too! So, the first rule of being an effective student is to attend classes. Besides, how else can you get your money's worth?

But okay, now that you've determined you will go to every class, what will you do?

# Benefiting from Lectures

Sometimes students think that if they come to class and "pay attention," they will remember what the instructor talked about; they think that if they take notes, they will miss much of what the instructor says. However, sitting and paying attention is difficult. For one thing, most people can think much faster than they can speak. While the instructor lectures at 80 words per minute, the student thinks at about 350 words per minute! The student should use this extra "thinking capacity" to focus on what the instructor is saying, but this rarely lasts more than five minutes at a time. Most of the time, this extra "thinking capacity" is used to daydream!

Daydreaming can be helpful in resolving our emotional problems, planning the course of our lives, and avoiding work. Often, it is motivated by the desire to avoid work. For whatever motive, however, daydreaming is not compatible with attending a lecture. Human beings simply cannot attend to more than one stimulus at one time. And you have to admit, your daydreams can be ever so much more interesting than your professor's lectures.

Benefiting from lecture notes is best achieved by taking notes. Use plenty of paper, and leave blank lines at regular intervals, or leave wide side margins. You will use these spaces later (they are not wasted!). If the instructor permits it, be brave and interrupt with questions if you do not understand what is being said. I try to stress to my students that, while I may know what I am talking about, it may be unclear to them—and if it's unclear to one student, it may well be unclear to other students. So, for the sake of the other students who didn't understand what I was talking about, each student should take on the responsibility of asking me to clarify what I said, or to expand in a way that will help them understand. Remember that lectures have a way of progressing and building on earlier information. It is important to understand each point, or later points will be lost. (But please, DO NOT ask the person sitting next to you what the professor said—it disrupts the class, disturbs your neighbor, and you are likely NOT to get an accurate response!)

When you take notes, write out the major points, and try to just make simple notes on the supporting minor points. If you miss something, and you cannot ask a question about it, approach the instructor immediately afterward, when it is likely to still be fresh in both your minds. DO NOT try to write down every word, and DO try to use abbreviations or symbols. I learned shorthand when I was a student, or, you can make up your own system!

Often my students will ask if they may tape record my lectures. Personally, I have no objection to having students do this. In fact, I did this my first term back in college, but I found it was terribly tedious trying to transcribe the lecture. The students for whom this may be particularly helpful are those who have visual, auditory, or motor impairments. However, do not ever tape record a lecture without first asking for and obtaining the professor's permission.

Within one or two hours after the lecture, on the same day, go back over your notes. Fill in the rest of the minor points. This often amounts to completing the sentence or other element. Then write brief summaries and any questions that you now have in the blank spaces (lines or margins) you left earlier (clever of you to leave those spaces!). These few minutes spent reviewing and organizing your notes will pay off in greatly improved memory. The questions you have, you can ask in class or during the instructor's office hours, which will yield two benefits: You will get the answers, and you will demonstrate you are a serious student, which will impress your instructor.

By the way, to get the most out of the lectures, complete the assigned reading BEFORE the class begins so you are familiar with the material. This will help you keep up with what the instructor is talking about, will reduce the amount of information you do not understand, and may bring up important questions for you to ask in class if the instructor does not talk about them.

One more thing about going to class, while this is not always true, I have found that typically my best students sit in front. And most students seem to have a need to have "their seat," while a few students have a need to move around, sitting in one seat one day and a different seat the next. It wasn't until my graduate school days that I realized why I needed "my seat"—as a student, we are being overwhelmed with new information, a stressful experience; we need some structure we can count on to reduce that stress. So, if you are one of those who likes to wander, be considerate of your classmates' needs for stress reduction.

## Reading for Learning

We all know how to read. You are proving it by reading these words. Hopefully, you also are realizing some ideas as a result of reading. If you are only reading words, please WAKE UP! STOP DAYDREAMING!

We can read a variety of things: newspapers, movie reviews, novels, magazines, and textbooks. Textbooks are unique and must be read with a strategy all their own.

There are many reading and studying strategies, and all of them work to an extent. Perhaps you learned one or more in the course of going to high school. Perhaps you even took a how-to-study course when you entered college. If so, you probably learned one or two of these systems. If you have one you like that works for you, keep it. If you are interested in learning a new one, read on.

# The PQ4R Method

One of the most successful and most widely used methods of studying written material was the SQ3R method, first developed at The Ohio State University. Researchers had noted that students who were more successful were more active readers. More recently, this method has been updated to the PQ4R Method, which adds an additional step. This method teaches the same skills that made many thousands of students successful. If you use this method when you read and study, you will be more successful, too. I have outlined the steps below, and the text describes this method in Chapter 13.

The P stands for PREVIEW. After you have read the overview or chapter outline and the list of learning objectives, you should survey the chapter in the text. This is also called skimming. Look at the headings and subheadings, and get the gist of the major points in this chapter. Check off each point in the outline of this Study Guide as you pass it in the pages of the text.

The Q stands for QUESTION. Reading is greatly enhanced if you are searching for the answers to questions. For this text, the Student Study Guide provides learning objectives that can serve as questions. For other texts, make up questions for yourself, based on the chapter overview or on your own survey of the chapter. Be sure that you have at least one question for each major unit in the chapter; you will be less efficient at studying those units for which you do not have questions.

The first of the four Rs is for READ. As you read, look for the answers to the questions you posed, or to the study or learning objectives furnished for you. When you find material that answers these questions, put a mark (X) or a "post-it" note in the margin next to that material. This will help now, since you are actively involved, and later, when you review. It is a good idea to wait to underline or highlight lines of text until after you have read the entire chapter at least once, so you will know what is and what is not most important. (In fact, although some "authorities" suggest you underline or highlight no more than 10% of what you are reading, I find that when most of us begin to underline or highlight, we wind up doing it to most of the chapter. (I suggest not doing it at all because it becomes too passive, which counteracts your attempts to read "actively.")

The second R stands for REFLECT. As you are reading, stop every so often and reflect on the material to increase its meaningfulness. This includes analyzing the material, thinking about how to apply it to your own life, interpreting the information, and connecting it with information you already have in your long-term memory.

The third R is for RECITE. One of the oldest classroom techniques in the world (Aristotle used it) is recitation. In the classroom version, the teacher asks the questions and the students answer them. Unless you can get your teacher to study with you regularly, you'll have to play both roles. Periodically stop in your reading and say aloud (if possible) what the author is telling you. Try to put it in your own words, but be sure to use technical terms as you learn them. If you are not in a situation where you can recite out loud, do it in writing. Just thinking it is not enough. When should you pause to recite? A good rule of thumb is that each time you come to the end of a major subheading, you should recite. One professor encourages his students to recite at least one sentence at the end of each paragraph, and two, three, or more sentences at the end of each subunit (when you come to a new heading).

People who do not use recitation usually forget half of what they read in one hour and another half of the half they remembered by the end of the day. People who use recitation often remember from 75 to 90 percent of what they studied. This technique pays off. By the way, if anyone questions why you are talking to yourself, tell him or her that a psychologist recommended it.

The fourth R is for REVIEW. You should review a chapter soon after you have studied it (using the PQ and first 3Rs). You should review it again the day or evening before a test. It is not usually helpful to cram the night before a test, and particularly not the day of the test! That type of studying does not produce good memory, and it is can make you more anxious during the test itself.

## Taking Tests

One of the things students fear most is failure. Failure signifies that things are not going well, and alerts us to the possibility that we may not achieve our goals. Unfortunately, many students see tests and exams as opportunities to fail. They prepare by becoming anxious and fearful, and they try to cram as much work as possible right before the exam. These students rarely do well on the exam. They often fail, thus accomplishing just what they feared.

Taking tests requires strategy and planning. First, it is helpful to know what type of tests you will have. Your instructor probably told you during the first class meeting, or it may be in the class syllabus or course outline. If you do not know, ask.

If you are going to be taking essay exams, the best way to prepare is by writing essays. Before you do this, it is a good idea to find out what types of questions the instructor asks, and what is expected in a response. Again, it is helpful to ask the instructor for this material. Perhaps you can even see some examples of essay questions from previous years—some instructors at some colleges have copies of their exams on file in the department office or in the library. By finding out what is expected, you can formulate a model against which you can evaluate your answers.

Now, using the learning objectives or some essay questions you wrote, actually sit down and write out the answers. I have prepared at least two essay questions for each chapter in this text. HINT: If you usually feel more anxious during a test, it may help you to practice writing your essays in the room in which the test will be given. Simply find a time when the room is vacant, and make yourself at home.

If your instructor gives multiple-choice tests, then you should practice taking multiple-choice tests. For each chapter, either use questions provided in the Student Study Guide or make up your own. You may find it helpful to work out an arrangement to pool questions with other students, thereby reducing the amount of work you have to do, and developing a network of friends. Or, you may ask your professor if he or she would entertain the idea of having students write some of the exam questions—some of my professors did that in my undergraduate classes, and it is something I sometimes have my students do.

Whichever way you do it, the important thing is to prepare for tests and exams. Preparation is about 95 percent of the secret to getting a good grade. (Yes, there is some actual luck or chance involved in test scores, as even your instructor will admit!) Preparation is not only a good study and review technique, but also helps to reduce anxiety.

# Dealing with Test Anxiety

Anxiety, when it occurs at low levels, can be a helpful response. In 1908, Yerkes and Dodson showed that the amount of anxiety that benefited performance was a function of the difficulty and complexity of the task. As the difficulty of the task rose, anxiety became less helpful and more likely to interfere with performance.

If you have ever been so anxious in a test situation that you were unable to do well, even though you knew the information, you have test anxiety. If you get your exams back, and you are surprised that you marked wrong answers when you knew the correct answers, or if you can only remember the correct answers after you leave the examination room, you, too, may have test anxiety.

## Strategy Number One: Effective Study

Use study habits that promote learning and make the best use of time. Strategies, such as scheduling your time and using the PQ4R system, reduce anxiety by increasing confidence. As you come to realize that you know the material, your confidence rises and anxiety retreats.

## Strategy Number Two: Relaxation

Each of us develops a unique pattern of relaxation. Some people relax by going to a specific place, either in person or mentally. Others relax by playing music, by being with friends, by using autogenic relaxation phrases, or by meditating. Whatever you do, be aware of it, and try to practice relaxation techniques. If you are good at relaxing, try thinking about those situations that make you anxious, and relax while you think of them. To do this, allow yourself to think only briefly (fifteen to thirty seconds at a time) of the situation that makes you anxious, and then relax again. After a number of such pairings, you will find that thinking about that situation no longer makes you anxious. At this point, you may be surprised to find that the situation itself also no longer produces anxiety. You may find it helpful to think about these anxiety-provoking situations in a sequence from those that produce very little anxiety to those that evoke more anxiety. Such a list, from low to high anxiety, might look something like this:

1. Your instructor announces that there will be a test in four weeks.
2. Your instructor reminds you of the test next week.
3. As you study, you see on the course outline the word *test*, and remember next week's test.
4. One of your friends asks you if you want to study together for the test, which is the day after tomorrow.
5. You choose not to go out with your friends because of the test tomorrow.
6. As you get up in the morning, you remember that today is the day of the test.
7. You are walking down the hall toward the classroom; thinking about what questions might be on the test.
8. The instructor enters the classroom, carrying a sheaf of papers in hand.
9. The instructor distributes the papers, and you see the word *test* or *exam* at the top.
10. After reading the first five questions, you have not been able to think of the answer to any of them.

If you work at it gradually and consistently, the pairing these types of thoughts (briefly) with relaxation and remembering to let go and relax after each one will dispel test anxiety and make test taking a more productive and successful experience.

## Strategy Number Three: Thinking Clearly

Most students who have test anxiety think in unclear and unproductive ways. They say to themselves things like: "I can't get these answers correct . . . I don't know this stuff . . . I don't know anything at all . . . . I'm going to fail this test . . . I'm probably going to flunk out of school . . . I'm just a dumb nerd." These thoughts share two unfortunate characteristics: they are negative and they are absolute. They should be replaced.

When we tell ourselves negative and absolute thoughts, we find it impossible to focus on the test material. The result is that we miss questions even when we know the answers. Our thinking prevents us from doing well.

A good strategy for replacing these negative and absolute thoughts is to practice thinking positive and honest thoughts, such as: "I may not know all the answers, but I know some of them . . . I don't know the answer to that right now, so I will go on to the next one and come back to that . . . I don't have to get them all right . . . I studied hard and carefully, and I can get some of them correct . . . I am a serious student, and have some abilities . . . I am prepared for this test, and know many of the answers . . . This test is important, but it is not going to determine the course of my entire life and if I don't do well, it doesn't mean I'm a horrible person or a dummy."

By thinking clearly, honestly, and positively, we quiet the flood of anxiety and focus on the task. Students who use this technique invariably do better on the tests. It takes practice to think clearly, but it is worth the effort. After a while, you will find that it becomes natural and does not take any noticeable effort. And as anxiety is reduced, more energy is available for studying and for doing well on examinations. The eventual outcome is more enjoyment with learning, better learning, more success in college, and the achievement of your goals.

## Strategy Number Four: Guided Imagery

Something I often do with my students before a test is to have them relax (see Strategy Two), close their eyes, and visualize themselves walking into a tall building. They go into the elevator in the building and take it to the top floor, which is fifty-six stories up. They walk out of the elevator, go to the stairwell, and climb to the top of the building. There is no railing on the top of the building. I direct them to walk over to the very edge of the building, put their toes at the very edge, then look down. I ask them to think about how they are feeling as they are looking down onto the street from the top of this building. I then tell them to back up, have the realization that they can fly—just spread out their arms and they can fly. Then they are directed back to the edge of the building, knowing that they can fly. They put their toes on the edge, look down, and then spread their arms and fly, eventually flying down to land safely on the ground below. Next I have them visualize themselves in the classroom; on the desk before them is their test. They look at the test and see themselves reading the questions saying, "I know that answer. Yes, I remember learning that." They visualize themselves being successful, answering all the questions correctly, and feeling good about themselves. Then I have them visualize getting their tests back, with a big "A" on the test.

Some students are much better able to visualize than others. You can try combining Strategy Two with this strategy to help you improve your visualization, since it can be an effective success strategy.

## Strategy Number Five: Do the Easy Ones First

A technique I learned while studying for the GRE (Graduate Record Exam) was to read each question and answer the ones I knew, then go back to the harder ones. Two things to watch out for on this: first, be sure you get the answers in the right place—sometimes when we skip a question or two, we wind up marking the wrong space, so check that your answer to question 10 is in space 10; second, you may find you're stumped by the first several questions—don't let that throw you, just keep going because there is bound to be one you jump on and say, "Yes! I know that one." Answer the easy ones first, then go back to the others after you've built up your confidence seeing you DO know "stuff." Also, always go back over the whole test to be sure you answered every question (the exception here is if you have a professor who takes more than one point off for wrong answers—in that case, it's better not to answer than to answer wrong, but I don't know anyone who does that).

## Strategy Number Six: State Dependent Learning

Research shows that we remember information best when we are in the same "state" we were in when we first learned the information. So, for example, you might remember a certain song when prompted by a specific stimulus (seeing someone who reminds you of your "first true love"); or, we will remember things we learned when we were particularly happy if we are again in that mood. This goes for physical contexts as well—so that we have an advantage if we take an exam in the same room where we learned the information in the first place. But it also goes to physical context in terms of our bodies—if you drink coffee or caffeine-laden sodas when you study, try to do the same before your exam. On the other hand, if you don't consume caffeine when you study, by all means, DO NOT suddenly have a cup of coffee before your exam. Because of the power of this phenomenon, you may want to create a particular mental context for yourself when you study so that you can put yourself into the same mental context when you take your exams.

## Strategy Number Seven: Take a Break

If you find yourself getting stressed out during the test, take a break. Put your pencil down, breath deeply, you may even want to put your head down on the desk (please, do not fall asleep!). Use the relaxation techniques or the guided imagery strategy; visualize yourself looking at the test and suddenly realizing that you DO know the answers to at least most of the questions. Then go back to taking the test.

Remember, that with all of these test-taking strategies, if you don't do the first one, none of the others will help! Passing the course requires that you actively study the material.

## Memory Techniques

No matter how much you read, it won't help you if you don't remember *what* you read. The most critical factor in remembering is being able to apply what you have learned. Of course, some things such as people's names, or certain dates, or statistical information are not easily applied to your life, so you'll have to use other techniques. But first, let's talk about the "easy way."

# Apply It to Your Life

If you can take the material you are learning and use it in your everyday life, you will remember it. Connect it with what you already know, either from life experience or other courses you have taken. Sometimes what you are learning fits nicely with what you already knew; sometimes it will contradict what you learned before. This is an opportunity to look at how the new information fits in with the old. For example, were there new research findings? Or, is it merely a difference of opinion? Make these associations—don't keep the information for any class neatly compartmentalized—if you do, you'll have a hard time trying to find it when you need it.

## Teach It to Someone Else!

When we start teaching something to someone else, we find we HAVE TO learn it, and by trying to explain the material to another person, we examine it and think about it differently. So, take the material you are learning in this class (or any class) and teach it to someone else. When they ask you questions, look them up and find the answers, or you can think them out together or ask someone else. As you explain these concepts to someone else (your children, your friends, or even your dog), you will suddenly see them in a totally different light.

## Mnemonic Techniques

Some things are just very difficult to apply to your own life. Dates, names, places, statistics, and such may not have a great deal of meaning for you. In that event, use the tricks that memory specialists use—mnemonics. There are many different types. For example, one famous mnemonic is an acronym for remembering the Great Lakes: HOMES = Huron, Ontario, Michigan, Erie, and Superior; or the colors of the rainbow is a man's name: ROY G. BIV = Red, Orange, Yellow, Green, Blue, Indigo, and Violet (if not for this "man," I'd never remember indigo!) You can make up your own acronyms by taking the first initial of any term, person, etc. It's easiest, though, if it's something that makes sense to you.

Another mnemonic technique is called the ***method of loci,*** which I understand is the technique medical students use to remember body parts. You list the things you need to remember, and then visualize yourself walking around a familiar place (like your living room), putting one item on a particular piece of furniture. Then, when you need to remember that item, you go through your "living room" to see where it is.

One other mnemonic technique is the story method. Take the information you need to remember and put it into a story.

## Be an "Information Dropper"

This is similar to the suggestion to teach, but it is less formal. Ask your friends to "indulge" you by listening to what you learned in your class. Then *tell* them what you are learning. You may, in fact, find that you have managed to help one of your friends by sharing this information!

## Rote Memory

If you can remember back to grade school when you learned to multiply, somehow the only way that seemed to happen was by repeating the multiplication tables over and over and over again. Personally, I think this is about the worst way to learn, but for some things (like multiplication tables), it works. The Flashcards that are included in each chapter of this Study Guide can help you learn through repeating the material you don't know until you are able to answer the questions posed without looking at the reverse side of the cards. Hopefully you will then go further and apply the information to other areas of your life.

## Most Important

Remember: Professors don't "teach" their students; rather, they facilitate learning so students end up teaching themselves. Although we try to motivate our students, keep them interested, and present information in a way that helps students to understand, the ultimate responsibility for learning rests with the students. Some students have learned *despite* their professors, others don't learn even with the very best of professors. So keep your goals in mind, study hard, ask questions, and aim for success!

# Further Resources

## Online Learning Center

http://www.mhhe.com/santrocka11

An expansive resource for students, this site includes:

- Self-assessment quizzes for each chapter
- Study tools, including crossword puzzles
- Links to relevant websites
- Adolescent Development Image Gallery
- Interactive scenarios

## McGraw-Hill Developmental Psychology Supersite

http://www.mhhe.com/developmental

This website provides such valuable resources as Interactive exercises, simulations, and links to some of the best developmental psychology sites on the Web.

**For those of you with "Print Disabilities,"** including blindness, visual impairment, learning disabilities or other physical disabilities, please check out the **Recording for the Blind and Dyslexic website** at **www.rfbd.org/** or call customer service at **(800) 221-4792.** This educational library has 77,000 taped titles including textbooks and reference and professional materials for people who cannot read standard print because of a disability.

We Want to Hear from You!

Help us to improve the quality of future supplements.
Take a moment to visit our website and share your thoughts
by completing our supplements feedback form.
Your feedback will greatly help us in the future.
The form is located at:
http://www.mhhe.com/developmental

# APA Style

For information on APA writing style and guidelines, please refer your students to the American Psychological Association's website at http://www.apa.org, or link to this site by visiting Santrock's *Adolescence* Online Learning Center at http://www.mhhe.com/santrocka11.

# Using the Internet

There are numerous possibilities or ways to use the Internet with *Adolescence* courses. In fact, the sheer vastness of available information is often overwhelming for both instructors and students alike. Most of you have some idea about how to search for information available on the Internet, but you need to have the critical thinking skills necessary to discern whether the information you are locating is valid and useful. The following five criteria may be helpful in assisting you with analyzing the appropriateness of information available on the Internet. Also, get familiar with Google (www.google.com). You can explore many areas with this tool.

1. **Accuracy**

2. **Authority**

3. **Objectivity**

4. **Currency**

5. **Coverage**

You can often struggle with search strategies or become easily frustrated if you cannot locate the type of information you want. There are several excellent tutorials available online that can assist in this process, and most libraries have resources designed to help students create more sophisticated searching methodologies. The following site may provide some assistance.

## Tutorial for Beginning Users:

http://www.lib.berkeley.edu/TeachingLib/Guides/Internet/FindInfo.html

This excellent guide, created by the library staff of the University of California at Berkeley, is a powerful starting place for instructors and students to learn more about using the Internet. The tutorial's first section provides information about how to access the Internet and use Netscape. The second part discusses how to search for information and includes a comparative chart of the best five search engines, explanations of meta-search tools, and convenient handouts for class exercises. The handouts section also includes PowerPoint slides and instructor's notes.

# ✧ Chapter 1    Introduction

**Learning Goals with Key Terms and Key People in Boldface**

1.0     **DESCRIBE THE HISTORICAL PERSPECTIVE ON ADOLESCENCE**

    A.     **Early History**

         1.1     Compare and contrast the views of Plato and Aristotle regarding adolescence.

         1.2     In which ways are Aristotle's views similar to the views of contemporary adolescent theorists?

         1.3     What are the similarities between the view Plato expressed concerning adolescence and views expressed by Jean-Jacques Rousseau?

    B.     **The Twentieth Century**

         1.4     What was the driving force behind the changing views of adolescence that emerged between 1890 and 1920?

         1.5     What factors led historians to label **G. Stanley Hall** the "father of the scientific study of adolescence"?

         1.6     What was Hall's **storm-and-stress view** concept of adolescence?

         1.7     How did the views of Charles Darwin influence the views of **G. Stanley Hall**?

         1.8     Why was **Margaret Mead**'s sociocultural view of adolescence considered pathbreaking in the early 1900s?

         1.9     What factors have led to a debate over the accuracy of Mead's findings?

         1.10     What is the **inventionsist view** of adolescence?

         1.11     Why do historians call the period of 1890 to 1920 the "age of adolescence"?

         1.12     How did the efforts to create a system of compulsory public education affect the concept of adolescence?

         1.13     How are schools, work, and economics important dimensions of the **inventionist view**?

         1.14     The focus on higher education becomes a prominent part of adolescence during which time period?

         1.14     Why do some historians suggest that changing laws, in effect, created adolescence?

         1.16     What challenges were presented to adolescents during the Great Depression and World War II?

         1.17     What factors combined in the 1960s and 1970s to challenge the position of prominence achieved by adolescents in the 1950s?

         1.18     Which females and individuals from ethnic minorities have contributed to the study of adolescents?

    C.     **Stereotyping Adolescents**

         1.19     What is a **stereotype**, and what are the contemporary stereotypes of adolescence?

         1.20     What is the purpose served by a **stereotype**?

         1.21     How have adolescents been portrayed during most of the 20<sup>th</sup> century?

         1.22     What did Joseph Adelson mean by the **adolescent generalization gap**?

    D.     **A Positive View of Adolescence**

         1.23     In what way did research by **Daniel Offer** and his colleagues challenge existing stereotypes of adolescence?

<table>
<tr><td></td><td>1.24</td><td>Do adolescents deserve the negative portrayal they get from adults today? Support your answer with information from the book and your own experience.</td></tr>
<tr><td></td><td>1.25</td><td>Researchers reviewing the progression of the field of psychology (including adolescence) over the last century reached what conclusions?</td></tr>
</table>

**2.0 DISCUSS TODAY'S U.S. ADOLESCENTS AND SOCIAL POLICY ISSUES INVOLVING ADOLESCENTS**

**A. Current Status of U.S. Adolescents**

2.1 Why is today the best of times and the worst of times for adolescents?

2.2 Is adolescence today less stable than it was several decades ago? Why?

2.3 How would you compare the status of adolescents and public attitudes toward them with that of adolescents of several decades ago?

2.4 What differences in development among adolescents make them a heterogeneous group?

**B. Social Contexts**

2.5 How do **contexts** of development influence adolescent development?

2.6 Why is the cultural context for U.S. adolescents changing today?

**C. Social Policy and Adolescents' Development**

2.7 What is **social policy,** and why do we need one that is concerned with adolescent development?

2.8 According to **Marian Wright Edelman,** how are today's politicians falling short in practicing what they preach, i.e., "family values?"

2.9 In the U.S., how have older generations been disproportionately benefiting from social policy?

2.10 Describe the position **Peter Benson** and his colleagues hold regarding the focus of social policy on youth today?

2.11 What is **generational inequity** and how does it relate to social policy issues?

2.12 In what ways generational inequality are more likely to challenge future generations?

2.13 Contrast the views of **Bernice Neugarten** with those of **Peter Benson.**

2.14 Why should one of America's foremost concerns be the well-being of adolescents?

2.15 Why is it important to not diminish the role of youth in future generations?

2.16 Why does **Reed Larson** believe that more adolescents need opportunities to extend their capacity for initiative?

**3.0 CHARACTERIZE THE CURRENT GLOBAL PERSPECTIVE ON ADOLESCENCE**

**A. The Global Perspective**

3.1 What is meant by a "Eurocentric" way of thinking?

3.2 What traditions remain for adolescents around the globe?

3.3 What are some ways that adolescents around the globe vary in the ways they develop?

3.4 Why are youth in the United States marrying later, while youth in some other countries are marrying earlier?

3.5 According to Brown and **Larson,** how has adolescent health and well-being changed in recent years?

3.6 What is the access to education for females around the world?

3.7 What are some differences between kids raised in Arab families and those being raised in typical American households?

3.8 Are schools around the world improving?

3.9 What is the role of peers in Western cultures?

**4.0 SUMMARIZE THE DEVELOPMENTAL PROCESSES, PERIODS, TRANSITIONS, AND ISSUES RELATED TO ADOLESCENCE**

**A. What Is Development?**

4.1 What do we mean when we speak of an individual's **development**?

**B. Processes and Periods**

4.2 What are the three major processes that shape adolescent development?

4.3    Differentiate between **cognitive processes** and **socioemotional processes** and their roles in adolescent development?

4.4    What are the three major developmental periods and their subperiods from conception to death?

4.5    What are the four (4) periods of childhood development?

4.6    What factors reflect the role of **biological processes** in the adolescent's development?

4.7    Why would it be inappropriate to suggest that a child enter **adolescence** as a blank slate?

4.8    What is **adolescence,** and what are its two periods?

4.9    Why do developmentalists no longer believe that change ends with adolescence?

4.10   How do cultural and gender differences impact when children enter adolescence?

4.11   Do adolescents enter **adulthood** at the same time?

4.12   What are the three periods of adult development?

4.13   What adjustments need to occur in **late adulthood**?

C.    **Developmental Transitions**

4.14   What does the saying "Adolescence begins in biology and ends in culture" mean?

4.15   What are some of the biological changes associated with adolescence?

4.16   Kenniston referred to which transitional period when he proposed the term **youth?**

4.17   Contrast **youth** and emerging adulthood.

4.18   Name the personal and social assets linked to well-being in adolescents?

4.19   Is there a specific age at which individuals become an adult?

D.    **Developmental Issues**

4.20   What are the three major issues of adolescent development?

4.21   What is the **nature-nurture issue** and how is it relevant to the concept of **maturation** and experience?

4.22   Differentiate between **continuity of development** and **discontinuity of development**.

4.23   Contrast the views of **nature** proponents with those of **nurture** proponents.

4.24   What are the main issues in **early-later experience issue** debate?

4.25   Which recent changes in the choices being made by young women are reflective of the role **nurture** plays?

4.24   How do beliefs about significant developmental experiences differ in various cultures?

4.25   How do nature differences influence differences between adolescent boys and girls?

4.26   Why do developmentalists usually refrain from taking extreme positions on developmental issues?

# Exercises

## KEY TERMS SENTENCE COMPLETION EXERCISE

Each key term is presented in the form of an incomplete sentence. Complete each sentence by either defining the term or giving an example of it. Compare your definitions with those given at the end of the study guide chapter.

1.    The **storm-and-stress view** of adolescence suggests that

_____

_____

2. According to the **inventionist view,** adolescence began

_____

_____

3. If someone invokes a common **stereotype,** he or she would view adolescents as

_____

_____

4. Evidence that an **adolescent generalization gap** exists is

_____

_____

5. Examples of **contexts** are

_____

_____

6. In the United States, **social policy** has resulted in

_____

_____

7. In the United States, the biggest threat of **generational inequity** stems from

_____

_____

8. **Development** is the

_____

_____

9. **Biological processes** affect a person by

_____

_____

10. The best evidence of changing **cognitive processes** in adolescence is

_____

_____

11. Confirmation of **socioemotional processes** in adolescence is

_____

_____

12. The **prenatal period** is from

_____

13. A child in its **infancy** is often seen as

_____

_____

14. **Early childhood** is marked by

_____

_____

15. During **middle and late childhood,** children

_____

_____

16. The change from childhood to **adolescence** involves

_____

_____

17. **Early adolescence** is characterized by

_____

_____

18. The activities that make up **late adolescence** are

_____

_____

19. You can tell that Susan is in **early adulthood** because she

_____

_____

20. **Middle adulthood** is marked by

_____

_____

21. A person in **late adulthood** might

_____

_____

22. According to Kenniston, **youth** is

_____

_____

23.     **Emerging adulthood** is represented by

_____

_____

24.     The **nature-nurture issue** refers to

_____

_____

25.     The **continuity–discontinuity issue** implies

_____

_____

26.     Theorists debating the **early-later experience issue** suggest

_____

_____


## KEY PEOPLE IN THE STUDY OF ADOLESCENCE

Match the name with the concept, issue, or topic related to adolescence with which they are associated.

| | | |
|---|---|---|
| ____ | 1. G. Stanley Hall | A. Studied teenagers in Samoa |
| ____ | 2. Margaret Mead | B. Coined the term "youth" |
| ____ | 3. Leta Hollingsworth | C. The father of the scientific study of adolescence |
| ____ | 4. Daniel Offer | D. His work challenged the negative stereotypes of adolescents |
| ____ | 5. Marian Wright Edelman | E. First used the term "gifted" and challenged the theory of male superiority |
| ____ | 6. Bernice Neugarten | F. Argued that adolescents need more opportunities to develop the capacity for initiative |
| ____ | 7. Kenneth & Mamie Clark | G. A child's rights advocate, who champions improvements in social policies affecting young people and their families |
| ____ | 8. Peter Benson | H. Believes that many segments of society, not just adolescents, are affected by inequities in our social and economic policies |
| ____ | 9. George Sanchez | I. Conducted research on the self-esteem of African-American children |
| ____ | 10. Reed Larson | J. Documented cultural bias in intelligence tests |
| ____ | 11. Kenneth Kenniston | K. Suggests that U.S. social policy for youth is too negatively focused. |


## "DR. DETAIL'S" MATCHING EXERCISE

Match the correct percentage with the appropriate statement or question.

| | | |
|---|---|---|
| 1. | From 1910 to 1930, the number of 10- to 15-year olds gainfully employed dropped by: | A. More than 70% |
| 2. | Between 1900 and 1930 the number of high school graduates increased by: | B. One-third |

6

3. Daniel Offer and his colleagues studied the self-images of adolescents around the world and found that _____ had a healthy self-image.     C.   75%

4. According to Jerome Kagan _____ of a group of children with an inhibited temperament at 2 years of age were not unusually shy at age 4.     D.   600%

5. This is the amount of college students who said that being an adult means accepting responsibility for the consequences of one's actions:     E.   73%

6. This is the amount of local TV coverage devoted to crime victimization, accidents, and violent crime involving adolescents.     F.   Two-thirds

7. This is the proportion of Asian Indian adolescents who accept their parents' choice of a marital partner for them.     G.   46%

8. Half a century ago, families with a breadwinner father, stay-at-home mother made up _____ of families.     H.   40%

9. About _____ of individuals in their late teens to early twenties move back into their parent's home at least once after having moved out.     I.   2 of 3

## ADOLESCENT MYTH AND FACT

**Which of the following statements regarding adolescents are true (T) and which are false (F)?**

1. We owe the beginnings of the scientific study of adolescence to G. Stanley Hall. T or F

2. The concept of adolescence was invented mainly as a by-product of the movement to create a system of compulsory public education. T or F

3. Once assigned, stereotypes are relatively easy to abandon or change. T or F

4. Psychologists who reviewing the development of the field of psychology (adolescence included) over the past century, suggested that a major concern about the field is that it is overly optimistic. T or F

5. Acting out and boundary testing are time-honored ways in which adolescents move toward accepting, rather than rejecting, parental values. T or F

6. According to Cohen and others (2003) adolescents represent a homogeneous group. T or F

7. By 2100, Latino adolescents are expected to outnumber White adolescents. T or F

8. The government has underserved adolescents more than other age groups. T or F

9. In developing countries, marriage occurs much later on average than it does in the United States or Europe. T or F

10. According to Plato, infants who were rocked frequently became better students. T or F

## HISTORICAL PERSPECTIVE
## SECTION REVIEW

1. How did the views proposed by Jean-Jacques Rousseau regarding adolescence advance those proposed by Plato and Aristotle?

_____

_____

2. According to Aristotle, what is the most important aspect of adolescence?

_____

_____

3. Compare and contrast Hall's storm-and-stress perspective of adolescence with Margaret Mead's sociocultural view.

_____

_____

4. Why were Hall's views regarding adolescence strongly influenced by Darwin?

_____

_____

5. What are some criticisms of Margaret Mead's research?

_____

_____

6. In what ways were Hall's views of adolescence impacted by the writings of Goethe and Schiller?

_____

_____

7. Describe the factors that led to the period between 1890 and 1920 being known as the "age of adolescence."

_____

_____

8. What accounted for the prominence adolescents gained in society from 1920 to 1950, and what factors would challenge this distinction?

_____

_____

9. How did Daniel Offer and his colleagues challenge the negative views of adolescents, and what empirical support did they find?

_____

_____

10. How did the protests of the Vietnam era and the Women's movement of the 1970's influence the roles of adolescents in our society?

_____

_____

KEY PEOPLE IN SECTION (describe the contributions of this individual to the study and understanding of adolescence).

**Plato** — _____

_____ .

**Aristotle** — _____

_____ .

**Jean-Jacques Rousseau** — _____

_____ .

**G. Stanley Hall** — _____

_____ .

**Charles Darwin** — _____

_____ .

**Margaret Mead** — _____

_____ .

**Leta Hollingworth** — _____

_____ .

**Kenneth and Mamie Clark** — _____

_____ .

**George Sanchez** — _____

_____ .

**Joseph Adelson** — _____

_____ .

**Daniel Offer** — _____

_____ .


## TODAY'S ADOLESCENTS
## SECTION REVIEW

1.    List three facts of contemporary life that makes today "the best of times" for adolescents.

_____

_____

2. List three facts of contemporary life that makes today "the worst of times" for adolescents.

_____

_____

3. Why might it be said that today's adolescents are growing up in a less stable environment than that of several decades ago?

_____

_____

4. Why are adolescents not considered a homogeneous group?

_____

_____

5. Why are contexts important in understanding adolescent development?

_____

_____

6. Why should the well-being of adolescents be one of the major concerns for makers of social policy?

_____

_____

7. Has discussion of 'family values' by politicians led to meaningful changes in government policies regarding adolescents?

_____

_____

8. What would be the risk associated with ignoring a problem like generation inequity?

_____

_____

9. How are advances in transportation and telecommunication affecting youth around the globe?

_____

_____

KEY PEOPLE IN SECTION (describe the contributions of this individual to the study and understanding of adolescence).

**Peter Benson** — _____

_____.

**Marian Wright Edelman —** _____

_____.

**Bernice Neugarten —** _____

_____.

**Reed Larson —** _____

_____.


## THE GLOBAL PERSPECTIVE
## SECTION REVIEW

1.    Around the world, adolescents vary in their experiences. However, explain how some adolescent traditions remain the same across cultures.

_____

_____

2.    With respect to gender, are there significant differences in the lives of females across the globe dependent upon which culture they happen to be born into? Explain.

_____

_____

3.    According to Brown and Larson, how has adolescent health and well-being changed in recent years?

_____

_____


## THE NATURE OF DEVELOPMENT
## SECTION REVIEW

1.    Complete the table by giving the name and a brief description of the eight periods of development corresponding to the given ages.

| Age | Name | Description |
|---|---|---|
| Prenatal | | |
| Birth to 18–24 months | | |
| 2 to 5–6 years | | |
| 6 to 10–11 years | | |
| 10–13 to 18–22 years | | |

| Late teens to early 20s and 30s | | |
| --- | --- | --- |
| 35–45 to 55–65 years | | |
| 60–70 years until death | | |

2. Explain why biological, cognitive, and socioemotional processes are unavoidably interwoven.

_____

_____

3. Is there a specific age at which an adolescent becomes an adult?

_____

_____

4. Which two factors require consideration when formulating a definition of adolescence?

_____

_____

5. Explain the nature/nurture issue in your own words, using any facet of adolescent physical, cognitive, or emotional development as an example.

_____

_____

6. Contrast the 'old' and 'current' view of adolescence as a transition into adulthood.

_____

_____

7. How does the continuity-discontinuity issue apply to today's youth?

_____

_____

8. Discuss the early-later experience issue from both the 'Western' and 'Eastern' (Asian) perspectives.

_____

_____

**KEY PEOPLE IN SECTION** (describe the contributions of this individual to the study and understanding of adolescence).

**Kenneth Kenniston —** _____

_____

## EXPLORATIONS IN ADOLESCENCE

1.    Have you ever been the target of a stereotype (race, gender, ethnicity, religion, social class, etc.)? Identify what type of stereotype it may have been, and consider how it may have changed your thinking. How has this affected you positively or negatively?

2.    In recent years, the covers of prominent magazines and many documentaries featured adolescents The tone of these discussions is becoming increasingly negative in that the shortfalls and pitfalls of adolescence are the general themes in nearly all cases. How might this influence today's children who are just starting to enter adolescence?

3.    Is the modern emphasis on education and career training creating a gap between cultures, or is it bringing cultures closer together?

## COGNITIVE CHALLENGE

1.    Imagine you could time-travel. How would your life, as an adolescent, have been different in each of these different time periods?

a.    1890 – 1920

_____

_____

b.    1920 – 1950

_____

_____

c.    1960 – 1980

_____

_____

2.    Choose any ethnic group other than your own, and imagine how your experiences would have been different in the following domains. Write the ethic group or culture that you choose on the line:

_____

a.    relationship with your parents

_____

_____

b.    relationship with your peers

_____

c.     high school experience

_____

_____

d.     your physical health and development

_____

_____

e.     your moral and spiritual development

_____

_____

f.     your intellectual development

_____

_____

g.     your dating behavior and romantic relationships

_____

_____

h.     the neighborhood in which you lived

_____

_____

i.     your family's socioeconomic status

_____

_____

j.     Would you be the focus of stereotypes, and if so, how would this affect your development?

_____

_____

3.     Referring to the list of areas in the previous question (2), which factors do you believe had the greatest impact on which you have become?

_____

_____

## ADOLESCENCE IN RESEARCH

Concerning Kenneth Kenniston's (1970) study of the transition from adolescence to adulthood, state the hypothesis, the research methods (if known), the research conclusions, and the implications and applications for adolescent development.

_____

_____

## ☒ COMPREHENSIVE REVIEW

1.    That these times are the best of times for today's adolescents is indicated by the observation that
      a.    crack cocaine is more addictive and deadly than marijuana.
      b.    individuals have longer life expectancies than ever before.
      c.    most families include a father who is the breadwinner, a mother, and children.
      d.    television transmits powerful messages about sex and violence.

2.    According to Plato, the distinguishing feature of the adolescent period was the development of
      a.    reason.                            c.    virtues and morals.
      b.    self-determination.                d.    conformity to societal standards.

3.    According to Aristotle, the most important aspect of adolescence is
      a.    emotional stability.               c.    self-determination.
      b.    virtues and morals.                d.    reasoning.

4.    Stanley Hall described adolescence as a period of
      a.    emotional stability.               c.    considerable upheaval.
      b.    passivity and conformity.          d.    gradual socioemotional development.

5.    The _____ marked the beginning of the scientific exploration of adolescence.
      a.    19$^{th}$ century                   c.    4$^{th}$ century
      b.    15$^{th}$ century                   d.    20$^{th}$ century

6.    G. Stanley Hall was strongly influenced by the views of
      a.    Rousseau.                          c.    Darwin.
      b.    Mead.                              d.    Freud.

7.    Rousseau is credited with having revived the notion that
      a.    adolescents, like children, are a blank slate.
      b.    development has distinct phases.
      c.    we are passive victims of our respective environments.
      d.    emotional development occurs exclusively in childhood.

8.    Margaret Mead proposed that adolescents develop easily into adulthood if their environments are appropriately designed after observing adolescents in
      a.    Samoa.                             c.    the Trobriand Islands.
      b.    the Philippines.                   d.    Mangia.

9.	The current view of Margaret Mead's research on Samoan adolescents is that
	a.	it was unbiased and error-free.
	b.	it supports the inventionist view rather than G. Stanley Hall's view of adolescence.
	c.	it exemplifies the adolescent generalization gap.
	d.	their lives are more stressful than Mead observed or suggested.

10.	Historians have described _____ as the "father of the scientific study of adolescence."
	a.	Daniel Offer	c.	Sigmund Freud
	b.	Jerome Kagan	d.	G. Stanley Hall

11.	Hall described adolescence as encompassing which age range?
	a.	11 to 19 years of age	c.	12 to 23 years of age
	b.	15 to 26 years of age	d.	7 to 16 years of age

12.	Because they believe it was during this period that the concept of adolescence was formed, historians now call this period the "age of adolescence."
	a.	1910 to 1940	c.	1920 to 1950
	b.	1890 to 1920	d.	1960 to 1980

13.	According to Hall, which of the following is NOT one of the sociohistorical circumstances at the beginning of the 20th century that led to the conceptualization of adolescence?
	a.	the appearance of youth groups.
	b.	increased need for skilled laborers.
	c.	dispersement of the population from urban to more rural areas.
	d.	the creation of age-graded schools.

14.	Which of the following factors did NOT contribute to the invention of the concept of adolescence?
	a.	child-saving legislation
	b.	increased adolescent employment during the Great Depression
	c.	the separation of work and the home
	d.	the creation of a system of compulsory education

15.	What event in the 1970's led to a change in both the description and the study of adolescence?
	a.	the assassination of John F. Kennedy
	b.	a man landing on the Moon
	c.	the end of the Vietnam War
	d.	the Women's Movement

16.	What historical event led to the increase in adolescent rebellion and protest?
	a.	the discovery of marijuana
	b.	the bombing of Pearl Harbor
	c.	the Vietnam War
	d.	the Great Depression

17.	In a recent analysis of local television coverage, the frequently reported topics involving youth were
	a.	awards and positive accomplishments.
	b.	community service.
	c.	crime victimization, accidents and violent juvenile crime.
	d.	sports accomplishments.

18. If you categorized all adolescents as rebellious, lazy, smart alecks, you would be using a(n)
    a. context.
    c. stereotype.
    b. inventionist view.
    d. generation gap view.

19. The term "adolescent generation gap" was coined by
    a. Daniel Offer
    c. Joseph Adelson
    b. Kenneth Kenniston
    d. Leta Hollingworth

20. Research by Daniel Offer and his colleagues in 1988 examined the self-images of adolescents around the world and had what effect on the belief that adolescents are highly stressed?
    a. It supported that belief.
    b. It challenged its accuracy.
    c. It showed depression to be a larger problem than stress.
    d. It was inconclusive and therefore had no impact.

21. As the world transitioned from the old century to the new one, psychological theorists looked back at the old century and concluded that
    a. psychology had become an overly grim science.
    b. very little had actually been accomplished in the 20th century.
    c. most psychological research had focused on positive situations and outcomes.
    d. Freud was the most influential researcher in the 20th century.

22. _____ conducted important research on adolescent development, mental retardation, and gifted children.
    a. Leta Hollingworth
    c. Kenneth Clark
    b. George Sanchez
    d. Daniel Offer

23. _____ was the first to document cultural bias in intelligence tests for children and adolescents.
    a. Leta Hollingworth
    c. Kenneth Clark
    b. George Sanchez
    d. Daniel Offer

24. A national government's actions that influence the welfare of its citizens defines the concept of
    a. family values.
    c. the inventionist viewpoint.
    b. generational inequity.
    d. social policy.

25. According to Marian Wright Edelman, president of the Children's Defense Fund, the most important function of our society should be
    a. eliminating violence.
    b. restructuring our educational system.
    c. parenting and nurturing the next generation.
    d. developing a healthy knowledge of the body and sexuality.

26. Peter Benson believes social policy for youth in the United States is too focused on
    a. minority youth.
    c. education.
    b. positive health practices.
    d. negative developmental deficits.

27. The concern that older members of the society benefit disproportionately more than younger members of the society in terms of national allocations of resources is the concept of
    a. generational inequity.
    c. the adolescent generalization gap.
    b. social policy.
    d. the storm and stress view.

28. Which of the following is NOT a major process contributing to the scientific study of development?
   a. cognitive
   b. biological
   c. socioemotional
   d. personal

29. This represents the pattern of change that begins at conception and continues throughout one's life span
   a. context
   b. adolescence
   c. development
   d. continuity

30. According to G. Stanley Hall, the dominant process of adolescent development would be
   a. biological.
   b. cognitive.
   c. sexual.
   d. socioemotional.

31. Alterations in an individual's thinking and intelligence suggest a change in
   a. cognitive processes.
   b. biological processes.
   c. context.
   d. socioemotional processes.

32. _____ is a period of extreme dependency upon adults.
   a. Toddlerhood
   b. Infancy
   c. Prenatal period
   d. Middle childhood

33. First grade typically marks the end of this period.
   a. prenatal period
   b. infancy
   c. toddlerhood
   d. early childhood

34. Developmentalists subdivide the period of development before adolescence into _____ periods.
   a. two
   b. six
   c. four
   d. eight

35. This developmental transition is marked by many biological changes, including the growth spurt.
   a. adolescence to adulthood
   b. infancy to childhood
   c. childhood to adolescence
   d. emerging adulthood

36. If Kenneth Kenniston is correct, a youth would be expected to
   a. live in several different places.
   b. be confused about sexual orientation.
   c. avoid dating.
   d. be unable to secure full-time employment.

37. The most widely recognized marker of entry into adulthood is
   a. the first sexual experience.
   b. the decision to get married.
   c. taking a job that is more or less permanent and fulltime.
   d. learning to drive a car.

38. Many developmentalists believe that humans progress through a number of defined stages in the course of their lives. John Santrock, the author of *Adolescence*, would say that these developmentalists see human development
   a. as discontinuous.
   b. as unstable.
   c. as dominated by environment.
   d. much as G. Stanley Hall did.

39. Which of the following is the best example of discontinuity in development?
   a. a seedling growing into an oak
   b. a worm growing into a night crawler
   c. a caterpillar becoming a butterfly
   d. a leaf falling from a tree

40. According to Jerome Kagan, _____ of children who show an inhibited temperament at age 2 are not unusually shy or fearful at age 4.
   a. two-thirds          c. one-half
   b one-third            d. nearly all

41. Many previously well-established differences between adolescent males and females are diminishing as females pursue careers in male-dominated areas and seek greater autonomy. This supports the
   a. social policy perspective.     c. nurture perspective.
   b. nature perspective.            d. context perspective.

42. Which of the following is not an important context in the lives of adolescents?
   a. music               c. school
   b family               d. peers


## ADOLESCENCE ON THE SCREEN

- *Cider House Rules* shows an orphaned boy whose identity search leads him back to what his foster father wanted for him.

- *The Talented Mr. Ripley* depicts a highly educated and charming sociopath.

- *Girl, Interrupted* concerns an adolescent's 1960s hospitalization in a private psychiatric facility.

- *October Sky* tells the story of budding rocket scientists in the 1950s in rural West Virginia.

- *Good Will Hunting* portrays the life and friends of a boy who grew up in foster homes and learned to be self-sufficient while working as a janitor and living in a lower socioeconomic class neighborhood.

- *Tumbleweeds* follows a displaced single mother and her teenage daughter as they move from place to place and live on a shoestring while the mother looks for a man who will give them a better life.

- *Liberty House* depicts the changing sociopolitical climate of the 1950s, including integration, interracial dating, and changing family structure and influence.

- *Of Hopscotch and Little Girls* is a powerful documentary film that explores the plight of girls growing up to be women in different cultures.

- *Daughters of the Dust* explores life and development on a barrier island off the coast of South Carolina. It focuses on the Gullah subculture, an isolated African-American group.

- *The Heart is a Lonely Hunter* shows the plight of adolescence in pre-WWII America.

- *A Walk to Remember* addresses the issues of peer pressure and youth views on mortality and achievement.

- *The Butterfly Effect* a young man develops a unique way of dealing with crises in his life, which leads to interesting outcomes.

## ADOLESCENCE IN BOOKS

- *You and Your Adolescent (Second Edition)*, by Laurence Steinberg (Harper Perennial, 1997), provides a broad, developmental overview of adolescence, with parental advice mixed in.

- *The Rise and Fall of the American Teenager,* by Thomas Hine (Avon, 1999), traces the evolution of American adolescence as a social invention shaped by the needs of the 20th century.

- *Preparing for Adolescence,* by James C. Dobson (Gospel Light/Regal Books, 1999), examines the preparation of children to handle the stresses of growing up today. It addresses such issues as self-confidence, handling group pressure, and feelings of inferiority.

- *Adolescence isn't Terminal*, by Kevin Leman (Tyndale House Publishing, 2002), examines such contemporary topics as peer pressure, dating and risky adolescent behaviors.

# Answer Key

## KEY TERMS

1.  **storm-and-stress view** G. Stanley Hall's concept that adolescence is a turbulent time charge with conflict and mood swings

2.  **inventionist view** The view that adolescence is a sociohistorical creation. Especially important in this view are the sociohistorical circumstances at the beginning of the 20th century, a time when legislation was enacted that ensured the dependency of youth and made their move into the economic sphere more manageable.

3.  **stereotype** A broad category that reflects our impressions and beliefs about people. All stereotypes refer to an image of what the typical member of a particular group is like.

4.  **adolescent generalization gap** Adelson's concept of widespread generalizations about adolescents based on information about a limited, highly visible group of adolescents.

5.  **contexts** Settings in which development occurs. These settings are influenced by historical, economic, social, and cultural factors.

6.  **social policy** A national government's course of action designed to influence the welfare of its citizens.

7.  **generational inequity** The unfair treatment of younger members of an aging society in which older adults pile up advantage by receiving inequitably large allocations of resources, such as Social Security and Medicare.

8.  **development** The pattern of change that begins at conception and continues through the life cycle. Most development involves growth, although it also includes decay (as in death and dying).

9.  **biological processes** Changes in an individual's physical nature and appearance.

10. **cognitive processes** Changes in an individual's thinking and intelligence.

11. **socioemotional processes** Changes in an individual's relationships with other people, emotions, personality, and social contexts.

12. **prenatal period** The time from conception to birth.

13. **infancy** The developmental period that extends from birth to 18 or 24 months.

14. **early childhood** The developmental period extending from the end of infancy to about 5 or 6 years of age; sometimes called the preschool years.

15. **middle and late childhood** The developmental period extending from about 6 to about 11 years of age; sometimes called the elementary school years.

16. **adolescence** The developmental period of transition from childhood to early adulthood; it involves biological, cognitive, and socioemotional changes.

17. **early adolescence** The developmental period that corresponds roughly to the middle school or junior high school years and includes most pubertal change.

18. **late adolescence** Approximately the latter half of the second decade of life. Career interests, dating, and identity exploration are often more pronounced in late adolescence than in early adolescence.

19. **early adulthood** The developmental period beginning in the late teens or early twenties and lasting into the thirties.

20. **middle adulthood** The developmental period that is entered at about 35 to 45 years and exited at about 55 to 65 years of age.

21. **late adulthood** The developmental period that lasts from about 60 to 70 years of age until death.

22. **youth** Kenniston's term for the transitional period between adolescence and adulthood that is a time of economic and personal temporariness.

23. **emerging adulthood** Occurs from approximately 18 to 25 years of age and is characterized by experimentation and exploration.

24. **nature-nurture issue** *Nature* refers to an organism's biological inheritance, *nurture* to environmental experiences. "Nature" proponents claim that biological inheritance is the most important influence on development; "nurture" proponents believe environmental experiences are the most important.

25. **continuity-discontinuity issue** Continuity is the gradual, cumulative change from conception to death, while discontinuity is development progressing through distinct stages in the life span.

26. **early-later experience issue** This issue focuses on the degree to which early experiences (especially early in childhood) or later experiences are the key determinants of development.

## KEY PEOPLE IN THE STUDY OF ADOLESCENCE

| | | | |
|---|---|---|---|
| 1. c | 4. d | 7. i | 10. f |
| 2. a | 5. g | 8. k | 11. b |
| 3. e | 6. h | 9. j | |

## "DR. DETAIL'S" MATCHING EXERCISE

| | | | | |
|---|---|---|---|---|
| 1. C | 3. E | 5. A | 7. F | 9. H |
| 2. D | 4. B | 6. G | 8. I | |

## ADOLESCENT MYTH AND FACT

| | | | |
|---|---|---|---|
| 1. T | | 6. F |
| 2. T | | 7. T |
| 3. F | | 8. T |
| 4. F | | 9. F |
| 5. T | | 10. F |

1.  Rousseau restored the belief that being a child or an adolescent is not the same as being an adult. He revived the belief that development has distinct phases.

2.  Self-determination and the ability to choose.

3.  Hall believed that adolescence is a turbulent time charged with conflict and mood swings. Mead believed that when a culture proves a smooth, gradual transition from childhood to adulthood, little storm and stress occurs.

4.  Hall believed genetically determined physiological factors control all development and environment plays a minimal role in development. He based this view on the scientific and biological dimensions of Darwin's views.

5.  Theorists currently state that Samoan adolescence is more stressful than Mead had suggested and that delinquency does occur. Her work has been criticized as biased and error-prone.

6.  Hall borrowed the labels of storm and stress from Goethe and Schiller, who incorporated those themes into their writing on the period.

7.  It is believed that during this time the concept of adolescence was invented. Adolescence was the result of changes in the law that changed the way adolescents lived.

8.  During the roaring '20s, adolescence took a turn for the better. The depression and war would soon challenge this new status; however, those who survived the war years received new distinction and responsibilities in its aftermath. This would again change in the 1960s because of unsettledness associated with the Vietnam War.

9.  In measuring the self-images of adolescents around the world, Offer and his colleagues found a healthy self-image in 73 percent of the adolescents studied.

10. Sociohistorical circumstances always have a major impact on in societal adjustments. Political unrest, distrust in authority, and dissatisfaction expressed by women and minorities on their roles in society all played a roles in the many policy changes that occurred during this time period.


## KEY PEOPLE IN SECTION

**Plato** — suggested that reasoning is not a characteristic of children, but rather makes its first appearance in adolescence.

**Aristotle** — argued that the most important aspect of adolescence is the ability to choose and that this self-determination becomes the hallmark of maturity.

**Jean-Jacques Rousseau** — is credited with restoring the belief that being a child or an adolescent is not the same as being an adult.

**G. Stanley Hall** — is credited as being the father of the scientific study of adolescence. Proposed the storm-and-stress view regarding adolescent mood swings.

**Charles Darwin** — famous evolutionary theorist. Hall applied his scientific and biological views to the study of adolescence.

**Margaret Mead** — studied adolescents on the South Sea island of Samoa. She concluded that the basic nature of adolescence is not biological, but rather sociocultural.

**Leta Hollingworth** — conducted important research on adolescent development, mental retardation, and gifted children. Was the first individual to use the term 'gifted' to describe youth who scored exceptionally high on intelligence tests.

**Kenneth and Mamie Clark** — conducted research on the self-esteem of African-American children.

**George Sanchez** — documented cultural bias in intelligence tests for children and adolescents.

**Joseph Adelson** — called the widespread stereotyping of adolescents so widespread as to represent an "adolescent generation gap."

**Daniel Offer** — found evidence contradicting the negative view of adolescence. Offer found 73 percent of adolescents around the world had healthy self-images.

## TODAY'S ADOLESCENTS
## SECTION REVIEW

1. computers; longer life expectancies; television, satellites, and air travel

2. crack cocaine; television images of violence and sex; contradictory messages about sex

3. high divorce rates; high adolescent pregnancy rates; increased geographic mobility of families; adolescent drug use.

4. The majority is successful; however, there is a large, growing minority who fined trouble and do not do well.

5. Without a reference to historic, economic, social, and cultural factors, there would be no basis by which to judge the behavior of adolescents today.

6. The future of youth is the future of society. If adolescents don't reach their full potential they will be able to contribute less to society.

6. Edelman doesn't believe that policies currently don't reflect the words of politicians. She believes that we need better health care, safer schools and neighborhoods, better parent education, and improved family support programs.

7. According to Edelman, while we hear a lot about family values, there has been little meaningful change in policies directed at families.

8. Not addressing generation inequity could result in alienation, distrust, and ill-will between the generations.

9. Modern transportation as well as the internet do provide some interesting options for adolescents. However, more often than not, they end up as a means for them to find new and different trouble.

## KEY PEOPLE IN SECTION

**Peter Benson** — his Search Institute has determined through research that a number of assets (e.g., family support) serve as a buffer to prevent adolescents from developing problems while making the transition to adulthood.

**Marian Wright Edelman** — president of the Children's Defense Fund and a tireless advocate of children's rights.

**Bernice Neugarten** — believed in developing a spirit of support for improving the range of options of all people in society.

**Reed Larson** — argued that adolescents need more opportunities (e.g., sports & art) to develop the capacity for initiative.

## THE GLOBAL PERSPECTIVE
## SECTION REVIEW

1.      Brown and Larson summarized these static traditions within the context of health, gender, family, school, and peers. While certain trend in style and music do catch on across the globe, traditions within family, school, gender, peers tend to remain rather unchanged.

2.      Gender issues are very different around the globe. Japan, the U.S. and the Philippines offer many opportunities to woman. But outside these regions, men have far greater access to education and resources.

3.      Fewer adolescents die from infectious diseases and malnutrition; however, there are more drug-related health concerns and more sexually transmitted infections within this population than before.

## THE NATURE OF DEVELOPMENT
## SECTION REVIEW

| Age | Name | Description |
|---|---|---|
| Conception to birth | Prenatal | Growth from a single cell to a complete organism |
| Birth to 18–25 months | Infancy | Dependency on adults; early psychological development |
| 2 to 5 – 6 years | Early childhood | Children learn to care for self, develop school readiness, and play with peers |
| 6 to 10–11 years | Middle and late childhood | Master reading, writing, and arithmetic; exposure to culture; self-control increases; achievement becomes a theme |
| 10–13 to 18–22 years | Adolescence | Biological, cognitive, and emotional changes; career interests, dating, and identity options explored in late adolescence |
| Late teens to early 20s and 30s | Early adulthood | Establish personal and economic independence; career development; starting a family |
| 35–45 to 55–65 years | Middle adulthood | Transmit values to the next generation; enhanced concerns about one's body; reflection on meaning of life |
| 60–70 years to death | Late adulthood | Adjusting to decreasing strength and health, retirement and reduced income; adapting to changing social roles; increased freedom; parenthood |

2.      Socioemotional processes shape cognitive processes, cognitive processes advance or restrict socioemotional processes, and biological processes influence cognitive processes.

3.      Is there a specific age at which an adolescent becomes an adult? Early adulthood usually begins in the late teens or early twenties and lasts through the thirties.

4.      A definition of adolescence requires a consideration of age and sociohistorical influences.

5.      For instance, nature influences physical differences between boys and girls, but nurture accounts for changing gender roles.

6.      The old view of adolescence was that it is a singular, uniform period of transition resulting in entry to the adult world. Current approaches emphasize a variety of transitions and events that define the period.

7.      It helps to refine the process of maturation and growth and makes it a more understandable process. Continuity is marked by continuous and gradual change. Whereas discontinuity is marked by distinct stages.

8.      The Western view is that early experiences (Freudian theory) are crucial in the proper development of a child. The Eastern view argues reasoning skills are essential for proper development. Reasoning skills develop later in life.

## KEY PEOPLE IN SECTION

**Kenneth Kenniston**—proposed that a transition occurs between adolescence and adulthood that can last two to eight years or longer.

**Jerome Kagan**—pointed out that even children who show the qualities of an inhibited temperament, which is linked to heredity, have the capacity to change their behavior.

**Jacqueline Eccles**—concluded that three types of assets are linked to well-being in adolescence and emerging adulthood: intellectual, psychological, and social.

## EXPLORATION IN ADOLESCENCE

No answers given—personal reflection

## COGNITIVE CHALLENGE

No answers given—personal reflection

## ADOLESCENCE IN RESEARCH

Kenniston tested the theory that adolescents enter adulthood abruptly. He hypothesized that the transition between adolescence and adulthood can last two to eight years, or longer. He coined the term **youth** to label that transitional period where there are many economic and personal uncertainties.

## ⊠ COMPREHENSIVE REVIEW

| | | | |
|---|---|---|---|
| **1.** b | **12.** b | **23.** b | **34.** c |
| **2.** a | **13.** c | **24.** d | **35.** c |
| **3.** c | **14.** b | **25.** c | **36.** a |

| 4. c | 15. d | 26. d | 37. c |
|------|-------|-------|-------|
| 5. a | 16. c | 27. a | 38. a |
| 6. c | 17. c | 28. d | 39. c |
| 7. b | 18. c | 29. c | 40. b |
| 8. a | 19. c | 30. a | 41. d |
| 9. d | 20. b | 31. a | 42. a |
| 10. d | 21. a | 32. b | |
| 11. c | 22. a | 33. d | |

# Chapter 2     The Science of Adolescent Development

**Learning Goals with Key Terms and Key People in Boldface**

**1.0**     **DESCRIBE THE MAJOR THEORIES OF DEVELOPMENT**

**A.**     **Theories of Development**
- 1.1    Identify are the four steps of the scientific method
- 1.2    Describe a theory.
- 1.3    What is a hypothesis?
- 1.4    Differentiate between a **theory** and an **hypothesis**.
- 1.5    What are the four major theoretical perspectives on human development?

**B.**     **Psychoanalytic Theories**
- 1.6    What does **psychoanalytic theory** describe?
- 1.7    How do psychoanalysts view behavior?
- 1.8    What are the id, ego, and superego?
- 1.9    What are defense mechanisms?
- 1.10    What is repression?
- 1.11    What did **Sigmund Freud** mean by his iceberg analogy?
- 1.12    How did **Peter Blos** and **Anna Freud** help to shape the understanding of adolescence?
- 1.13    How did Anna Freud view the role of adolescent defense mechanisms?
- 1.14    What are the characteristics of Freud's oral, anal, phallic, genital, and latency stages of psychosexual development?
- 1.15    What did Freud mean by the Oedipus complex?
- 1.16    What was the feminine-based criticism of Freud's theory?
- 1.17    Contrast **Erik Erikson's** views on development from those of Freud?
- 1.18    How do *psychosocial* stages differ from *psychosexual* stages?
- 1.19    What are the characteristics of Erikson's eight life span stages—trust versus mistrust, autonomy versus shame and doubt, initiative versus guilt, industry versus inferiority, identity versus identity confusion, intimacy versus isolation, generativity versus stagnation, and integrity versus despair?
- 1.20    What are the primary contributions of **psychoanalytic theories** of adolescent development?
- 1.21    What are the main criticisms of **psychoanalystic theories**?

**C.**     **Cognitive Theories**
- 1.22    What are the three major theories of cognitive development?
- 1.23    What are the characteristics of **Piaget's** stages of cognitive development—the sensorimotor, preoperational, concrete operational, and formal stages?
- 1.24    According to Piaget, which two processes, underlie the cognitive construction of the world?
- 1.25    How does the cognitive theory of **Lev Vygotsky** differ from that of **Piaget**?
- 1.26    How has **Vygotsky's** view stimulated interest in the view that knowledge is situated and collaborative?
- 1.27    Does **Vygotsky's** theory account for developmental differences across cultures?
- 1.28    What is the main emphasis of the **information-processing theory?**
- 1.29    Which two processes are central to the **information-processing theory**?
- 1.30    What are the primary contributions of the cognitive theories of adolescent development?

1.31    What are the main criticisms of the cognitive theories?

   **D.**   **Behavioral and Social Cognitive Theories**

1.32    What do **behavioral** and **social cognitive** theories emphasize?

1.33    What is the main emphasis of **behaviorism?**

1.34    What role does the mind play in development according to **Skinner**?

1.35    According to behaviorists, can the rearranging of experiences impact development?

1.36    Who are the architects of the contemporary version of **social cognitive theory**?

1.37    What is the essence of **Bandura's social cognitive theory?**

1.38    What are the primary contributions of the **behavioral and social cognitive theories** of adolescent development?

1.39    What are the main criticisms of the **behavioral** and **social cognitive theories?**

   **E.**   **Ecological, Contextual Theories of Development**

1.40    How does **Urie Brofenbrenner's ecological, contextual theory** explain adolescent development?

1.41    What are the characteristics of the five systems that make up Brofenbrenner's ecological theory—the **microsystem, mesosystem, exosystem, macrosystem,** and **chronosystem**?

1.42    What are the primary contributions of the **ecological, contextual theory** of adolescent development?

1.43    What are the main criticisms of the **ecological, contextual theory**?

   **F.**   **An Eclectic Theoretical Orientation**

1.44    What is meant by an **eclectic theoretical orientation**?

**2.0   EXPLAIN HOW RESEARCH ON ADOLESCENT DEVELOPMENT IS CONDUCTED**

   **A.**   **Types of Research**

2.1    Explain the role of **descriptive research** in studying adolescent behavior.

2.2    What skills does scientific observation require?

2.3    What role does a **laboratory** play in research?

2.4    What are some drawbacks of **laboratory** research?

2.5    How does **naturalistic observation** differ from scientific observation in general?

2.6    What is the role of interviews and surveys in adolescent research?

2.7    What are some problems with using surveys and interviews?

2.8    What is a **standardized test**?

2.9    What are some advantages and criticisms of **standardized tests**?

2.10   Describe the **experience sampling method (ESM)**.

2.11   How are physiological measures used in assessing adolescent development?

2.12   What are **case studies**?

2.13   What is the goal of **correlational research**?

2.14   Why does correlation not equal causation?

2.15   What does **experimental research** allow us to conclude about behavior?

2.16   What is the difference between the **independent variable** and the **dependent variable**?

2.17   What are the functions of the experimental group and the control group?

2.18   Why is it important to have both experimental and control groups when conducting research?

2.19   What is the value of random assignment?

   **B.**   **Time Span of Research**

2.20   What is the difference between **cross-sectional research** and **longitudinal research**?

2.21   What is the value of **longitudinal research**?

   **C.**   **The Field of Adolescent Development Research**

2.22   Why were researchers so neglectful of adolescence until recently?

2.23   What is the role played by journals and professional meetings in the distribution of scientific information about adolescence?

**3.0    DISCUSS TWO RESEARCH CHALLENGES IN ADOLESCENT DEVELOPMENT**

**A.    Conducting Ethical Research**

3.1    What are two challenges faced by researchers in adolescent development?

3.2    What ethical considerations guide researchers?

3.3    Why did the American Psychological Association (APA) adopt a code of ethics?

3.4    What are the four main issues in ethical guidelines designed to protect subjects from harm?

3.5    What is meant by informed consent?

**B.    Minimizing Bias**

3.6    What is a gender bias, and what role can it play in research?

3.7    What do ethnicity and culture have to do with research into adolescent development?

3.8    What is **ethnic gloss**?

3.9    What research errors can ethnic gloss result in?

# Exercises

## KEY TERMS COMPLETION EXERCISE

Each key term is presented in the form of an incomplete sentence. Complete each sentence by either defining the term or giving an example of it. Compare your definitions with those given at the end of the study guide chapter.

1.    A **theory** can be helpful to

_____

_____

2.    **Hypotheses** are used to

_____

_____

3.    According to **psychoanalytic theory** the personality is

_____

_____

4.    **Erikson's theory** addresses development from

_____

_____

5.    The four stages in **Piaget's theory** are

_____

_____

6. **Vygotsy's theory** is a sociocultural cognitive theory that emphasizes

_____

_____

7. According to **information-processing theory,**

_____

_____

8. **Social cognitive theories** emphasize

_____

_____

9. **Ecological, contextual theory** consists of

_____

_____

10. A therapist applying an **eclectic theoretical orientation** might try

_____

_____

11. **Descriptive research** is a

_____

_____

12. A **laboratory** is often used in conducting

_____

_____

13. A **naturalistic observation** is done

_____

_____

14. **Standardized tests** are useful in

_____

_____

15. The **experience sampling method (ESM)** can be used to

_____

_____

16. You might use a **case study** when you are

_____

_____

17. In **correlational research,** the goal is to

_____

_____

18. The goal of **experimental research** is to

_____

_____

19. In research, the **independent variable** is

_____

_____

20. In research, the **dependent variable** is

_____

_____

21. **Cross-sectional research** involves

_____

_____

22. **Longitudinal research** involves

_____

_____

23. **Ethnic gloss** can result in

_____

_____

## KEY PEOPLE IN THE STUDY OF ADOLESCENCE

Match the name with the concept, issue, or topic related to adolescence with which they are associated.

| | | |
|---|---|---|
| ____ | 1. Sigmund Freud | A. Associated with social cognitive theory |
| ____ | 2. Peter Blos | B. Eight psychosocial stages |
| ____ | 3. Anna Freud | C. Four cognitive stages |
| ____ | 4. Karen Horney | D. Five systems in which adolescents develop |
| ____ | 5. Nancy Chodorow | E. Associated with behaviorism |
| ____ | 6. Erik Erikson | F. Proposed a sociocultural cognitive theory that emphasized developmental analysis, the role of language, and social relations. |

| | | | |
|---|---|---|---|
| ___ | 7. Jean Piaget | G. | Five psychosexual stages |
| ___ | 8. B. F. Skinner | H. | Believed that regression is a normal aspect of puberty |
| ___ | 9. Albert Bandura | I. | Believed that women define themselves in terms of relationships |
| ___ | 10. Lev Vygotsky | J. | Believed that defense mechanisms are the key to understanding adolescent adjustment |
| ___ | 11. Urie Bronfenbrenner | K. | Believes that thinking is information processing |
| ___ | 12. Robert Siegler | L. | Associated with the first feminist-based criticism of Freud's theory |
| ___ | 13. Walter Mischel | M. | Used ESM and found that adolescents experienced emotions that were more extreme and more fleeting than those of their parents |
| ___ | 14. Reed Larson & Maryse Richards | N. | Initially labeled cognitive social learning theory |

## "DR. DETAIL'S" MATCHING EXERCISE

Match the stage with the correct developmental information associated with that stage across each of the following theories.

### Freud's Psychosexual Stages

| | | | |
|---|---|---|---|
| ___ | 1. Genital stage | A. | Between 1 and 3 yrs. Pleasure involves the anus and the process of eliminating. |
| ___ | 2. Oral stage | B. | Occurs between age 6 and puberty. The child focuses on intellectual development while repressing sexual interest. |
| ___ | 3. Phallic stage | C. | Goes from puberty onward. The source of sexual pleasure now becomes someone outside of the family. |
| ___ | 4. Latency stage | D. | First 18 months of life. Pleasure centers around the mouth. |
| ___ | 5. Anal stage | E. | Occurs between ages 3 and 6. Pleasure focuses on the genitals. |

### Erikson's Eight Life-Span Stages

| | | | |
|---|---|---|---|
| ___ | 1. Autonomy vs. Shame and Doubt | A. | Experienced during late adulthood, when people look back and evaluate what they have done with their lives. |
| ___ | 2. Identity vs. Identity Confusion | B. | Experienced during middle adulthood. This stage marks what a person has done to help the next generation. |
| ___ | 3. Trust vs. Mistrust | C. | Experienced during early adulthood. Individuals face the developmental task of forming intimate relationships with others. |
| ___ | 4. Integrity vs. Despair | D. | Experienced during the adolescent years. A time when the individual needs to find out who they are. |
| ___ | 5. Intimacy vs. Isolation | E. | Experienced in the elementary school years. Success in school brings a sense of pride; failure brings about a sense of not being good enough. |
| ___ | 6. Initiative vs. Guilt | F. | Experienced in the first year of life. A sense of well-being depends upon whether or not one's needs are being met. |
| ___ | 7. Generativity vs. Stagnation | G. | Experienced between ages 1 and 3. Is a stage in which infants begin to discover that their behavior is their own. |
| ___ | 8. Industry vs. Inferiority | H. | Experienced during the preschool years. Children are asked to accept responsibility for their bodies, their behavior, their toys, and their pets. |

## Piaget's Stages of Cognitive Development

____ 1. Concrete Operational stage    A. Infants construct an understanding of the world by coordinating sensory experiences with physical actions.

____ 2. Preoperational stage    B. Children begin to represent the world with words, images, and drawings.

____ 3. Formal Operational stage    C. A child in this stage is likely not to be able to imagine the steps needed to complete an algebraic equation.

____ 4. Sensorimotor stage    D. The child begins to think in more abstract and logical terms.


## Bronfenbrenner's Ecological, Contextual Theory

____ 1. Chronosystem    A. Includes the person's family, peers, school, and neighborhood.

____ 2. Microsystem    B. The relation of family experiences to school experiences, school experiences to work experiences, and family experiences to peer experiences.

____ 3. Macrosystem    C. Experiences in another social setting influence what the individual experiences in an immediate context.

____ 4. Mesosystem    D. Involves the culture in which a person lives.

____ 5. Exosystem    E. Involves the patterning of environmental events and transactions over the life course and sociohistorical circumstances.


## ADOLENCENT MYTH AND FACT

Which of the following statements regarding adolescents are true (T) and which are false (F)?

1. No single theory has yet been able to account for all aspects of adolescent development. T or F

2. Psychoanalytic theories describe human development in terms reflecting on the conscious mind. T or F

3. Freud conceptualized personality as a mountain with all but the 'peak' in plain sight. T or F

4. The ego consciously resolves conflict between the id and the superego using defense mechanisms. T or F

5. Repression is the foundation on which all other defense mechanisms rest. T or F

6. One advantage of psychoanalytic theories is that they are easily tested scientifically. T or F

7. Both Piaget's and Vygotsky's ideas remained virtually unknown to American scholars until the 1960's. T or F

8. In Bandura's view, the environment can determine a person's behavior. This view conflicts with Skinner's view. T or F

9. Those who adopt an eclectic theoretical orientation tend to prefer one theoretical approach to adolescent development. T or F

10. Descriptive research methods cannot prove what causes a phenomenon. T or F

11. In research, correlation always means causation. T or F

12. A correlation coefficient of -1.00 indicates a total lack of correlation. T or F

13. Experimental research is the only reliable method of establishing cause and effect. T or F

# THEORIES OF ADOLESCENT DEVELOPMENT
## SECTION REVIEW

1.  Label each stage of the scientific method, and describe what would be done in each stage of a scientific study of mentoring.

| Number | Name | Description |
|--------|------|-------------|
| One | | |
| Two | | |
| Three | | |
| Four | | |

2.  Differentiate between a theory and an hypothesis.

    _____

    _____

3.  What are the four major theoretical perspectives on human development?

    _____

    _____

## PSYCHOANALYTIC THEORIES

1.  According to Freud, the personality has three structures. Explain the role of each of these structures.

    _____

    _____

2.  How did Freud come to conceptualize the personality to be like an iceberg?

    _____

    _____

3.  How do psychoanalysts view behavior?

    _____

    _____

4.  Explain the role ego defense mechanisms have in protecting the personality.

    _____

    _____

5.	How did Anna Freud view the role of adolescent defense mechanism?

_____

_____

6.	Compare the views of Anna Freud with those of Peter Blos.

_____

_____

7.	Contrast Erik Erikson's views on development with those of Freud.

_____

_____

8.	Discuss some of the criticisms of Freud's views.

_____

_____

9.	For each of the Freudian stages, state the age and focus of development and pleasure.

| Stage | Age | Focus of Development/Pleasure |
|-------|-----|-------------------------------|
| Oral | | |
| Anal | | |
| Phallic | | |
| Latency | | |
| Genital | | |

10.	For each of the Erikson stages, provide the age range and focus of psychosocial development.

| Stage | Age | Focus of Development |
|-------|-----|----------------------|
| Trust vs. mistrust | | |
| Autonomy vs. shame and doubt | | |
| Initiative vs. guilt | | |
| Industry vs. inferiority | | |
| Identity vs. identity confusion | | |

| | | |
|---|---|---|
| Intimacy vs. isolation | | |
| Generativity vs. stagnation | | |
| Integrity vs. despair | | |

## COGNITIVE THEORIES

1.  Compare and contrast cognitive theories with psychoanalytic theories.

    _____

    _____

2.  According to Piaget, which two processes underlie the cognitive construction of the world?

    _____

    _____

3.  What occurs in the Formal Operations Stage that differentiates it from Piaget's other stages?

    _____

    _____

4.  Does Vygotsky's theory account for developmental differences across cultures?

    _____

    _____

5.  For each of Piaget's cognitive stages, state the age and identify the manner in which the child/adolescent thinks and understands the world.

| Stage | Age | Way of Thinking and Understanding |
|---|---|---|
| Sensorimotor | | |
| Preoperational | | |
| Concrete operational | | |
| Formal operational | | |

6.  Why have Vygotsky's views on adolescence become an important addition to the understanding of adolescent cognitive development?

    _____

    _____

7. What are the primary contributions of cognitive theories to the understanding of adolescent development?

_____

_____

8. What are the main criticisms of the cognitive theories?

_____

_____

9. Which two processes is central to the information-processing theory?

_____

_____

## BEHAVIORAL AND SOCIAL COGNITIVE THEORIES

1. In Skinner's view, what is development?

_____

_____

2. Contrast Skinner's view with that of Albert Bandura?

_____

_____

3. What role does empirical research play in studying development from both the social cognitive and behavioral perspectives?

_____

_____

4. What are some of the contributions of the behavioral and social cognitive theories of development?

_____

_____

5. According to behaviorists, how can the rearranging of experiences impact development?

_____

_____

6. Describe some of the criticisms of the behavioral and social cognitive theories of development?

_____

_____

# ECOLOGICAL, CONTEXTUAL THEORY

1.  What are some of the contributions of ecological, contextual theory to the overall understanding of adolescent development?

    _____

    _____

2.  What does it mean to say someone follows an eclectic theoretical orientation?

    _____

    _____

3.  Describe the five systems in Bronfenbrenner's ecological theory.

| System | Description |
|---|---|
| Microsystem | |
| Mesosystem | |
| Exosystem | |
| Macrosystem | |
| Chronosystem | |

KEY PEOPLE IN SECTION (describe the contributions of this individual to the study and understanding of adolescence).

**Sigmund Freud —** _____

_____.

**Peter Blos —** _____

_____.

**Anna Freud —** _____

_____.

**Karen Horney —** _____

_____.

**Nancy Chodorow —** _____

_____.

**Erik Erikson —** _____

_____ .

**Jean Piaget —** _____

_____ .

**Lev Vygotsky —** _____

_____ .

**Robert Siegler —** _____

_____ .

**B.F. Skinner —** _____

_____ .

**Albert Bandura —** _____

_____ .

**Walter Mischel —** _____

_____ .

**Urie Bronfenbrenner —** _____

_____ .

## RESEARCH ON ADOLESCENT DEVELOPMENT
## SECTION REVIEW

1.  What are some common types of descriptive research methods?

    _____

    _____

2.  What skills are required for scientific observation?

    _____

    _____

3.  What is a laboratory?

    _____

    _____

4.  What are some drawbacks to laboratory research?

    _____

    _____

5.  What is a benefit of naturalistic observation?

    _____

6.     What is a problem encountered with surveys and interviews?

_____

_____

7.     What are advantages and disadvantages of standardized tests?

_____

_____

8.     What led to an increase of research studies on the brain activities of adolescents?

_____

_____

9.     When is it appropriate to use case studies in conducting research?

_____

_____

10.    What is the goal of correlational research?

_____

_____

11.    Compare and contrast independent and dependant variables used in research studies.

_____

_____

12.    Why were researchers so neglectful of adolescence until recently?

_____

_____

## TIME SPAN OF RESEARCH

1.     Identify some strengths and limitations of cross-sectional research studies?

_____

_____

2.     What are some positives and drawbacks of longitudinal research studies?

_____

_____

# THE FIELD OF ADOLESCENT DEVELOPMENT RESEARCH

1.      Explain the role played by journals in the advancement of scientific theory.

      _____

      _____

2.      Explain which information goes in respective sections of a journal article.

| Section | Description |
|---|---|
| Abstract | |
| Introduction | |
| Method | |
| Results | |
| Discussion | |
| References | |

## FACING UP TO RESEARCH CHALLENGES
## SECTION REVIEW

## CONDUCTING ETHICAL RESEARCH

1.      Explain the importance of informed consent, confidentiality, debriefing and deception in conducting ethical research?

      _____

      _____

## MINIMIZING BIAS

1.      How might gender be a bias that influences the choice of theory, questions, hypotheses, participants, and research design?

      _____

      _____

2.      Define ethnic gloss, and discuss its implications regarding adolescent research?

      _____

      _____

3.      What do we mean when we refer to minorities as "noise" in research data?

      _____

      _____

## EXPLORATIONS IN ADOLESCENCE

Find an article in a research journal (such as *Developmental Psychology, Child Development, Journal of Research on Adolescence, Journal of Early Adolescence,* or *Journal of Youth and Adolescence*) about any topic in the text. Then look for an article on the same subject in either a newspaper or are a magazine. Compare how the research article on the topic differs from the newspaper or magazine article. How do the nature, type, and quality of information presented in the articles differ?

## COGNITIVE CHALLENGE

In the chapter, we were given a brief look at the lives of Jean Piaget and Erik Erikson. From that look at their lives, we get a glimpse at what factors might have led them to formulate the theories they did. In looking back at your life (childhood, adolescence, college experience), what kind of theory could you formulate, and what factors would contribute to this?

## ADOLESCENCE IN RESEARCH

Concerning the studies conducted by Crowley and others (2001) and Tenenbaum and others (2002) on gender bias in research into parenting styles, state the hypothesis, the research methods (if known), the research conclusions, and the implications for adolescent development.

 COMPREHENSIVE REVIEW

1. Which of the following is NOT one of the 4 major theoretical perspectives on human development noted in the chapter?
   a. cognitive      c. behavioral
   b. nomothetic      d. contextual

2. Sigmund Freud developed his ideas about psychoanalytic theory
   a. while being held in a Nazi detention camp.
   b. while reviewing the published theories of Erik Erikson.
   c. from work he did with mental patients.
   d. while studying to become a medical doctor.

3. Which of the following is NOT one of Freud's three structures of the personality?
   a. ego      c. superego
   b. repression      d. id

4. Billy never lies about anything regardless of the consequences. Billy is strongly influenced by his
   a. id.      c. superego.
   b. ego.      d. ego-ideal.

5. Feeling guilty over adolescent sexual exploration is a result of
   a. ego.      c. superego.
   b. libido.      d. id.

6.      According to Freud, this is the most powerful of the defense mechanisms.
        a.      autonomy              c.      Oedipus complex
        b.      latency               d.      repression

7.      Unconsciously hating your younger brother might be an example of
        a.      ego-centrism.         c.      the Oedipus complex.
        b.      repression.           d.      id-ideals.

8.      According to Peter Blos and Anna Freud,
        a.      it is permissible to make generalizations about the role of defense mechanisms in adolescent development because of small or clinical samples of subjects.
        b.      research on adolescent defense mechanisms should be nonsexist.
        c.      defense mechanisms are a normal aspect of adolescent development.
        d.      Sigmund Freud's original analysis of the role of defense mechanisms in adolescent development has been confirmed many times.

9.      Louella believes all boys have "cooties." She devotes herself to athletics and caring for various pets. A psychoanalyst would say Louella is
        a.      behaving normally for someone in the latency stage.
        b.      being overly controlled by her superego.
        c.      experiencing unconscious conflicts between her ego and id.
        d.      fixated at the phallic stage of development.

10.     Max tells his mom, "When I grow up I'm going to marry you." Freud might consider this an example of
        a.      repression.           c.      latency.
        b.      the Oedipus complex.  d.      the id.

11.     Horney and Chodorow criticized Freud for
        a.      his conceptualization of the Oedipus complex.
        b.      the male-bias reflected in his theories.
        c.      discussing children's sexuality too extensively in his theories.
        d.      ignoring sexuality in the elderly.

12.     _____ believed that the problems of youth are rooted in "love objects" in an adolescent's past.
        a.      Peter Blos            c.      Sigmund Freud
        b.      Anna Freud            d.      Erik Erikson

13.     The decision to get married might indicate that Johnny is in which of Freud's psychosexual stages?
        a.      latency               c.      genital
        b.      oral                  d.      phallic

14.     According to Sigmund Freud, the discovery of sexual pleasure occurs in which psychosexual stage?
        a.      oral                  c.      genital
        b.      phallic               d.      latency

15.     An infant left to cry in her crib for long periods of time might, according to Erikson, develops
        a.      autonomy.             c.      initiative.
        b.      guilt                 d.      mistrust.

16. Sheree changed her major three times in college, and now that she has graduated, she still cannot decide what type of job she wants. Erik Erikson would describe Sheree as going through a period of
    a. shame and doubt.           c. despair.
    b. identity confusion.        d. generativity and stagnation.

17. Whereas Freud believed the primary motivator for humans was sexual, Erikson believed it was
    a. wealth.                    c. education.
    b. self-orientation.          d. social.

18. According to Erikson, in the _____ stage we reach our peak in enthusiasm towards learning.
    a. identity vs. identity confusion   c. industry vs. inferiority
    b. trust vs. mistrust                d. intimacy vs. isolation

19. According to Mavis Hetherington, disruption in a family following a divorce peaks at _____ year(s).
    a. 5                          c. 1
    b. 2                          d. 3

20. Piagetian called internalized mental actions that allow children to do mentally what they previously did physically
    a. schemas.                   c. operations.
    b. cognitions.                d. themes.

21. Diana often finds herself daydreaming about boys and wondering what her life will be like when she gets married. According to Piaget, Diana is likely in the
    a. sensorimotor stage.        c. concrete operational stage.
    b. preoperational stage.      d. formal operational stage.

22. Which of the following is NOT emphasized by the behavioral and social cognitive theories as being important in the understanding of adolescent development?
    a. environmental experiences  c. unconscious thoughts
    b. observable behaviors       d. personal/cognitive factors

23. The information processing approach emphasizes
    a. the quality of thinking and memory skills among adolescent of different ages.
    b. overcoming age related problems or "crises."
    c. age appropriate expressions of sexual energy.
    d. perception.

24. Denise received a big promotion at her job that requires her to travel away from home quite often. Although her pay raise initially excited her family, gradually Denise's husband and teenage children became greatly bothered by her extended absences. This example matches which of Bronfenbrenner's 5 ecological systems?
    a. microsystem                c. macrosystem
    b. mesosystem                 d. exosystem

25. The culture in which the adolescent lives is part of which of Bronfenbrenner's systems?
    a. microsystem                c. chronosystem
    b. macrosystem                d. exosystem

26. Which of the following is NOT a drawback of laboratory research?
    a. It is almost impossible to conduct research without the subject knowing they are being studied.

b. The setting allows for control of more variables.

c. It is an unnatural setting.

d. Some aspects of adolescent development are nearly impossible to examine in a laboratory.

27. Sam is shy when around his friends, teachers, and family. Skinner would suggest this behavior is
   a. modeled after his father's behavior.     c. repressed.
   b. learned.                                  d. ecological.

28. One of the strong points of behavior theory is its
   a. belief that cognitive processes are irrelevant for understanding development.
   b. emphasis on the relationship between environmental stimuli and adolescent behavior.
   c. emphasis on reducing adolescent behavior to fine-grained elements.
   d. emphasis on the role of information processing as a mediator between behavior and environment.

29. From B. F. Skinner's point of view, the best way to explain adolescent behavior is to
   a. pay attention to the external consequences of that behavior.
   b. pay attention to the self-produced consequences of that behavior.
   c. focus on adolescent cognitive interpretation of environmental experiences.
   d. identify the biological processes that determine adolescent maturation.

30. The frequent finding that adults who abuse their children and adolescents typically comes from families in which they themselves were abused supports which theory of development?
   a. Freudian psychoanalytic theory     c. ecological theory
   b. information processing theory       d. social cognitive theory

31. A researcher who takes the best aspect from many theories in constructing a research model could be said to be applying
   a. ecological theory.                  c. eclectic theory.
   b. information processing theory.      d. social cognitive theory.

32. A major strength of ecological theory is its framework for explaining
   a. environmental influences on development.
   b. biological influences on development.
   c. cognitive development.
   d. affective processes in development.

33. Many developmentalists have chosen to subscribe to an eclectic viewpoint because
   a. they cannot afford to subscribe to all the other viewpoints; the annual dues are too high.
   b. none of the current theories is completely correct.
   c. they believe not enough data have been collected to begin proposing a definitive theory.
   d. each major theory has valid points and flaws.

34. An investigator interested in gender differences in helping behavior spends three hours a day in the mall watching who opens doors for shoppers burdened with packages. The investigator is using the _____ method of data collection.
   a. naturalistic observation            c. correlational
   b. experimental                        d. case studies

35. Which of the following is TRUE about correlation research?
   a. Correlation means causation.
   b. Correlation ranges from 0 to +1.00.

c. Correlation does not mean causation.

d. A correlation of -.40 is less than a correlation of +.20.

36. _____ is NOT a section typically found in a research article published in a journal?

a. discussion          c. results

b. statistical design    d. method

37. A psychologist treats Brent's irrational fear of balloons. The assessment of Brent's problem and his treatment is an example of a(n)

a. hypothesis.          c. case study.

b. correlational research.  d. context.

38. Experiments involve _____ independent and dependent variables?

a. one                c. three

b. two                d. four

39. The experimental factor that is manipulated in an experiment is the

a. independent variable.   c. control group.

b. dependent variable.    d. method.

40. The factor that is measured as the result of an experiment is the

a. independent variable.   c. control group.

b. dependent variable.    d. method.

41. Assigning participants to experimental and control groups by chance is

a. naturalistic observation.  c. random assignment.

b. longitudinal research.    d. experimental research.

42. In conducting her research on adolescent self-esteem, Professor Radcliff collected information from 14-year-old students in 20 different states. This is an example of

a. case study research.    c. cross-sectional research.

b. longitudinal research.   d. correlational research.

43. When Clint was in pre-school, he participated in a large study on temperament. The same researchers would subsequently observe Clint's behavior again in the 5th grade, the 10th grade, and when he turned 30 years old. Clint was likely a subject in which type of study?

a. case study research.    c. cross-sectional research.

b. longitudinal research.   d. correlational research.

44. Which of the following is NOT an important topic in research ethics?

a. informed consent       c. confidentiality

b. naturalistic observation  d. debriefing

## ADOLESCENCE ON THE SCREEN

- *Good Will Hunting* shows an adolescent named Will (played by Matt Damon) in treatment for attachment problems brought on by his being abandoned by his biological parents and abused by his foster parents. Will's therapist Sean (played by Robin Williams) uses a psychodynamic treatment model.

- *Ordinary People* portrays a surviving son's guilt and suicidal depression over what he feels was his role in his brother's death. He pulls through with the help of hospitalization and a psychodynamic therapist whom he trusts.

- *American Flyers* portrays a youngest son's difficulty in following in the steps of a highly successful older brother who is dying.

## ADOLESCENCE IN BOOKS

Two recent biographies about Erikson and Freud demonstrate how individual life events — as well as historical events, time, and place — influenced their theories:

- *Freud: A Life for Our Time*, by Peter Gay (W.W. Norton, 1998), is a balanced and comprehensive biography of Sigmund Freud that places his theories in the context of the times.

- *Identity's Architect: A Biography of Erik H. Erikson*, by Lawrence J. Friedman (Simon & Schuster, 1999), traces the origins of Erikson's concern with identity and identity crises to his early life experiences.

- *Self-efficacy in Changing Societies*, by Albert Bandura (Cambridge University Press, 1997), looks at changing views of self in adolescents across time.

# Answer Key

## KEY TERMS

1. **theory** An interrelated, coherent set of ideas that helps to explain and make predictions.

2. **hypotheses** Specific assumptions and predictions that can be tested to determine their accuracy.

3. **psychoanalytic theory** Describes development as primarily unconscious — that is, beyond awareness — and is heavily colored by emotion.

4. **Erikson's theory** Eight stages of development that unfold as we go through the life span. Each stage consists of a unique developmental task that confronts individuals with a crisis that must be faced.

5. **Piaget's theory** States that individuals actively construct their understanding of the world and go through four stages of cognitive development.

6. **Vygotsky's theory** A sociocultural cognitive theory that emphasizes developmental analysis, the role of language, and social relations.

7. **information-processing theory** Emphasizes that individuals manipulate information, monitor it, and strategize about it. Central to this approach are the processes of memory and thinking.

8. **social cognitive theories** Emphasis is placed on the importance of studying environmental experiences and observable behavior. Social cognitive theorists emphasize person/cognitive factors in development.

9. **ecological, contextual theory** Bronfenbrenner's view of development, involving five environmental systems — microsystem, exosystem, ecosystem, macrosystem, and chronosystem. These emphasize the role of social contexts in development.

10. **eclectic theoretical orientation** Rather than following any one theoretical approach, these scientists select whatever is considered the best from each theory.

11. **descriptive research** Has the purpose of observing and recording behavior.

12.  **laboratory**  A controlled setting with many of the complex factors of the real world removed.

13.  **naturalistic observation**  Observation made in the "real world" outside the laboratory.

14.  **standardized tests**  Commercially prepared tests that assess performance in different domains. A standardized test often allows researchers to compare an adolescent's performance to other adolescents of the same age.

15.  **experience sampling method (ESM)**  Involves providing participants with electronic pagers and beeping them at random times, at which time they are asked to report on various aspects of their lives.

16.  **case study**  An in-depth look at an individual.

17.  **correlation research**  Describes the strength of the relationship between two or more events or characteristics.

18.  **experimental research**  Allows researchers to appropriately determine the causes of behavior.

19.  **independent variable**  The manipulated, influential, experimental factor.

20.  **dependent variable**  The factor that is measured in an experiment.

21.  **cross-sectional research**  Research that studies all people at one time.

22.  **longitudinal research**  Involves studying the same individuals over a period of time, usually several years or more.

23.  **ethnic gloss**  Using an ethnic label such as African American or Latino in a superficial way that portrays an ethnic group as being more homogeneous than it really is.

## KEY PEOPLE IN THE STUDY OF ADOLESCENCE

| | | | |
|---|---|---|---|
| 1. G | 4. L | 7. C | 10. F |
| 2. H | 5. I | 8. E | 11. D |
| 3. J | 6. B | 9. A | 12. K |
| | | | 13. N |
| | | | 14. M |

## "DR. DETAIL'S" MATCHING EXECISE

*Freud's Psychosexual Stages*

| | |
|---|---|
| 1. C | 4. B |
| 2. D | 5. A |
| 3. E | |

*Erikson's Eight Life-Span Stages*

| | | | |
|---|---|---|---|
| 1. G | 3. F | 5. C | 7. B |
| 2. D | 4. A | 6. H | 8. E |

*Piaget's Stages of Cognitive Development*

| | |
|---|---|
| 1. C | 3. D |
| 2. B | 4. A |

*Bronfenbrenner's Ecological, Contextual Theory*

| | | |
|---|---|---|
| 1. E | 3. D | 5. C |
| 2. A | 4. B | |

# ADOLENCENT MYTH AND FACT

| | | | |
|---|---|---|---|
| 1. | T | 7. | T |
| 2. | F | 8. | F |
| 3. | F | 9. | F |
| 4. | F | 10. | T |
| 5. | T | 11. | F |
| 6. | F | 12. | F |
| | | 13. | T |

## THEORIES OF ADOLESCENT DEVELOPMENT
## SECTION REVIEW

| Number | Name | Description |
|---|---|---|
| One | Conceptualize the problem | Identify the problem; develop hypothesis that mentoring will improve achievement of adolescents from impoverished backgrounds. |
| Two | Collect information (data) | Conduct the mentoring program for six months and collect data before and after program begins. |
| Three | Draw conclusions | Analyze the data that show improvement over period of program; conclude that mentoring helped increase achievement. |
| Four | Revise research conclusions and theory | Research will increase likelihood that mentoring will be considered an important component to help improve achievement of low-income adolescents. |

2.   A theory is an interrelated, coherent set of idea that helps to explain observations and make predictions. An hypothesis is an assumption and/or prediction that can be tested for accuracy.

3.   Psychoanalytic, cognitive, behavioral and social cognitive, and ecological/contextual.

## PSYCHOANALYTIC THEORIES

1.   *Id* — consists of instincts, which are an individual's reservoir of psychic energy. *Ego*—the structure of the personality that deals with the demands of reality. *Superego*—the moral branch of the personality.

2.   Freud felt that most of our personality exists below our level of awareness. Just as an iceberg's greatest mass exists below the surface of the water and is out of sight.

3.   Psychoanalysts believe behavior is merely a surface characteristic, and to truly understand development, we have to analyze the symbolic meanings of behavior and the deep inner workings of the mind.

4.   Ego defense mechanisms are unconscious methods the ego uses to distort reality and protect itself from anxiety.

5.  She believed the problems of adolescence are not rooted in the id; rather they reside in the "love objects" in the adolescent's past. She developed the idea that defense mechanisms are key to understanding these adjustment problems.

6.  Blos stated that regression is actually not defensive at all during adolescence; rather it is an integral, normal, inevitable, and universal part of puberty. Anna Freud developed the idea that defense mechanisms are key to understanding adolescent adjustment.

7.  Erikson recognized Freud's contributions but believed Freud misjudged some important dimensions of human development. In contrast to Freud, Erikson proposed a series of psychosocial stages. For Freud, the primary motivation for human behavior was sexual, whereas Erikson argued it was social.

8.  Most contemporary psychoanalytic theorists place less emphasis on sexual instincts and more emphasis on cultural experiences as determinants of an individual's development. Most theorists today also argue that conscious thought makes up more of the iceberg than Freud envisioned. Lastly, Freud's theories have been viewed as too focused on males.

9.

| Stage | Age | Focus of Development/pleasure |
|---|---|---|
| Oral | 0–1 1/2 years | Pleasure focused on the mouth; sucking reduces tension. |
| Anal | 1 1/2–3 years | Pleasure involves the anus; eliminative functions reduce tension. |
| Phallic | 3–6 years | Pleasure focuses on the genitals; child discovers self-manipulation is enjoyable. |
| Latency | 6 years–puberty | Child represses interest in sexuality and develops social and intellectual skills |
| Genital | Adolescence–adulthood | Sexual pleasure is focused on those outside of the family. |

10.

| Stage | Age | Focus of Development |
|---|---|---|
| Trust vs. mistrust | Infancy | Feeling of physical comfort and minimal amount of fear and apprehension. |
| Autonomy vs. shame and doubt | 1–3 years | Begin to assert independence or autonomy in behavior. |
| Initiative vs. guilt | 3–5 years | Engage in active, purposeful behavior to cope with challenges of the world. |
| Industry vs. inferiority | 6 years–puberty | Direct energy toward mastering knowledge and intellectual skills. |
| Identity vs. identity confusion | 10–20 years | Finding out who they are, what they are about, and where they are going in life. |
| Intimacy vs. isolation | 20s and 30s | Forming intimate relationships. |
| Generativity vs. stagnation | 40s and 50s | Assist younger generation in developing and leading useful lives. |
| Integrity vs. despair | 60s to death | Look back and evaluate life's accomplishments. |

## COGNITIVE THEORIES

1.  Whereas psychoanalytic theories stress the importance of adolescents' unconscious thoughts, cognitive theories emphasize their conscious thoughts.

2.     Organization and adaptation. We organize our experiences and adapt our thinking to include new ideas.

3.     In formal operations, hypothetical or abstract thinking is possible. This greatly increases the thinking capacity of the child in this stage.

4.     Vygotsky believed that the development of memory, attention, and reasoning involves learning to use the inventions of society, such as language, mathematical systems, and memory strategies.

5.

| Stage | Age | Way of Thinking and Understanding. |
|---|---|---|
| Sensorimotor | Birth–2 | Coordinates sensory experiences with physical actions. |
| Preoperational | 2–7 | Uses words and images to represent the world. |
| Concrete operational | 7–11 | Reason logically about concrete events and classify objects. |
| Formal operational | 11–adulthood | Reasons in abstract, idealistic, and logical ways. |

6.     Vygotsky's theory stimulated considerable interest in the view that knowledge is situated and collaborative. That is to say, that within our communities we are immersed in an environment rich with knowledge.

7.     They present a positive view of development. They emphasize the individual's active construction of understanding. They underscore the importance of examining developmental changes in children's thinking. The information-processing approach offers detailed descriptions of cognitive processes.

8.     There is skepticism about the pureness of Piaget's stages. The cognitive theories do not give adequate attention to individual variations in cognitive development. The information processing does not give an adequate description of developmental changes in cognition. Psychoanalytic theorists argue that the cognitive theories do not give enough credit to unconscious thought.

9.     The processes of memory and thinking are central to the information-processing theory. According to I-P theory, adolescents develop a gradually large capacity for processing information, and this allows them to acquire increasingly complex knowledge and skills.

## BEHAVIORAL AND SOCIAL COGNITIVE THEORIES

1.     For Skinner, development is behavior.

2.     Bandura believes observational learning is a key aspect of how we learn. This adds a cognitive component that differs from Skinner's views.

3.     Like Skinner's behavioral approach, the social cognitive approach emphasizes the importance of empirical research in studying development.

4.     An emphasis on the importance of scientific research. A focus on the environmental determinants of behavior. An underscoring of the importance of observational learning. An emphasis on person and cognitive factors.

5.     Since behaviorists believe that development is learned and often changes based on environmental encounters, it makes sense that rearranging experiences can change development (e.g., shy >> outgoing; aggressive >> docile).

6.     Too little emphasis on cognition. Too much emphasis on environmental determinants. Inadequate attention to developmental changes. Too mechanical, and inadequate consideration of the spontaneity and creativity of humans.

# ECOLOGICAL, CONTEXTUAL THEORY

1.  A systematic examination of macro and micro dimensions of environmental systems. Attention to connections between environmental settings. Consideration of sociohistorical influences on development.

2.  An eclectic theoretical orientation does not follow any one theoretical approach, but rather selects and uses whatever is considered the best in each theory.

3.

| System | Description |
|---|---|
| Microsystem | family, peers, school, neighborhood |
| Mesosystem | school and parents; parents and friends |
| Exosystem | lack of facilities for a handicapped person |
| Macrosystem | ethnic or racial group |
| Chronosystem | wider range of gender roles for men and women |

## KEY PEOPLE IN SECTION

**Sigmund Freud**—a medical doctor who specialized in neurology; he developed his ideas about psychoanalytic theory from work with mental patients.

**Peter Blos**—a British psychoanalyst who felt that regression during adolescence is actually not defensive at all, but rather a normal part of puberty.

**Anna Freud**—Sigmund's daughter Anna developed the idea that defense mechanisms are the key to understanding adolescent adjustment.

**Karen Horney**—developed a model of women with positive feminine qualities and self-evaluation; she was a critic of Sigmund Freud's male oriented theories.

**Nancy Chodorow**—a Freud critic; she noted that many more women than men define themselves in terms of their relationships with others.

**Erik Erikson**—developed the theory that people develop in psychosocial stages; Erikson emphasized developmental changes throughout the human life span.

**Jean Piaget**—proposed that individuals actively construct their understanding of the world and go through four stages of cognitive development.

**Lev Vygotsky**—proposed a sociocultural cognitive theory that emphasizes developmental analysis, the role of language, and social relations.

**Robert Siegler**—leading expert on children's information processing, and believes that thinking is information processing.

**B.F. Skinner**—to Skinner, development is behavior; the mind, conscious or unconscious, is not needed to explain behavior and development.

**Albert Bandura**—believes that observational learning is a key aspect of how we learn.
**Walter Mischel**—along with Bandura, he is an architect of the contemporary version of social cognitive theory, which Mischel initially labeled *cognitive social learning theory*.

**Urie Bronfenbrenner**—proposed a strong environmental view of children's development that is receiving increased attention today: Ecological, Contextual Theory.

## RESEARCH ON ADOLESCENT DEVELOPMENT
## SECTION REVIEW

### TYPES OF RESEARCH

1. Observation, surveys, interviews, standardized tests, experience sampling, physiological measures, and case studies.

2. Must be systematic, know what you are observing, and know where to observe.

3. A controlled setting that removes many of the complex factors present in the "real world."

4. It is almost impossible to conduct research without the participants' knowing that they are being studied. The lab setting is unnatural. People willing to come to a lab might not represent the real population of people. Some adolescent behaviors are not able to be studied in a lab setting.

5. Behavior observed is more likely to reflect real behavior, as opposed to lab setting.

6. Participants tend to answer in a way they think is socially acceptable or desirable rather than saying what they really think.

7. Advantage — they provide information about individual difference among people. Problem — they do not always predict behavior or performance in a non-test situation.

8. The development of neuroimaging techniques.

9. When for practical or ethical reasons, the unique aspects of an individual's life cannot be duplicated and tested in other individuals. A case study is most relevant when the phenomenon being studied is rare and you want an in-depth look at the individual being studied

10. The goal is to describe the strength of the relationship between two or more events or characteristics.

11. The independent variable is the manipulated, influential factor in an experiment. The dependent variable is measured as the result of an experiment.

12. For most of the 20$^{th}$ century experiences in childhood were thought to be so critical (because of the heavy influence of Freud) that later experiences, such as those occurring in adolescence, were believed to have little impact.

### TIME SPAN OF RESEARCH

1. The cross-sectional study's main advantage is that the researcher does not have to wait for the children to grow older. However, a disadvantage is that this approach provides no information about the stability of the children's and adolescent's feelings or attitudes over time.

2. A positive is that you can evaluate how the individual children and adolescents change as they get older. However, this approach is costly and time consuming.

# THE FIELD OF ADOLESCENT DEVELOPMENT RESEARCH

1. Journals are the main outlets for the vast amount of research being conducted on adolescence.

2. Explain which information goes in respective sections of a journal article?

| Section | Description |
|---|---|
| Abstract | A brief summary that appears at the beginning of the article. |
| Introduction | Introduces the problem or issue that is being studied. |
| Method | Consists of a clear description of the participants evaluated in the study, the measures used, and the procedures that were followed. |
| Results | Reports the analysis of the data collected. Might be difficult for nonprofessionals to understand. |
| Discussion | Presents the author's conclusions, inferences, and interpretation of what was found. Statements are usually made about whether the hypotheses presented in the introduction were supported, limitations of the study, and suggestions for future research. |
| References | Gives a bibliographic listing for every source cited in the article. |

# FACING UP TO RESEARCH CHALLENGES
# SECTION REVIEW

## CONDUCTING ETHICAL RESEARCH

1. Informed consent means that the participants' legal guardians have been told what participation will entail and any risks that might be involved. Confidentiality means that researchers are responsible for keeping all of the data they gather completely confidential, and, when possible, completely anonymous. Debriefing consists of informing participants of the purpose and methods used in a study after the study has been completed.

## MINIMIZING BIAS

1. Because most of the early research opportunities in developmental psychology went to men, they tended to study what they were most familiar with, which was males. This means that many hypotheses have not been adequately tested with female participants even to this day.

2. Ethnic gloss means using an ethnic label in a superficial way that makes an ethnic group look more homogeneous than it really is.

3. Because their scores often didn't fit neatly into measures of central tendency (the normal curve or distribution), they were often viewed as 'outlyers' or confounds in the data (i.e., noise).

## EXPLORATIONS IN ADOLESCENCE

Individual assignment—various articles and responses could be appropriate.

## COGNITIVE CHALLENGE

Individual reflection—no answers provided.

## RESEARCH IN ADOLESCENCE

The hypothesis was that parents would be more likely to engage boys in exploratory talk. The setting was a science museam, and the outcome appeared to suggest a clear example of a gender bias that encourages boys more than girls in science.

## ☒ COMPREHENSIVE REVIEW

| | | | |
|---|---|---|---|
| 1. b | 12. b | 23. a | 34. a |
| 2. c | 13. c | 24. d | 35. c |
| 3. b | 14. b | 25. b | 36. b |
| 4. c | 15. d | 26. b | 37. c |
| 5. c | 16. b | 27. b | 38. a |
| 6. d | 17. d | 28. b | 39. a |
| 7. b | 18. c | 29. a | 40. b |
| 8. c | 19. c | 30. d | 41. c |
| 9. a | 20. c | 31. c | 42. c |
| 10. b | 21. d | 32. a | 43. b |
| 11. b | 22. c | 33. d | 44. b |

# ✦ Chapter 3    Puberty, Health, and Biological Foundations

Learning Goals with Key Terms and Key People in Boldface

**1.0    DISCUSS THE DETERMINANTS, CHARACTERISTICS, AND TIMING OF PUBERTY**

**A.    Determinants of Puberty**

1.1    What is **puberty**?

1.2    What role does heredity play in puberty?

1.3    What are **hormones**, and what is their role in **puberty**?

1.4    Name the two classes of **hormones**, and how do they affect males and females differently?

1.5    What is testosterone, and what role does it play in male development?

1.6    Explain the role of the endocrine system in puberty?

1.7    What are the different endocrine glands, and what are their functions?

1.8    How does the endocrine system work?

1.9    How does the negative feedback system in the endocrine system work?

1.10    What are the two phases of **puberty** linked to hormonal changes?

1.11    What role is played **menarche** and **spermarche** with regards to a girl's or boy's entry into gonadarche?

**B.    Growth Spurt**

1.12    What physical changes coincide with the growth spurt?

**C.    Sexual Maturation**

1.13    What is the order of physical changes during sexual maturation?

**D.    Secular Trends in Puberty**

1.14    To what does the term secular trends refer?

1.15    What is a likely contributor to the earlier maturation of girls today?

1.16    What are the five pubertal stages of male and female sexual development?

**E.    Psychological Dimensions**

1.17    What accounts for adolescents' preoccupation with their bodies?

1.18    What are some gender differences in adolescents' perception of their bodies?

1.19    How do hormones affect behavior in adolescents?

1.20    What is the typical reaction of young girls to **menarche?**

1.21    What effect does early or late maturation have on a developing boy or girl?

1.22    Are the effects of puberty exaggerated?

**F.    Pubertal Timing and Health Care**

1.23    What can be done to help off-time maturers who are at risk for health problems?

**2.0    DESCRIBE THE DEVELOPMENTAL CHANGES IN THE BRAIN DURING ADOLESCENCE**

**A.    Neurons**

2.1    What are **neurons?**

2.2    Identify the three basic parts of the **neuron?**

2.3    How do **neurons** change in adolescence?

2.4    What are synapses?

2.5    What is meant by synaptic "blooming and pruning?"

2.6    What determines the timing and course of synaptic overproduction and retraction?

    **B.**    **Brain Structure**
- 2.7    Identify the four lobes of the brain?
- 2.8    Name recent technological advances have allowed for more in-depth study of the adolescent brain?
- 2.9    What role might the amygdala play in adolescent thought processes?
- 2.10    What is the significance of increased synaptic density in the brain?

    **C.**    **Experience and Plasticity**

**3.0**    **EXPLAIN THE CONTRIBUTIONS OF EVOLUTION, HEREDITY, AND ENVIRONMENT TO ADOLESCENT DEVELOPMENT**

    **A.**    **The Evolutionary Perspective**
- 3.1    What is adaptive behavior?
- 3.2    Which behaviors does **evolutionary psychology** emphasize?

    **B.**    **The Genetic Process**
- 3.3    What are **chromosomes**?
- 3.4    Define **DNA**
- 3.5    What is the nature of **genes**?
- 3.6    What is the difference between a **genotype** and **phenotype**?
- 3.7    What physical traits are included in **phenotypes?**
- 3.8    Would measured introversion-extroversion be predictable from knowledge of the specific genes?
- 3.9    What are the research methods of **behavior genetics?**
- 3.10    How is the influence of heredity on behavior studied?
- 3.11    What is a **twin study?**
- 3.12    How do **twin studies** examine the difference between identical twins and fraternal twins?
- 3.13    What are some issues that develop as a result of **twin studies?**
- 3.14    What is an **adoption study?**
- 3.15    What is the basis of the enthusiasm regarding the study of molecular genetics?
- 3.16    What is a genome?
- 3.17    What is the importance of the Human Genome Project?

    **C.**    **Heredity-Environment Interaction**
- 3.18    Behavior geneticist Sandra Scarr identified which three ways heredity and environment are correlated?
- 3.19    What distinguishes Scarr's concepts of **passive genotype-environment correlations, evocative genotype-environment correlations,** and **active (niche-picking) genotype-environment correlations?**
- 3.20    What is the difference between **shared environmental influences** and **nonshared environmental influences?**
- 3.21    What are the most reasonable conclusions we can make about the interaction of heredity and environment?
- 3.22    Why are the views of Judith Harris both intriguing and controversial?

# Exercises

## KEY TERMS COMPLETION EXERCISE

This exercise presents each key term in the form of an incomplete sentence. Complete each sentence by either defining the term or giving an example of it. Compare your definitions with those given at the end of the study guide chapter.

1. One of the early signs of **puberty** is

_____

_____

2. **Hormones** play a major role in

_____

_____

3. Testosterone is an **androgen** that

_____

_____

4. Estradiol is an **estrogen** that

_____

_____

5. Suzy is probably entering **menarche** because

_____

_____

6. John is probably entering **spermarche** because

_____

_____

7. **Neurons** are made up of

_____

_____

8. **Basal metabolism rate (BMR)** gradually declines

_____

_____

9. **Evolutionary psychology** is the study of

_____

_____

10. **Chromosomes** play a major role in

_____

_____

11. **DNA** is responsible for

_____

12. **Genes** determine

_____

_____

13. A **genotype** is a

_____

_____

14. A girl's **phenotype** can be observed in her appearance by

_____

_____

15. The study of **behavior genetics** might involve

_____

_____

16. In a **twin study,** a comparison is made between

_____

_____

17. In an **adoption study,** researchers seek

_____

_____

18. **Passive genotype-environment correlations** lead parents to

_____

_____

19. **Evocative genotype-environment correlations** might explain Tom's happiness because

_____

_____

20. **Active (niche-picking) genotype-environment correlations** might explain why athletic boys seek out

_____

_____

21. Examples of **shared environmental influences** are

_____

_____

22. Example of **nonshared environmental influences** are

_____

_____

23. The **epigenetic view** is

_____

_____


## KEY PEOPLE IN THE STUDY OF ADOLESCENCE

Match the person with the event or concept in adolescent development with which they are associated.

___ 1. Sandra Scarr

___ 2. Laurence Steinberg

___ 3. Roberta Simmons and Dale Blyth

___ 4. Robert Plomin

___ 5. David Moore

___ 6. Albert Bandura

___ 7. Mihalyi Csikszentimalyi and Jennifer Schmidt

___ 8. David Buss

___ 9. Charles Nelson

A. Argued that the prefrontal cortex of adolescents haven't developed to the point where they can control their strong emotions.

B. Described three ways that heredity and environment are correlated.

C. Studied the effects of being an early or late maturing male or female.

D. Wrote the book *The Dependent Gene*.

E. Rejected "one-sided evolution" in which social behavior is seen as the product of evolved biology.

F. Found that common rearing and environment accounts for little of the variation in adolescents' personality.

G. Felt that evolution shapes our physical features, decision making, aggressive behaviors, fears, and mating behaviors.

H. Argued that evolution has programmed humans to act in predictable ways from puberty into early adulthood.

I. Argued that the reward and pleasure aspects of the limbic system may also be involved in adolescents' difficulty in controlling their behavior.


## "DR. DETAIL'S" PUZZLE

*Down*
1. The main class of female hormones.
2. Powerful chemical substances secreted by the endocrine glands and carried through the body by the bloodstream.
3. The way an individual's genotype is expressed in observed and measurable characteristics.
4. The nervous system's basic units.

*Across*
1. A girl's first menstrual period.
2. The main class of male sex hormones.
3. A period of rapid physical maturing involving hormonal and bodily changes.
4. A person's genetic heritage.
5. A boy's first ejaculation of semen.

## ADOLESCENT MYTH AND FACT

**Which of the following statements regarding adolescents are true (T) and which are false (F)?**

1.  Puberty cannot be distinguished from adolescence. T or F

2.  Androgens are found only in males, and estrogen is found only in women. T or F

3.  African American girls typically experience puberty earlier than white girls. T or F

4.  At the beginning of adolescence, girls tend to be taller than boys. T or F

5.  Girls, in their teen years, have more positive body images than boys. T or F

6.  Increased estrogen levels are linked with aggression in girls. T or F

7.  Increased androgen levels in boys are linked with increases in aggression. T or F

8.  Late-maturing females tend to be shorter and stockier than early-maturing females. T or F

9.  Early-maturing girls are more likely to achieve a college education than late-maturing females. T or F

10. Most recent research suggested that the overall effects of early or late maturation are not great. T or F

11. The brain quits growing prior to adolescence. T or F

12. The earlier a brain injury occurs, the more likely is a successful recovery. T or F

13. Scientists have recently discovered that people can generate new brain cells throughout their entire lives. T or F

14. Neuroscientists believe that during development there is a biological "window of opportunity" when learning is easy, effective, and readily retained. T or F

15. Humans take longer to become reproductively mature than any other mammal. T or F

16. When first fertilized, a human cell (egg) weighs one twenty-millionth of an ounce. T or F

17. Human genes only rarely work independently, they are more likely to interact or collaborate with other genes. T or F

## PUBERTY
## SECTION REVIEW

1.  How can puberty be distinguished from adolescence?

_____

2.    How is the emergence of puberty timed, and what can have an impact on it?

_____

_____

3.    Differentiate between the two classes of hormones, and how they specifically affects males and females.

_____

_____

4.    What physical changes in boys is testosterone associated with?

_____

_____

5.    Describe the endocrine system's role in puberty?

_____

_____

6.    Contrast the functions of the hypothalamus and pituitary gland.

_____

_____

7.    How does the endocrine system work?

_____

_____

8.    Describe the role of the negative feedback system in the endocrine system.

_____

_____

9.    Identify the two phases of puberty linked with hormonal changes?

_____

_____

10.   Discuss the association between body weight and physical maturation?

_____

_____

11.   What is the order of appearance of physical changes in females?

_____

_____

12.     Explain what is meant by secular trends.

_____

_____

13.     Describe some aspects of the physical preoccupation boys and girls have with their changing bodies.

_____

_____

14.     What types of behaviors have been linked with increases or suppression of the hormone system?

_____

_____

15.     Identify some advantages and disadvantages of being an "early" or "late" maturing adolescent?

_____

_____

16.     If puberty and development are unusually late, what steps can be taken to help the adolescent?

_____

_____


KEY PEOPLE IN SECTION (describe the contributions of this individual to the study and understanding of adolescence).

**Roberta Simmons and Dale Blyth** — _____

_____.

THE BRAIN
SECTION REVIEW

1.     Identify the three basic parts of the neuron?

_____

_____

2.     How do neurons change in adolescence?

_____

_____

3.     Contrast the process of "blooming" and "pruning" in adolescent neurological development.

_____

_____

4.      Match the lobe of the brain with its primary function.

     ___    1.  Occipital lobe                A.  Involved in bodily sensations

     ___    2.  Parietal lobe                   B.  Involved in hearing

     ___    3.  Temporal lobe                C.  Involved in the control of voluntary muscles, personality, and intelligence

     ___    4.  Frontal lobe                  D.  Involved in visual functioning

5.      Describe recent discoveries scientists made using MRIs to examine the growing brains of children.

_____

_____

6.      How has the conceptualization of "left-brained" or "right-brained" individuals helped to perpetuate misinformation?

_____

_____

# EVOLUTION, HEREDITY, AND ENVIRONMENT
# SECTION REVIEW

1.      Identify the difference between genotypes and phenotypes, and discuss how genotypes and phenotypes affect development.

_____

_____

2.      Explain adaptive behavior in terms of evolutionary psychology.

_____

_____

3.      Explain Bandura's concerns about the "biologizing" of psychology.

_____

_____

4.      In the study of adolescence, what has been learned from twin studies and adoption studies?

_____

_____

5.      Why does behavior geneticist Robert Plomin maintain that shared environment accounts for little of the variation in adolescent's personalities or interests?

_____

_____

6.      What was the cause of the most recent nature-nurture controversy?

_____

_____

7.     Explain the epigenetic view.

_____

_____


KEY PEOPLE IN SECTION (describe the contributions of this individual to the study and understanding of adolescence).

**Sandra Scarr** — _____

_____

**Robert Plomin** — _____

_____

**Charles Darwin** — _____

_____

**Judith Harris** — _____

_____

**David Buss** — _____

_____

**Stephen Jay Gould** — _____

_____


## EXPLORATIONS IN ADOLESCENCE

Which of the following most closely resembles you?

Early maturing male      ___
Late maturing male       ___
Early maturing female    ___
Late maturing female     ___

Depending upon which you checked, how might your life (e.g., experiences, opportunities, dating, sports, leadership experiences, etc.) have been affected by how early or late you matured?

_____

_____

_____

_____


## COGNITIVE CHALLENGE

Looking at the following characteristics, first circle whether you believe nature or nurture is more responsible for these characteristics in you. Then briefly explain your reasoning.

| | | |
|---|---|---|
| **Height** | (nature \| nurture) | _____ |
| **Weight** | (nature \| nurture) | _____ |
| **Skin color** | (nature \| nurture) | _____ |
| **Temperament** | (nature \| nurture) | _____ |
| **Intelligence** | (nature \| nurture) | _____ |
| **Humor** | (nature \| nurture) | _____ |
| **Hair color** | (nature \| nurture) | _____ |
| **Athleticism** | (nature \| nurture) | _____ |
| **Age at maturation** | (nature \| nurture) | _____ |
| **Academic ability** | (nature \| nurture) | _____ |

## ADOLESCENCE IN RESEARCH

Concerning the research about early and late maturation by Simmons and Blyth (1987), state the hypothesis, the research methods (if known), the research conclusions, and the implications and applications for adolescent development.

_____

_____

_____

_____

_____

_____

## ⊠ COMPREHENSIVE REVIEW

1. _____ is a period of rapid physical maturation involving hormonal and bodily changes that take place primarily in early adolescence.
   - a. Menarche
   - b. Heredity
   - c. Adolescence
   - d. Puberty

2. Of the following, which has NOT been identified as a trigger for puberty?
   - a. hormones
   - b. caffeine consumption
   - c. weight
   - d. body fat

3. _____ are the main class of male sex hormones.
   a. Estrogens                    c. Neurons
   b. Androgens                    d. Spermarche

4. _____ are the main class of female sex hormones.
   a. Estrogens                    c. Menarche
   b. Androgens                    d. Spermarche

5. Levels of sex hormones are regulated by the
   a. endocrine regulator system.    c. gonadotropin feedback system.
   b. negative feedback system.      d. testosterone regulator system.

6. Which household appliance is the negative feedback system most similar to?
   a. television set               c. stove
   b. toaster                      d. furnace

7. Which of the following is NOT monitored by the hypothalamus?
   a. sex                          c. hearing
   b. eating                       d. drinking

8. _____ is the only time during development in which growth is faster than during puberty.
   a. Toddlerhood                  c. Infancy
   b. Middle childhood             d. Young adulthood

9. Two of the most noticeable aspects of female pubertal change are
   a. a deeper voice and dense muscles.
   b. armpit hair and height.
   c. pubic hair and breast development.
   d. a deeper voice and weight gain.

10. _____ refers to patterns seen over time, and especially across generations.
    a. Secular trends              c. Historical eras
    b. Generation gaps             d. Temporal units

11. On average, females enter puberty at an earlier age than males, and as a result,
    a. women are typically shorter than men.
    b. fifth- and sixth-grade girls are usually taller than boys.
    c. girls and boys do not get along well during puberty.
    d. boys are more muscular, and girls have more fat.

12. Sue started her menstrual period about two years earlier than Mary, even though both girls are very healthy. A likely explanation for this event is that
    a. Sue is an athlete.
    b. Sue has greater body mass than Mary.
    c. Mary has greater body mass than Sue.
    d. Sue has better genes than Mary.

13. Which of the following is one known marker of male pubertal transition?
    a. sexual daydreams            c. increased aggression
    b. wet dreams                  d. running faster

14. The most likely reason for the dissatisfaction seen in pubertal girls regarding their changed bodies is that
    a.  most don't like being tall.
    b.  not dislike increased attention from boys.
    c.  most are bothered by increases in body fat.
    d.  most fear becoming too muscular.

15. Emily and Ervin are fraternal twins, and both are in the sixth grade. Ervin gets angry because people tease him about his sister being taller than he. His parents can legitimately tell Ervin that
    a.  although his sister is taller, his sexual maturation is more advanced.
    b.  his sister is probably taller because she doesn't eat as much junk food.
    c.  he needn't worry, because he'll probably catch up with or surpass his sister's height by the end of the eighth grade.
    d.  since his sister was taller than he was during childhood, she'll be taller than he is during adolescence.

16. The most likely reason for the pubertal increase in body image and self-esteem in boys is that
    a.  they have more interest in girls.
    b.  they receive more interest from girls.
    c.  they have rapidly increasing muscle mass.
    d.  they enjoy having deeper voices.

17. After their initial menstrual period, all girls told
    a.  no one.                    c.  their mother.
    b.  their best friend.         d.  their school nurse.

18. In the Berkeley Longitudinal Study, males who matured early
    a.  perceived themselves as more successful in peer relations.
    b.  perceived themselves more negatively because of additional parental pressure.
    c.  were perceived by peers as unattractive due to the accompanying occurrence of acne.
    d.  perceived themselves more negatively because they were "ahead of the others."

19. In a college course in human sexuality, Jill was asked to describe her initial reactions to menarche. She described the experience very negatively, emphasizing discomfort and messiness. Jill probably was
    a.  well prepared for the event.
    b.  unlikely to tell her mother about the event.
    c.  an early maturer.
    d.  on time in her pubertal development.

20. Jonathan is just entering puberty. The first of many changes that he is likely to notice is
    a.  a minor voice change.
    b.  growth of hair in the armpits.
    c.  appearance of straight pubic hair.
    d.  increase in penis and testicle size.

21. Jenny is just entering puberty. The first of many changes that she is likely to notice is
    a.  growth of hair in the armpits.   c.  increase in breast size.
    b.  increase in hip width.           d.  significant increase in height.

22. The layer of fat cells that encases most axons is called
    a.  the nucleus                c.  dendrites.
    b.  the terminal button        d.  the myelin sheath.

23. Which of the following parts of the brain is most involved with hearing?
    a. parietal lobe          c. frontal lobe
    b. auditory lobe          d. temporal lobe

24. Which type of technology has recently dramatically advanced the study of the adolescent brain?
    a. the "living autopsy"   c. the MRI
    b. the EEG                d. PET scans

25. Stephanie is a late-maturing female. She has an increased probability of
    a. being tall and thin.
    b. being shorter and stockier.
    c. having a clear complexion.
    d. having to visit a dermatologist for acne treatment.

26. According to researcher Charles Nelson,
    a. adolescent brains are like turbo-charged cars without driving skills.
    b. growth in the limbic system leads to increases in risk-taking behavior.
    c. enriched environments lead to heavier brains.
    d. children who grow up in un-stimulating environments show less brain activity on EEGs.

27. Which of the following is not one of the three basic parts of a neuron?
    a. cell body              c. occipital lobe
    b. axon                  d. dendrites

28. What role does the myelin sheath play in the functioning of a neuron?
    a. It carries information away from the cell body to other cells.
    b. It receives information from other cells.
    c. It helps to insulate the axon and speeds transmission.
    d. It provides the neuron with nutrition.

29. Which role does the axon play in the functioning of a neuron?
    a. It carries information away from the cell body to other cells.
    b. It receives information from other cells.
    c. It helps to insulate the axon and speeds transmission.
    d. It provides the neuron with nutrition.

30. Which role does the dendrite play in the functioning of a neuron?
    a. It carries information away from the cell body to other cells.
    b. It receives information from other neurons.
    c. It helps to insulate the axon and speeds transmission.
    d. It provides the neuron with nutrition.

31. Which lobe of the brain is involved in visual functioning?
    a. temporal              c. parietal
    b. frontal               d. occipital

32. Which lobe of the brain is involved in bodily sensations?
    a. temporal              c. parietal
    b. frontal               d. occipital

33. Which lobe of the brain is most involved in personality?
    a.   temporal                         c.   parietal
    b.   frontal                          d.   occipital

34. If the total existence of the Earth is represented by the calendar, humans would have existed since
    a.   September.                       c.   early December.
    b.   November.                        d.   the last moments of December.

35. The _____ human cell structure has a double helix shape or appearance.
    a.   gene                             c.   genome
    b.   chromosome                       d.   DNA

36. One of the biggest surprises of the Human Genome Project was
    a.   that humans have a remarkably similar gene structure to spiders.
    b.   that there are over 1 million human genes.
    c.   that humans only have about 30,000 genes.
    d.   that humans are NOT as similar to apes as once believed.

37. _____ is the unique arrangement of chromosomes and genes inherited by each adolescent; whereas
    _____ is the adolescent's observed characteristics.
    a.   Phenotype; genotype             c.   Genotype; reaction range
    b.   Phenotype; reaction range       d.   Genotype; phenotype

38. _____ is the area concerned with the degree and nature of the hereditary basis of behavior.
    a.   Genetic psychology             c.   Behavior genetics
    b.   Behavioral psychology          d.   Developmental genetics

39. A behavioral geneticist comparing the IQs of monozygotic twins with those of dizygotic twins is applying the
    a.   twin-study method.             c.   kinship method.
    b.   family-of-twins method.        d.   habitability method.

40. Sandra Scarr proposed all the following heredity-environment interactions except
    a.   passive genotype-environmental interactions.
    b.   heritable genotype-environmental interactions.
    c.   evocative genotype-environmental interactions.
    d.   active genotype-environmental interactions.

## ADOLESCENCE ON THE SCREEN

■   *My Left Foot* addresses how a boy deals with physical deformity.

■   *Trainspotting* depicts the decadent lifestyle of Scottish teenagers bent on self-destruction through heroin addiction.

■   *Ordinary People* tells of an adolescent boy's struggle with suicidal tendencies arising out of the guilt he feels for an accident that took his young brother's life.

■   *Antonia's Line* is a longitudinal portrayal of the transformation from early adolescence to womanhood, and life's decisions involved.

■   *The Body Beautiful* is a generative example of how our various bodily and social identities are built and given meaning concurrently.

- *Daughters of the Dust* portrays life and development on a barrier island among the Gullah subculture, an isolated African-American culture off the coast of South Carolina.

- *Rain* tells the story of a 13-year-old girl who becomes increasingly aware of problems in her parents' marriage, while at the same time beginning to discover her own sexuality.

## ADOLESCENCE IN BOOKS

- *The What's Happening to My Body? Book for Boys,* by Lynda Madaras & D. Ssveddra (Newmarket, 1991), is written for parents and focuses on how to help boys cope with pubertal transitions.

- *You're in Charge*, by Niels Lauersen & Eileen Stukane (Fawcett, 1993), is written for teenage girls and describes the changing female body.

# Answer Key

## KEY TERMS

1. **puberty** A period of rapid physical maturation involving hormonal and bodily changes that occur primarily in early adolescence.

2. **hormones** Powerful chemical substances secreted by the endocrine glands and carried through the body by the bloodstream.

3. **androgen** The main class of male sex hormones.

4. **estrogen** The main class of female sex hormones.

5. **menarche** A girl's first menstruation.

6. **spermarche** A boy's first ejaculation of semen.

7. **neurons** Are the nervous system's basic units.

8. **basal metabolism rate (BMR)** Is the minimum amount of energy an individual uses in a resting state.

9. **evolutionary psychology** An approach that emphasizes the importance of adaptation, reproduction, and "survival of the fittest" in explaining behavior.

10. **chromosomes** Threadlike structures that contain deoxyribonucleic acid, or DNA.

11. **DNA** A complex molecule that contains genetic information.

12. **gene** The units of hereditary information, which are short segments composed of DNA.

13. **genotype** A person's genetic heritage; the actual genetic material.

14. **phenotype** The way an individual's genotype is expressed in observed and measurable characteristics.

15. **behavior genetics** The study of the degree and nature of behavior's hereditary basis.

16. **twin study** A study in which the behavioral similarity of identical twins is compared with the behavioral similarity of fraternal twins.

17. **adoption study** A study in which investigators seek to discover whether, in behavior and psychological characteristics, adopted children and adolescents are more like their adoptive parents, who provided a

home environment, or their biological parents, who contributed to their heredity. Another form of adoption study is to compare adoptive and biological siblings.

18. **passive genotype-environment correlations** Occur when parents who are genetically related to the child provide a rearing environment for the child.

19. **evocative genotype-environment correlations** Occur when the adolescent's genotype elicits certain types of physical and social environments.

20. **active (niche-picking) genotype-environment correlations** Occur when adolescents seek out environments they find compatible and stimulating.

21. **shared environmental influences** Adolescents common environmental experiences that are shared with their sibling, such as their parents' personalities and intellectual orientation, the family's social class, and the neighborhood in which they live.

22. **nonshared environmental influences** The adolescent's own unique experiences, both within a family and outside the family that are not shared by another sibling.

23. **epigenetic view** The epigenetic view emphasizes that development is the result of an ongoing, bidirectional interchange between heredity and the environment.

## KEY PEOPLE IN THE STUDY OF ADOLESCENCE

| | | |
|---|---|---|
| 1. B | 4. F | 7. H |
| 2. I | 5. D | 8. G |
| 3. C | 6. E | 9. A |

## "DR. DETAIL'S" PUZZLE

*Down*
1. estrogens
2. hormones
3. phenotype
4. neurons

*Across*
1. menarche
2. androgens
3. puberty
4. genotype
5. spermarche

## ADOLENCENT MYTH AND FACT

| | | | | | |
|---|---|---|---|---|---|
| 1. F | 7. T | 13. T |
| 2. F | 8. F | 14. F |
| 3. T | 9. F | 15. T |
| 4. T | 10. T | 16. T |
| 5. F | 11. F | 17. T |
| 6. F | 12. T | |

## PUBERTY
## SECTION REVIEW

1. Puberty ends long before adolescence does.

2. It is programmed into the genes, but the environment can influence it.

3. Androgen plays an important role in male pubertal development. Estrogen plays an important role in female pubertal development.

4. Testosterone is associated with the development of external genitals, increase in height, and change in voice.

5. The endocrine system's role in puberty involves the interaction of the hypothalamus, the pituitary gland, and the gonads.

6. The hypothalamus monitors eating, drinking, and sex. The pituitary gland controls growth and regulates other glands.

7. The pituitary gland sends a signal via gonadotropins to the appropriate gland to manufacture the hormone. Then the pituitary gland, through interaction with the hypothalamus, detects when the optimal level of hormones is reached and responds by maintaining gonadotropin secretion.

8. It works in the body like a thermostat-furnace system.

9. Andrenarche and gonadarche.

10. Some researchers believe that a child must reach a critical mass before puberty starts. Some have proposed a body weight of 106 pounds $\pm$ 3 pounds. Others have suggested that body fat, as a proportion of one's entire weight, must reach a certain target.

11. First breasts enlarge or pubic hair appears. Later, hair appears in the armpits, height increases, and the hips become wider.

12. The term refers to patterns over time, especially across generations.

13. Girls in puberty are less happy with their bodies and have more negative body images when compared to boys, who are pleased to see their muscles develop.

14. Hormonal factors are thought to account for at least part of the increase in negative and variable emotions (e.g., depression or aggression) that characterize adolescents.

15. Early maturing boys perceived themselves more positively and had more successful peer relations. Early maturing girls had a similar outcome to early boys, but not as pronounced. Some are cognitively not ready for social activities. Late maturing boys faced many challenges, but they developed a strong sense of identity; perhaps due to adversity. Late maturing girls develop at a better pace and tend to grow to be tall and slender, which can be socially advantageous.

16. A physician may recommend hormonal treatment.

## KEY PEOPLE IN SECTION

**Roberta Simmons and Dale Blyth** — developed a longitudinal studied of early and late maturing males and females.

## THE BRAIN
## SECTION REVIEW

1. The dendrite, cell body, and axon.

2. Much of the neuron does not change; however, axons develop throughout adolescence.

3. Blooming is the development of new connections, whereas pruning is where connections between neurons are eliminated. Blooming and pruning in the brain appears to very a great deal by section.

4.    1. D        2. A        3. B        4. C

5.    MRIs have shown the significant changes that the brain goes through between ages 3 and 15. Some areas dramatically gain 'material' in a short period of time, while other areas appear to 'purge' unneeded cells,

6.    The conceptualization of "right" and "left-brained" individuals has oversimplified the acquiring of specific skills in the developing brain.

## EVOLUTION, HEREDITY, AND ENVIRONMENT
## SECTION REVIEW

1.    A genotype is a person's genetic heritage, the actual genetic material. A phenotype is the way an individual's genotype is expressed and observed.

2.    In evolutionary conceptions of psychology, adaptive behavior is a modification of behavior that promotes an organism's survival in the natural habitat.

3     Bandura has complained about the biologizing of psychology. While he acknowledges the influence of evolution on human adaptation and change, he rejects what he calls "one-sided evolutionism" in which social behavior is seen as a by-product of evolved biology. Bandura believes that evolutionary pressures favored biological adaptations that encouraged the use of tools, allowing humans to manipulate, alter, and construct new environmental conditions. In time, humans' increasingly complex environmental innovations produced new pressures that favored the evolution of specialized brain systems to support consciousness, thought, and language.

4.    Twin and adoption studies are often used to study heredity's influence on behavior.

5.    Plomin has noted that even when living under the same roof, experiences are often very different.

6.    Judith Harris's recent book, *The Nurture Assumption*, dramatically downplays the role parents play in the development of their child's personality. This caused much new debate on nature versus nurture.

7.    The epigenetic view emphasizes that development is the result of ongoing, bi-directional interchange between heredity and the environment.

## KEY PEOPLE IN SECTION

**Sandra Scarr**—describes three ways heredity and environment are correlated: passively, evocatively, and actively.

**Robert Plomin**—believes that common rearing accounts for little of the difference in adolescents' personality or interests.

**Charles Darwin**—noted that most species reproduce at rates that would cause enormous increases in their population and yet populations remain nearly constant.

**Judith Harris** her provocative book, *The Nurture Assumption*, ignited the most recent nature-nurture controversy.

**David Buss**—his ideas on evolutionary psychology have produced a wave of interest in how evolution can explain human behavior.

**Stephen Jay Gould**—concluded that in most domains, human biology allows for a broad range of cultural possibilities.

# EXPLORATIONS IN ADOLESCENCE

No answers provided—individual reflection and response.


# COGNITIVE CHALLENGE

No answers provided—individual reflection and response.


# ADOLESCENCE IN RESEARCH

This longitudinal study followed more than 450 individuals in Milwaukee, Wisconsin, for 5 years from sixth to tenth grade. Researchers interviewed students individually and obtained their achievement test scores and grade point averages were obtained. The researchers found that early-maturing girls had more problems in school, were more independent, and were more popular with boys when compared to late-maturing girls.

## ⊠ COMPREHENSIVE REVIEW

| | | | |
|---|---|---|---|
| 1. d | 11. b | 21. c | 31. d |
| 2. b | 12. b | 22. d | 32. c |
| 3. b | 13. b | 23. d | 33. b |
| 4. a | 14. c | 24. c | 34. d |
| 5. b | 15. c | 25. a | 35. d |
| 6. d | 16. c | 26. a | 36. c |
| 7. c | 17. c | 27. c | 37. d |
| 8. c | 18. a | 28. c | 38. c |
| 9. c | 19. c | 29. a | 39. a |
| 10. a | 20. d | 30. b | 40. b |

# ✦ Chapter 4    Cognitive Development

**Learning Goals with Key Terms and Key People in Boldface**

**1.0**    **DISCUSS THE COGNITIVE DEVELOPMENTAL VIEW OF ADOLESCENCE**

    **A.**    **Piaget's Theory**

        1.1     What is Piaget's theory of cognitive processes?

        1.2     Define a **schema**?

        1.3     What roles do **assimilation** and **accommodation** play in cognitive development?

        1.4     What did Piaget mean by **equilibration**?

        1.5     What are names and defining characteristics of Piaget's four stages of cognitive development?

        1.6     How does an infant learn about the world in the **sensorimotor stage**?

        1.7     What happens in the **preoperational stage**?

        1.8     Identify the characteristics of the **concrete operational stage**?

        1.9     What did Piaget mean by **operations**?

        1.10   Detail the characteristics of **conservation and classification**?

        1.11   What are the indicators of the **formal operational stage**?

        1.12   Explain **hypothetical-deductive reasoning**?

        1.13   What were Piaget's main contributions to understanding cognitive development?

        1.14   What are the major criticisms of Piaget's theory?

        1.15   What are the distinctions between **early formal operational thought** and **late formal operational thought**?

        1.16   What principles of Piaget's theory of cognitive development can be applied to education?

        1.17   What were Piaget's main contributions, and has the theory withstood the test of time?

        1.18   Who are the **neo-Piagetians** who expanded and modified Piaget's theory?

        1.19   How strong is the evidence for a fifth, **postformal** stage of cognitive development?

    **B.**    **Vygotsky's Theory**

        1.20   What were Vygotsky's main contributions to cognitive developmental theory?

        1.21   What did Lev Vygotsky mean by the **zone of proximal development (ZPD)?**

        1.22   How do the concepts of **scaffolding, cognitive apprenticeship, tutoring, cooperative learning,** and **reciprocal teaching** contribute to cognitive development and learning?

        1.23   Why do we say that Piaget and Vygotsky both were proponents of **constructivism**?

        1.24   What is the difference between a cognitive constructivist approach and a **social constructivist approach**?

**2.0**    **DESCRIBE THE INFORMATION-PROCESSING VIEW OF ADOLESCENCE?**

    **A.**    **Cognitive Resources**

        2.1     Identify two things that, as they increase, likely influence developmental changes.

        2.2     What do increases in processing information influence?

    **B.**    **Mechanisms of Change**

        2.3     What, according to Robert Siegler, are the three main characteristics of the information processing approach to cognitive development?

        2.4     Identify the components of thinking, change mechanisms, and self-modification?

        2.5     Define encoding?

        2.6     What does automaticity refer to?

    C.    **Attention and Memory**

      2.7    What are **attention** and **memory**, and why are they such important adolescent cognitive processes?

      2.8    What are the functions of short-term memory and long-term memory?

      2.9    Why do many theorists choose to apply the concept of working memory?

      2.10    How is long-term memory different from working memory?

    D.    **Decision Making and Thinking**

      2.11    What do we know about adolescent decision-making ability?

      2.12    How is adolescent decision making different from that of children?

    E.    **Expertise**

      2.13    What determines whether someone is considered an expert or not?

    F.    **Metacognition and Self-Regulatory Learning**

      2.14    What is **metacognition**?

      2.15    How can adolescents develop better learning strategies?

      2.16    Describe **self-regulatory learning**?

      2.17    What are five characteristics of self-regulatory learners?

      2.18    How can teachers or parents help students become self-regulatory learners?

**3.0    SUMMARIZE THE PSYCHOMETRIC/INTELLIGENCE VIEW OF ADOLESCENCE**

    A.    **The Psychometric/Intelligence View**

      3.1    What does the **psychometric/intelligence view** emphasize?

      3.2    What did Huxley mean when he used the word intelligence?

      3.3    What is the traditional definition of **intelligence**?

    B.    **Intelligence Tests**

      3.4    What was the first valid intelligence test and why was it developed?

      3.5    What was Binet's concept of **mental age (MA)**?

      3.6    What is an **intelligence quotient (IQ)**?

      3.7    What is a **normal distribution**?

      3.8    What are the Wechsler scales and what kind of IQ scores do they yield?

      3.9    How are the Wechsler and Stanford-Binet scales similar or different?

      3.10    How are intelligence tests misused?

    C.    **Multiple Intelligences**

      3.11    What was the concept of general intelligence and what are its origins?

      3.12    Explain Spearman's two-factor theory.

      3.13    What were Thurstone's 7 primary mental abilities?

      3.14    According to Howard Gardner, what are the eight types of intelligence?

      3.15    What are the components of Sternberg's **triarchic theory of intelligence**?

      3.16    How are Gardner's and Sternberg's theories different, and how are they the same?

    D.    **Controversies and Cultural/Ethnic Comparisons in Intelligence**

      3.17    How strong is the effect of heredity on intelligence?

    E.    **Controversies and Issues in Intelligence**

      3.18    Is nature or nurture more important in determining intelligence?

      3.19    Why is intelligence increasing around the globe?

      3.20    Are there cultural differences in intelligence?

      3.21    What are the characteristics of **culture-fair tests**?

      3.22    Are intelligence tests culturally biased?

      3.23    What controversy did the publication of the book, The Bell Curve, by Herrnstein and Murray caused?

      3.24    What are the appropriate uses of intelligence tests? What uses are inappropriate?

      3.25    Does gender influence intelligence?

**4.0    EXPLAIN HOW SOCIAL COGNITION IS INVOLVED IN DEVELOPMENT**

**A.    Adolescent Egocentrism**

    4.1    What is **adolescent egocentrism** and what types of thinking does it include?

    4.2    What does David Elkind believe brings on adolescent egocentrism?

    4.3    What is an **imaginary audience**?

    4.4    What is the **personal fable**?

**B.    Perspective Taking**

    4.5    What is perspective taking, and how does it influence adolescent egocentrism?

**C.    Implicit Personality Theory**

    4.6    What is **implicit personality theory**?

    4.7    Do adolescents conceptualize an individual's personality differently than children?

**D.    Social Cognition in the Rest of the Text**

    4.8    What areas of adolescent development have been influenced by the concept of social cognition?

# Exercises

## KEY TERMS

This exercise presents each key term in the form of an incomplete sentence. Complete each sentence by either defining the term or giving an example of it. Compare your definitions with those given at the end of the study guide chapter.

1.    Piaget's interest in **schemas**

    _____

    _____

2.    **Assimilation** occurs when

    _____

    _____

3.    Suzy demonstrates **accommodation** when she

    _____

    _____

4.    **Equilibration** is a mechanism

    _____

    _____

5.    You can tell that Jeannine is in the **sensorimotor stage** because

    _____

    _____

6. Jared has now entered the **preoperational stage** in that he

_____

_____

7. In the **concrete operational stage,** children can engage in

_____

_____

8. You can tell that Ramon is in the **formal operational stage** because

_____

_____

9. **Hypothetical-deductive reasoning** is used to

_____

_____

10. **Neo-Piagetians** argue that

_____

_____

11. **Post-formal thought** is most likely seen in

_____

_____

12. The **zone of proximal development (ZPD)** refers to

_____

_____

13. **The social constructivist approach** is

_____

_____

14. Alex is good at **critical thinking** because

_____

_____

15. **Creativity** is the ability to

_____

_____

16. An example of **convergent thinking** is

_____

_____

17. An example of **divergent thinking** is

_____

_____

18. Cognitive psychologists define **metacognition** as

_____

_____

19. **Self-regulatory learning** consists of

_____

_____

20. The **psychometric/intelligence view** emphasizes

_____

_____

21. Some experts describe **intelligence** as

_____

_____

22. **Mental age (MA)** is an individual's

_____

_____

23. William Stern created the **intelligence quotient (IQ),** which refers to

_____

_____

24. A **normal distribution** is

_____

_____

25. **Emotional intelligence** was proposed as a

_____

_____

26. **Heritability** is seen as

_____

27.     What are examples of **culture fair tests?**

_____

_____

28.     Chris is going through a stage of **adolescent egocentrism** that is leading him to

_____

_____

29.     The **Triarchic Theory of Intelligence** suggests that

_____

_____

## KEY PEOPLE IN THE STUDY OF ADOLESCENCE

Match the name with the concept, issue, or topic related to adolescence with which they are associated.

| | | |
|---|---|---|
| ___ | 1. Jean Piaget | A. Multiple intelligences |
| ___ | 2. Lev Vygotsky | B. Mental age (MA) |
| ___ | 3. Nathan Brody | C. Four stages of cognitive development |
| ___ | 4. Annamarie Palincsar & Ann Brown | D. General intelligence |
| ___ | 5. Robert Siegler | E. Triarchic theory of intelligence |
| ___ | 6. Robbie Case | F. Zone of proximal development |
| ___ | 7. Peter Salovey & John Mayer | G. Felt that intelligence tests can predict school and job success |
| ___ | 8. J.P. Guilford | H. Information processing view |
| ___ | 9. Mihalyi Csikszentmihalyi | I. Reciprocal teaching |
| ___ | 10. Michael Pressley | J. Automaticity |
| ___ | 11. Robert Serpell | K. Creativity |
| ___ | 12. Alfred Binet | L. Developed a test that measures emotional intelligence |
| ___ | 13. William Stern | M. Strategies |
| ___ | 14. David Wechsler | N. Primary abilities related to intelligence |
| ___ | 15. Charles Spearman | O. Developed IQ tests with several subscales |
| ___ | 16. L. L. Thurstone | P. Emotional intelligence |
| ___ | 17. Robert Sternberg | Q. Imaginary audience & personal fable |
| ___ | 18. Howard Gardner | R. Cognitive development occurs as new generations collaborate with old generations |
| ___ | 19. Daniel Goleman | S. Authors of *The Bell Curve* |
| ___ | 20. David Elkind | T. Convergent & divergent thinking |
| ___ | 21. K. Warner Schaie | U. Intelligence quotient (IQ) |
| ___ | 22. Richard Herrnstein & Charles Murray | V. Studied intelligence in rural African communities |
| ___ | 23. Barbara Rogoff | W. Suggested that formal operations probably marks the end of adult gains in scientific thinking |

81

# "DR. DETAIL'S" TERM MATCHING EXERCISE

Match the term with the correct definition.

| | | | |
|---|---|---|---|
| ____ | 1. Operations | A. | Refers to changing the level of support over the course of a teaching session |
| ____ | 2. Conservation | B. | An expert stretches and supports the novice's understanding of and use of the culture's skills |
| ____ | 3. Classification | C. | The retention of information over time |
| ____ | 4. early formal operational thought | D. | Emphasis is on the individual's cognitive construction of knowledge and understanding |
| ____ | 5. late formal operational thought | E. | May appear during the middle adolescent years |
| ____ | 6. Scaffolding | F. | Involves students taking turns leading a small-group discussion |
| ____ | 7. cognitive apprenticeship | G. | Mental actions that allow the individual to do mentally what was done before physically |
| ____ | 8. cooperative learning | H. | Limited capacity memory where information is retained for 30 seconds unless rehearsed |
| ____ | 9. reciprocal teaching | I. | Emphasizes that individuals actively construct knowledge and understanding |
| ____ | 10. Constructivism | J. | Emphasis is on collaboration with others to produce knowledge and understanding |
| ____ | 11. cognitive constructivist approach | K. | Piaget's term for an individual's ability to recognize that the length, number, mass, quantity, area, weight, and volume of objects and substances do not change through transformations that alter their appearance |
| ____ | 12. social constructivist approach | L. | Involves students working in small groups to help each other learn |
| ____ | 13. Memory | M | Adolescent's have increased ability to think hypothetically |
| ____ | 14. short-term memory | N. | Piaget's concept of concrete operational thought, in which children systematically organize objects into hierarchies of classes and subclasses |
| ____ | 15. working memory | O. | Knowing about one's own (and others') knowing |
| ____ | 16. long-term memory | P. | A sense that adolescents have that they are unique, untouchable, and that no one else can understand them |
| ____ | 17. meta-knowing skills | Q. | Mental workbench where information is manipulated and assembled to help make decisions |
| ____ | 18. imaginary audience | R. | A relatively permanent memory system |
| ____ | 19. personal fable | S. | Adolescents believe they are the main actors in an imagined play, and all others are in the audience |
| ____ | 20. Encoding | T. | The ability to process information with little or no effort |
| ____ | 21. Automaticity | U. | The process by which information gets into memory |

# ADOLESCENT MYTH AND FACT

Which of the following statements regarding adolescents are true (T) and which are false (F)?

1.  Piaget's theory is the best known and most widely discussed theory of adolescent cognitive development. T or F

2.  In Piaget's theory, a person's cognition is quantitatively different in one stage compared with another. T or F

3.  Formal operational thought is a homogeneous stage of development. T or F

4.  Not all adolescents are full-fledged formal operational thinkers. T or F

5.  Most contemporary developmentalists agree that children's cognitive development is not as stage-like Piaget suggested. T or F

6.  Research has shown postformal thought to be a qualitatively more advanced stage than formal operational thought. T or F

7.  Cognitive psychologist Robert J. Sternberg believes that most school programs that teach critical thinking are doing an appropriate job. T or F

8.  All highly intelligent adolescents also are creative. T or F

9.  Motivation and effort alone can produce expertise. T or F

10. Talent alone can produce an expert. T or F

11. Intelligence cannot be directly measured. T or F

12. If misapplied or misused, IQ scores can become self-fulfilling prophecies. T or F

13. In their book, *The Bell Curve*, Herrnstein and Murray suggested that shortcomings of welfare, poverty, and crime might doom a large proportion of the underclass. T or F

14. African American students do more poorly when they think they are being evaluated; whereas if they think the test doesn't count they perform about the same as White students. T or F

15. Adolescent egocentrism is believed to be strongly linked with development of a *personal fable*. T or F

# PIAGET'S THEORY
# SECTION REVIEW

1.  Using any event or experience of your choice, describe how an existing schema changed because of disequilibrium, assimilation, and accommodation.

    _____

    _____

2.  Compare and contrast *assimilation* and *accommodation*.

    _____

    _____

3.   How do children apply the mechanism, equilibration, in everyday life?

_____

_____

4.   List and discuss the four stages of cognitive development according to Piaget.

_____

_____

5.   Compare and contrast *conservation* and *classification*.

_____

_____

6.   What were Piaget's main contributions to developmental theory?

_____

_____

7.   How has Piaget's theory withstood the test of time?

_____

_____

8.   What are some criticisms of Piaget's theory?

_____

_____

9.   Some developmentalists believe that formal operational thought consists of two subperiods. What are these?

_____

_____

KEY PEOPLE IN SECTION (describe the contributions of this individual to the study and understanding of adolescence).

**David Elkind —** _____

_____.

**Robbie Case —** _____

_____.

**K. Warner Schaie —** _____

_____.

**William Perry —** _____

_____.

# VYGOTSKY'S THEORY
## SECTION REVIEW

1.  Fill in the boxes with the descriptions comparing the views of Piaget and Vygotsky.

| Topic | Vygotsky | Piaget |
|---|---|---|
| Constructivism | | |
| Stages | | |
| View on Education | | |
| Teaching Implications | | |

2.  What did Vygotsky mean by the zone of proximal development?

    _____

    _____

3.  Explain how each of these contemporary cognitive concepts would be utilized in a high school classroom.
    a.  scaffolding

    _____

    _____

    b.  cognitive apprenticeship

    _____

    _____

    c.  tutoring

    _____

    _____

    d.  cooperative learning

    _____

    _____

    e.  reciprocal teaching

    _____

    _____

4.  Contrast the cognitive constructivist approach and social constructiveness approach.

    _____

5.      What are some criticisms of Vygotsky's theory or approach?

_____

_____


KEY PEOPLE IN SECTION (describe the contributions of this individual to the study and understanding of adolescence)

**Barbara Rogoff —** _____

_____.

**Ann Brown and Annemarie Palincsar —** _____

_____.


## THE INFORMATION-PROCESSING VIEW
## SECTION REVIEW

1.      Describe the three main characteristics of the information-processing approach.

_____

_____


2.      Describe the following types of memory:

   a.     short-term memory

_____

   b.     working memory

_____

   c.     long-term memory

_____

3.      How competent are adolescents at making decisions?

_____

_____

4.      What are some cognitive changes that allow for improved critical thinking in adolescence?

_____

_____

5.      Compare and contrast convergent and divergent thinking.

_____

_____

6.      Outline strategies to help adolescents become more creative.

_____

_____

7.      How might short-term memory be used in problem solving?

_____

_____

8.      What are critical thinking skills that Sternberg believes adolescents need in everyday living?

_____

_____

9.      What are the characteristics of self-regulatory learners?

_____

_____

KEY PEOPLE IN SECTION (describe the contributions of this individual to the study and understanding of adolescence)

**Robert Siegler** — _____

_____.

**Robbie Case** — _____

_____.

**Robert Sternberg** — _____

_____.

**J.P. Guilford** — _____

_____.

**Mark Strand** — _____

_____.

**Michael Pressley** — _____

_____.

**Barry Zimmerman, Sebastian Bonner, and Robert Kovach** — _____

_____.

# THE PSYCHOMETRIC/INTELLIGENCE VIEW
## SECTION REVIEW

1.      Calculate the following I.Q.s using Stern's formula ($IQ=MA/CA \times 100$).

   a. MA = 10, CA = 8 _____
   b. MA = 5, CA = 9 _____
   c. MA = 15, CA = 12 _____

2.      How do the Wechsler scales differ from the tests developed by Binet?

   _____

   _____

3.      What is meant by a normal distribution?

   _____

   _____

4.      Match the skills indicative of each of Gardner's eight frames of mind with the profession or vocation they are most likely to be associated with.

   ___    1.   scientists, engineers, accountants       A.   verbal skills
   ___    2.   farmers, botanists, landscapers          B.   intrapersonal
   ___    3.   teachers and mental health               C.   mathematical
               professionals
   ___    4.   surgeons, dancers, athletes              D.   naturalist
   ___    5.   composers and musicians                  E.   spatial
   ___    6.   theologians and psychologists            F.   interpersonal
   ___    7.   authors, journalists, speakers           G.   bodily-kinesthetic
   ___    8.   architects, artists, sailors             H.   musical

5.      Describe how each of components of Sternberg's triarchic theory of intelligence would be utilized in writing a book report.

   _____

   _____

6.      According to the Mayer-Salovey-Caruso Emotional Intelligence Test, emotional intelligence involves four main areas:

   _____

   _____

7.      Summarize the status of the following debates about intelligence:

   a.      Nature and nurture

   _____

   _____

b.   Ethnicity and culture

_____

_____


c.   Use and misuse of intelligence tests

_____

_____


8.   How strong is the effect of heredity on intelligence?

_____

_____


**KEY PEOPLE IN SECTION** (describe the contributions of this individual to the study and understanding of adolescence).

**Aldous Huxley** — _____

_____

**Alfred Binet** — _____

_____.

**Theophile Simon** — _____

_____.

**William Stern** — _____

_____.

**Lewis Terman** — _____

_____.

**David Wechsler** — _____

_____.

**Charles Spearmman** — _____

_____.

**L.L. Thurstone** — _____

_____.

**Robert Sternberg** — _____

_____ .

**Howard Gardner** — _____

_____ .

**Daniel Goleman** — _____

_____ .

**Nathan Brody** — _____

_____ .

**John Carroll** — _____

_____ .

**Robert Serpell** — _____

_____ .

**Elena Grigorenko** — _____

_____ .

**Richard Herrnstein and Charles Murray** — _____

_____ .

## SOCIAL COGNITION
## SECTION REVIEW

1.    Do you have a personal fable? What does it consist of? Do you think that it is important to have a personal fable? Why or why not?

_____

_____

2.    Can the imaginary audience lead adolescents to make bad decisions?

_____

_____

3.    How is perspective taking involved in the development of adolescent egocentrism?

_____

4.  Do adolescents conceptualize an individual's personality differently than children do?

_____

_____


5.  In what three ways do adolescents interpret personality differently than other children?

_____

_____


KEY PEOPLE IN SECTION (describe the contributions of this individual to the study and understanding of adolescence).

**David Elkind —** _____

_____.


# EXPLORATIONS IN ADOLESCENCE

How can the *imaginary audience* and *personal fable* affect you in a positive, or negative way?
  a.   imaginary audience

_____

_____


  b.   personal fable

_____

_____


# COGNITIVE CHALLENGE

If you could go back to high school and restructure the courses and curriculum there, how could you add more critical opportunities?

_____

_____


# ADOLESCENCE IN RESEARCH

Concerning Siegler's 1998 research regarding adolescent information-processing, state the hypothesis, the research methods (if known), the research conclusions, and the implications and applications for adolescent development.

_____

1. According to Jean Piaget, the fundamental ways in which adolescents adapt their thinking entails
   a. conservation and classification.
   b. social information processing and perspective taking.
   c. the imaginary audience and the personal fable.
   d. assimilation and accommodation.

2. _____ are used in actively constructing the world of an adolescent.
   a. Norms                     c. Equilibration
   b. Schemas                   d. Beliefs

3. When he learned the value of money, Kenny initially thought that a nickel was worth more than a dime. Recently, as he has begun to buy items, Kenny has come to realize the value of a dime. The process by which Kenny adapted his schema is
   a. assimilation.             c. equilibration.
   b. accommodation.            d. metacognition.

4. Piaget believed that there is considerable movement between states of cognitive equilibrium and disequilibrium as assimilation and accommodation work in concert to produce cognitive change. He called this
   a. assimilation.             c. equilibration.
   b. accommodation.            d. metacognition.

5. In which of Piaget's cognitive stages do we see the beginnings of symbolic thought.
   a. sensorimotor stage        c. preoperational stage
   b. formal operations stage   d. concrete operational stage

6. Which of the following is NOT a stage of cognitive development according to Piaget?
   a. sensorimotor              c. concrete operational
   b. preoperational            d. informal operational

7. When children begin representing their worlds in images and words, they are in which stage of cognitive development?
   a. sensorimotor              c. concrete operational
   b. preoperational            d. informal operational

8. According to Piaget, in the _____ individuals begin to do mentally what was previously done physically.
   a. formal operations stage   c. preoperational stage
   b. sensorimotor stage        d. concrete operational stage

9. Jimmy can systematically organize his marbles into different categories and qualities. Piaget would call this process
   a. perspective taking.       c. organization.
   b. classification.           d. conservation.

10. Unlike the concrete operational child, the formal operational adolescent can demonstrate
    a.   assimilation.                          c.   conservation ability.
    b.   reversible mental operations.          d.   hypothetical-deductive reasoning.

11. Compared to the early formal operational problem solver, the late formal operational solver
    a.   derives her hypothesis from the problem data.
    b.   looks for a general hypothesis to explain what has happened.
    c.   is satisfied with general statements about cause and effect.
    d.   searches for necessary and sufficient conditions to explain the results.

12. Late in his career, Piaget concluded that formal operational thought is achieved by _____ years of age.
    a.   11 to 15                              c.   15 to 20
    b.   20 to 25                              d.   7 to 12

13. _____ believe that cognitive development is more specific in many respects than Piaget described.
    a.   Piagetians                           c.   Competency-based developmentalists
    b.   Neo-Piagetians                        d.   Information processing developmentalists

14. A general criticism of Piaget's theory is it tends to underestimate the importance of ____ in cognitive development.
    a.   culture and education                c.   authority and mystery
    b.   arts and entertainment               d.   sexuality and role playing

15. A review of formal operational thought revealed that ____ out of every ____ eighth grade students is a formal operational thinker.
    a.   1; 4                                 c.   1; 2
    b.   1; 3                                 d.   4; 5

16. Which of the following is NOT a criticism of Piaget's theory?
    a.   His theory assumes developmental synchrony, but that is often not the case.
    b.   Some cognitive abilities emerge earlier than Piaget thought.
    c.   Some children can be trained to perform at a higher level.
    d.   Piaget's theory focuses too much on childhood sexual development.

17. Conservation of number has been demonstrated as early as age
    a.   7                                    c.   5
    b.   3                                    d.   1

18. Tasks too difficult for an individual that can be mastered with the help of more skilled individuals defines what?
    a.   Jean Piaget called it hypothetical-deductive reasoning.
    b.   Lev Vygotsky called it the zone of proximal development.
    c.   Kurt Fisher called them abstract relations.
    d.   Neo-Piagetians called it social information.

19. _____ was considered a genius at observing children.
    a.   Sigmund Freud                        c.   Jean Piaget
    b.   Lev Vygotsky                         d.   William Perry

20. The leading proponent of the neo-Piagetian viewpoint was
    a. K. Warner Schaie     c. William Perry
    b. Robbie Case     d. Lev Vygotsky

21. Adolescent egocentrism is represented by two types of thinking referred to as
    a. the imaginary audience and the personal fable.
    b. the abiding self and the transient self.
    c. narcissism and the imaginary audience.
    d. the indestructible self and the transient self.

22. According to Mayer (2003), _____ represent changes in the way individuals process information.
    a. changes in mood and temperament
    b. ·changes in attention and memory
    c. changes in memory and retrieval
    d. changes in organization and learning skills

23. The teacher tells Marty to think of how many different sculptures he can make out of snow. This is an exercise in
    a. magical thinking     c. artistic thinking
    b. convergent thinking     d. divergent thinking

24. _____ reported he was terrified of taking IQ tests as a child?
    a. Howard Gardner     c. Robert Sternberg
    b. Theophile Simon     d. David Wechsler

25. _____ is credited with developing the concept of mental age (MA)?
    a. William Stern     c. Alfred Binet
    b. Theophile Simon     d. David Wechsler

26. _____ is credited with developing the formula for calculating I.Q. (IQ = MA/CA x 100)?
    a. William Stern     c. Alfred Binet
    b. Theophile Simon     d. David Wechsler

27. Which of the following is NOT one of Howard Gardner's eight types of intelligence?
    a. verbal skills     c. cooking skills
    b. musical skills     d. naturalist skills

28. _____ is a kind of mental "workbench" where individuals manipulate and assemble information when they make decisions.
    a. working memory     c. long-term memory
    b. short-term memory     d. flashbulb memory

29. The ability to solve problems and adapt to everyday experiences defines
    a. creativity.     c. intelligence.
    b. critical thinking.     d. culture.

30. _____ devised his own IQ test at age 13 and used it to assess his classmates in school.
    a. David Wechsler     c. Robert Sternberg
    b. Alfred Binet     d. Theophile Simon

31. Which of the following is NOT one of the four content areas measured by the Stanford-Binet?
   a.   short-term memory                c.   long-term memory
   b.   verbal reasoning                  d.   quantitative reasoning

32. The _____ is generally considered to be a culture-fair test?
   a.   Stanford-Binet test
   b.   Wechsler test
   c.   Raven Progressive Matrices test
   d.   Kaufman Assessment Battery for Children

33. While taking an IQ test, a series of numbers is read aloud to a student, and the student is asked to repeat them as quickly as possible. This exercise assesses
   a.   long-term memory.                 c.   digital memory.
   b.   short-term memory.                d.   conceptual memory.

34. According to Brody (2000), IQ in the sixth grade correlates about _____ with the number of years of education an individual will eventually obtain.
   a.   .20                               c.   .60
   b.   .40                               d.   .80

35. Which of the following is NOT one of the seven primary mental abilities noted in Thurstone's Multiple-Factor Theory?
   a.   verbal comprehension
   b.   naturalist skills
   c.   word fluency
   d.   reasoning

36. One of the main advantages of the Wechsler scales over the Binet test is that the Wechsler scales include measures that are
   a.   progressive.                      c.   not verbal.
   b.   culturally specific.              d.   screen for brain damage.

37. In Spearman's *two-factor theory*, g stands for _____ and s stands for _____.
   a.   generality; specialization
   b.   general intelligence; specific abilities
   c.   gestalt; Spearman
   d,   goodness of fit; special traits

38. Which of the following individuals did NOT propose a theory of intelligence?
   a.   L.L. Thurstone                    c.   Charles Spearman
   b.   Lewis Terman                      d.   Howard Gardner

39. The type or aspect of intelligence measured by the Binet and Wechsler tests is most closely matched to the aspect Sternberg calls
   a.   componential intelligence.        c.   contextual intelligence.
   b.   experiential intelligence.        d.   tacit knowledge.

40. According to Howard Gardner,
   a.   it is better to administer intelligence tests to individuals than to groups.
   b.   intelligence is best defined in terms of eight types.
   c.   individuals have a general intelligence rather than various specific intelligences.

d.      intelligence is best defined in terms of three main components.

41.    In addition to the question of whether intelligence is primarily inherited, another important question about intelligence concerns
a.      the arbitrary distinction between aptitude and achievement tests.
b.      cultural and ethnic differences in test scores.
c.      using the computer as a model for information processing.
d.      the emotional and social adjustment of gifted individuals.

42.    Intelligence tests that are explicitly designed to minimize the differences between ethnic groups are called
a.      bias liberated.                      c.      socially equitable.
b.      culture fair.                         d.      psychometrically equivalent.

43.    A psychology professor asks his students to think of as many uses as possible for a paper clip. The professor is encouraging
a.      brainstorming.                      c.      convergent thinking.
b.      divergent thinking               d.      ideational originality.

44.    Which of the following is NOT one of Gardner's eight types of intelligence?
a.      verbal skills                        c.      bodily-kinesthetic skills
b.      perceptual speed                 d.      musical skills

45.    In Sternberg's view of analytical intelligence, the basic unit of analytical intelligence is
a.      a schema                            c.      $g$
b.      a component                       d.      $s$

46.    If children took the 1932 Stanford-Binet IQ test today, the average score would be
a.      80                                      c.      120
b.      100                                     d.      140

## ADOLESCENCE ON THE SCREEN

- *Phenomenon* explores the problems that come with high levels of intelligence.

- *Little Man Tate* depicts the education of a young child prodigy.

- *Searching for Bobby Fischer* depicts parents facing the dilemma of raising a gifted chess prodigy.

## ADOLESCENCE IN BOOKS

- *Teaching and Learning Through Multiple Intelligences (Second Edition)*, by Linda Campbell, Bruce Campbell, and Dee Dickonson (Allyn & Bacon, 1999), provides applications of Gardner's eight intelligences to classrooms.

- *How People Learn*, by Committee on Developments in the Science of Learning (National Academy Press, 1999), describes the current state of knowledge about how children and youth think and learn.

- *Creating Minds*, by Howard Gardner (New York: Basic Books, 1993), proposes that intelligence can be divided into seven basic forms.

# Answer Key

## KEY TERMS

1. **schema** Piaget's theory of a concept or framework that exists in the individual's mind to organize and interpret information.

2. **assimilation** Occurs when individuals incorporate new information into existing knowledge.

3. **accommodation** Occurs when individuals adjust to new information.

4. **equilibration** A mechanism in Piaget's theory that explains how children or adolescents shift from one stage of thought to the next. The shift occurs as they experience cognitive conflict or a disequilibrium in trying to understand the world. Eventually, the child or adolescent resolves the conflict and reaches a balance or equilibrium.

5. **sensorimotor stage** Piaget's first stage of development, lasting from birth until about 2 years of age. In this stage, infants construct an understanding of the world by coordinating sensory experiences with physical, motoric actions.

6. **preoperational stage** Piaget's second stage, which lasts from about 2 years of age until 7 years of age. In this stage children begin to represent their world with words, images, and drawings.

7. **concrete operational thought** Piaget's third stage, which lasts from about 7 years of age until 11 years of age. In this stage, children can perform operations. Logical reasoning replaces intuitive thought as long as the child can apply the reasoning to specific or concrete examples.

8. **formal operational thought** Piaget's fourth and final stage of cognitive development, which he believes emerges between 11 to 15 years of age. It is characterized by abstract, idealistic, and logical thought.

9. **hypothetical-deductive reasoning** Piaget's term for adolescents' ability, in the formal operational stage, to develop hypotheses, or best guesses, about ways to solve problems; they then systematically deduce, or conclude the best path to follow in solving the problem.

10. **neo-Piagetians** They believe Piaget got some things right, but they argue that his theory needs considerable revisions. In their revision, they give more emphasis to information processing that involves attention, memory, and strategies; they also seek to provide more precise explanations of cognitive changes.

11. **postformal thought** Postformal thought involves understanding that the correct answer to a problem requires reflective thinking and can vary from one situation to another, and that the search for truth is often an ongoing, never-ending process.

12. **zone of proximal development (ZPD)** Vygotsky's concept that refers to the range of tasks that are too difficult for individuals to master alone but that can be mastered with the guidance or assistance of adults or more skilled peers.

13. **social constructivist approach** Emphasizes the social contexts of learning and the construction of knowledge through social interaction.

14. **critical thinking** Thinking reflectively, productively, and evaluating the evidence.

15. **creativity** The ability to think about something in novel and unusual ways and come up with unique solutions to problems.

16. **convergent thinking** According to Guilford, a pattern of thinking in which individuals produce one correct answer; characteristic of the terms on conventional intelligence tests.

17. **divergent thinking** According to Guilford, a pattern of thinking in which individuals produce many answers to the same question; more characteristic of creativity than convergent thinking.

18. **metacognition** Cognition about cognition, or "knowing about knowing."

19. **self-regulatory learning** Consists of the self-generation and self-monitoring of thoughts, feelings, and behaviors to reach a goal.

20. **psychometric/intelligence view** Emphasizes the importance of individual differences in intelligence. Many advocates of this view also argue that intelligence should be assessed with intelligence tests.

21. **intelligence** Mental ability related to verbal and problem-solving skills, and the ability to adapt to and learn from life's everyday experiences. Not everyone agrees on what constitutes intelligence.

22. **mental age (MA)** Developed by Binet, an individual's level of mental development relative to others.

23. **intelligent quotient (IQ)** A person's tested mental age divided by chronological age, multiplied by 100.

24. **normal distribution** A symmetrical distribution of values or scores with a majority of scores falling in the middle of the possible range of scores and few scores appearing toward the extremes of the range; a distribution that yields what is called a "bell-shaped curve."

25. **emotional intelligence** A form of social intelligence that involves the ability to monitor one's own and others' feelings and emotions, to discriminate among them, and to use this information to guide one's thinking and action.

26. **Heritability** The fraction of the variance in a population that is attributed to genetics.

27. **culture-fair tests** Tests of intelligence that attempt to be free of cultural bias.

28. **adolescent egocentrism** The heightened self-consciousness of adolescents, which is reflected in their belief that others are as interested in them as they are in themselves.

29. **Triarchic Theory of Intelligence** Sternberg proposed that there are three main types of intelligence: analytical, creative, and practical.

## KEY PEOPLE IN THE STUDY OF ADOLESCENCE

| | | | |
|---|---|---|---|
| 1. c | 7. l | 13. u | 19. p |
| 2. f | 8. t | 14. o | 20. q |
| 3. g | 9. k | 15. d | 21. w |
| 4. i | 10. m | 16. n | 22. s |
| 5. h | 11. v | 17. e | 23. r |
| 6. j | 12. b | 18. a | |

## "DR. DETAIL'S" TERM MATCHING EXERCISE

| | | | |
|---|---|---|---|
| 1. g | 7. b | 13. c | 19. p |
| 2. k | 8. l | 14. h | 20. u |
| 3. n | 9. f | 15. q | 21. t |
| 4. m | 10. i | 16. r | |
| 5. e | 11. d | 17. o | |
| 6. a | 12. j | 18. s | |

## ADOLENCENT MYTH AND FACT

| | | | |
|---|---|---|---|
| 1. | T | 9. | F |
| 2. | F | 10. | F |
| 3. | F | 11. | T |
| 4. | T | 12. | T |
| 5. | T | 13. | T |
| 6. | F | 14. | T |
| 7. | F | 15. | T |
| 8. | F | | |

## PIAGET'S THEORY
## SECTION REVIEW

1. No answer provided—personal reflection. However, the answer should describe the preexisting schema, the disequilibrium that resulted as the result of the new information or experience, indicate the new information that was assimilated, and state how the old schema accommodated the new information.

2. Assimilation occurs when individuals incorporate new information into existing knowledge. Accommodation occurs when individuals adjust to new information.

3. Equilibration is a mechanism in Piaget's theory that explains how children or adolescents shift from one state of thought to the next. The shift occurs as they experience cognitive conflict or a disequilibrium in trying to understand the world. Eventually, the child or adolescent resolves the conflict and reaches a balance, or equilibrium of thought.

4. Sensorimotor stage — infants construct an understanding of the world by coordinating sensory experiences with physical, motoric actions.
   Preoperational stage — children begin to represent their world with words, images, and drawings.
   Concrete operational thought — children can perform operations. Logical reasoning replaces intuitive thought as long as the reasoning can be applied to specific or concrete examples.
   Formal operational stage — characterized by abstract, idealistic, and logical thought.

5. Conservation is Piaget's term for an individual's ability to recognize that the length, number, mass, quantity, area, weight, and volume of objects and substances do not change through transformations that alter their appearance.

   Classification is Piaget's concept of concrete operational thought, in which children systematically organize objects into hierarchies of classes and subclasses.

6. Piaget was the foundation for much of the current field of cognitive development.

7. Piaget's theory has withstood the test of time quite well. However, it has not gone unchallenged, in particular by those with specific criticisms (neo-Piagetions).

8. Questions have been raised regarding these areas: *Estimates of children's competence* — abilities are probably too fluid to be measured in Piaget's fashion; *Stages* — Piaget's theory assumes developmental synchrony, which is not consistent; *Training children to reason at a higher level* — it would appear that if properly trained, children can skip whole stages; *Culture and education* — these exert more influence on development than Piaget envisioned.

9. Early Formal Operational Thought – In this early period, flights of fantasy may submerge reality and the world may be viewed to subjectively or idealistically.

   Late Formal Operational Thought – Through accommodation, adolescents begin to adjust to the upheaval they have experienced. Thought during this stage more closely resembles reality.

# KEY PEOPLE IN SECTION

**David Elkind**—proposed communication and interaction with the environment in applying cognitive development to education.

**Robbie Case**— Canadian developmental psychologist that believes more precise description of changes within each stage needs to be carried out.

**K. Warner Schaie**—concluded that it is unlikely that adults go beyond the powerful methods of scientific thinking characteristic of the formal operations stage.

**William Perry**—said that younger adolescents tend to view the world in terms of polarities (i.e., right. wrong, or good/bad).

## VYGOTSKY'S THEORY
## SECTION REVIEW

1.

| Topic | Vygotsky | Piaget |
|-------|----------|--------|
| Constructivism | Social constructivist | Cognitive constructivist |
| Stages | No general stages of development proposed | Strong emphasis on stages — sensorimotor, preoperational, concrete operational, and formal operational |
| View on Education | Education plays a central role in helping children learn the tools of the culture | Education merely refines the child's cognitive skills that already have emerged. |
| Teaching Implications | Teacher is facilitator and guide, not director; establishes learning opportunities for children to learn with teacher and more skilled peers | Teacher is facilitator and guide, but not director; teacher provides support for children to explore their world and discover knowledge |

2. Zone of proximal development refers to the range of tasks that are too difficult for an individual to master alone, but can be mastered with the guidance of adults or skilled peers.

3. a. Scaffolding involves direct teaching, with less guidance provided by teacher or more advanced peer as student learns more.

   b. Cognitive apprenticeship involves an adult or expert modeling thinking strategies and allowing students to anticipate or complete the expert's next step or idea.

   c. Tutoring involves a cognitive apprenticeship between an adult or more skilled adolescent. Fellow students are more effective tutors, and peer tutoring also benefits the tutor.

   d. Cooperative learning involves working and learning in small groups.

   e. Reciprocal teaching involves students taking turns leading a small group discussion. The teacher gradually assumes a less active role, letting the student assume more initiative.

4. In a cognitive constructivist approach, emphasis is on the individual's cognitive construction of knowledge and understanding. In a social constructivist approach emphasis is on collaboration with others to produce knowledge and understanding.

5. Some say his emphasis on collaboration and guidance has potential pitfalls. Also, the emphasis on guidance might lead to laziness in adolescents who may come to expect help when they could have done something on their own.

# KEY PEOPLE IN SECTION

**Barbara Rogoff**—felt that cognitive development occurs as new generations collaborate with older generations in varying forms of interpersonal engagement.

**Ann Brown and Annemarie Palincsar**—used reciprocal teaching to improve students' abilities to enact certain strategies to improve their reading comprehension.

# THE INFORMATION-PROCESSING VIEW
# SECTION REVIEW

1.  Thinking, change mechanisms, and encoding.

2.  Short-term memory — is a limited-capacity memory system in which information is retained for as long as 30 seconds.
    Working memory — is a kind of "mental workbench" where information is manipulated and assembled to help make decisions, solve problems, and comprehend written and spoken language.
    Long-term memory — is a relatively permanent memory system that holds huge amounts of information for a long period.

3.  Compared to children, young adolescents are more likely to generate options that will lead to appropriate decisions.

4.  Increased speed and capacity of information processing, which free cognitive resources for other purposes. More breadth of content knowledge in a variety of domains. Increased ability to construct new combinations of knowledge. A greater range and more spontaneous use of strategies or procedures for applying or obtaining knowledge.

5.  Convergent thinking produces one correct answer and is characteristic of the kind of thinking required on a conventional intelligence test. Divergent thinking produces many answers to the same question and is more characteristic of creativity.

6.  a. Have adolescents engage in brainstorming and come up with as many meaningful ideas as possible.
    b. Provide adolescents with environments that stimulate creativity.
    c. Don't overcontrol.
    d. Encourage internal motivation.
    e. Foster flexible and playful thinking.
    f. Introduce adolescents to creative people.
    g. Talk with adolescents about creative people or have them read about them.

7.  In experiments, Sternberg saw that younger children often stopped processing information required to solve an analogy early in the process before they had all of the information needed. This was different than the approach used by the older kids. Sternberg felt the younger kids had overextended their short-term memories.

8.  The critical thinking skills that Sternberg believes adolescents need in everyday life include: recognizing that problems exist, defining the problems clearly, handling problems with no single right answer or any clear criteria for the point at which the problem is solved, making decisions on issues of personal relevance, obtaining information, thinking in groups, and developing long-term approaches to long-term problems.

9.  Self regulatory learners (1) set goals for extending their knowledge and sustaining their motivation; (2) are aware of their emotional make-up and have strategies for managing their emotions; (3) periodically

monitor their progress toward a goal; (4) fine tune or revise their strategies based on the progress they are making; and (5) evaluate obstacles that may arise and make the necessary adaptations.

## KEY PEOPLE IN SECTION

**Robert Siegler** — developed views related to information processing.

**Robbie Case** — believed adolescents process information differently than children.

**Robert Sternberg** — developed the triarchic theory of intelligence.

**J.P. Guilford** — made the distinction between convergent and divergent thinking in creativity.

**Mark Strand** — Poet Laureate who said that his most creative moments come when he loses a sense of time and is absorbed in what he is doing.

**Michael Pressley** — felt the key to education is helping students learn a rich repertoire of strategies that result in solutions to problems.

**Barry Zimmerman, Sebastian Bonner, and Robert Kovach** — developed a model of turning low-self-regulatory students into students who engaged in adopting specific, positive learning goals.

## PSYCHOMETRIC/INTELLIGENCE VIEW
## SECTION REVIEW

1.   a.   125
     b.   55
     c.   125

2.   Wechsler has both verbal and performance subscales, whereas the tests developed by Binet are predominantly verbally loaded.

3.   A normal distribution is a symmetrical bell-shaped curve with a majority of the focus cases falling in the middle of the range of possible scores.

4.   **1.** C;   **2.** D;   **3.** F;   **4.** G;   **5.** H;   **6.** B;   **7.** A;   **8.** E.

5.   Analytical—Analyze the book's main themes.
     Creative—Generate new ideas about how the book might have been written better.
     Practical—Think about how the book's themes can be applied to real life.[

6.   Developing emotional self-awareness; managing emotions; reading emotions; and, handling relationships.

7.   a.   Nature and nurture—Heredity is an important part of intelligence.
     b.   Ethnicity and culture—There are ethnic differences in the average scores on standardized intelligence tests between African American and White American adolescents, but the differences are believed to be the result of environmental factors such as social, economic, and educational opportunities.
     c.   Use and misuse of intelligence tests—Intelligence tests can lead to stereotypes and expectations about adolescents and should not be used as the main or sole characteristic of competence. Further, intelligence tests do not take into account the many domains of intelligence, such as those described by Sternberg and Gardner.

**8.**     Correlations of .70 and above show strong genetic influence. The APA suggests that for late adolescence the rate is .75.

## KEY PEOPLE IN SECTION

**Aldous Huxley** — said that children are remarkable for their curiosity and intelligence.

**Alfred Binet** — developed the concept of mental age (MA).

**Theophile Simon** — Binet's student and collaborator in developing the 1905 test.

**Lewis Terman** — was involved in forming and revising Binet's test.

**William Stern** — created the concept of the intelligence quotient (IQ).

**David Wechsler** — developed several IQ tests with multiple subscales.

**Charles Spearman** — said that people have both a general intelligence (*g*), and a specific types of intelligence (*s*).

**L.L. Thurstone** — identified primary mental abilities: verbal comprehension, number ability, word fluency, spatial visualization, associative memory, reasoning, and perceptual speed.

**Robert Sternberg** — developed the triarchic theory of intelligence.

**Howard Gardner** — identified eight types of intelligence.

**Daniel Goleman** — argues that emotional intelligence is more important than IQ when predicting an adolescent's competence.

**Nathan Brody** — argued that people who excel at one type of intellectual task are likely to excel in other intellectual tasks.

**John Carroll** — conducted an extensive examination of intellectual abilities and concluded that they are all related to each other.

**Robert Serpell** — studied concepts of intelligence in African communities since the 1970s.

**Elena Grigorenko** — studied the concept of intelligence in rural African people.

**Richard Herrnstein and Charles Murray** — sparked controversy by publishing the controversial book on intelligence, *The Bell Curve*.

## SOCIAL COGNITION
## SECTION REVIEW

1. No answer provided—personal reflection.
2. Yes. Popular examples suggest that they may lead to acts of violence, among other things.
3. The link between perspective taking and adolescent egocentrism likely occurs because advances in perspective taking cause young adolescents to be acutely concerned about what others think.
4. Adolescents are more likely to interpret an individual's personality in the way that many personality theorists do, as opposed to children.
5.    1.    When adolescents are given information about another person, they are more likely to consider both previously acquired information and current information, rather than relying only on the information at hand — as children do.
      2.    Adolescents are more likely to detect the situational or contextual variability in personality, rather than thinking that personality is always stable.

3.  Rather than merely accepting surface traits as a valid description of someone's personality, adolescents are more likely than children to look for deeper causes of personality.

## KEY PEOPLE IN SECTION

**David Elkind** — believes that adolescent egocentrism can be dissected into two types of social thinking — imaginary audience and personal fable.

## EXPLORATIONS IN ADOLESCENCE

No answer provided—personal reflection.

## COGNITIVE CHALLENGE

No answer provided—personal reflection.

## ADOLESCENCE IN RESEARCH

His hypothesis is that thinking is very flexible allowing individual's to adapt and adjust to many changes in their circumstances. He described three main characteristics of the information-processing view. 1. An emphasis on thinking as information processing. 2. An emphasis on mechanisms of change (encoding, automaticity, strategy construction, and generalization). 3. An emphasis on self-modification (i.e., prior knowledge is a base built upon).

## ⊠ COMPREHENSIVE REVIEW

| | | |
|---|---|---|
| 1. d | 19. c | 37. b |
| 2. b | 20. b | 38. b |
| 3. b | 21. a | 39. a |
| 4. c | 22. b | 40. b |
| 5. a | 23. d | 41. b |
| 6. d | 24. c | 42. b |
| 7. b | 25. c | 43. b |
| 8. d | 26. a | 44. b |
| 9. b | 27. c | 45. b |
| 10. d | 28. a | 46. c |
| 11. d | 29. c | |
| 12. c | 30. c | |
| 13. b | 31. c | |
| 14. a | 32. c | |
| 15. b | 33. b | |
| 16. d | 34. c | |
| 17. b | 35. b | |
| 18. b | 36. c | |

# ✧ Chapter 5   The Self, Identity, Emotions, and Personality

**Learning Goals with Key Terms and Key People in Boldface**

**1.0   DESCRIBE THE DEVELOPMENT OF THE SELF IN ADOLESCENCE**

    **A.   Self-Understanding**

        1.1      What is **self-understanding**?

        1.2      What causes contradictions within the self?

        1.3      What are the dimensions of adolescents' **self-understanding**?

        1.4      What is the difference between the real and ideal self, and the true and false self?

        1.5      What is meant by **possible self**?

        1.6      What is social comparison?

        1.7      What does it mean to be self-conscious and self-protective?

        1.8      What is self-integration?

        1.9      What is meant by adolescents having multiple selves?

    **B.   Self-Esteem and Self-Concept**

        1.10    What is **self-esteem**?

        1.11    What is **self-concept**?

        1.12    How do researchers measure an adolescent's **self-esteem**?

        1.13    What is Harter's Self-Perception Profile for Adolescents?

        1.14    Why is it good to use multiple measures to assess **self-esteem**?

        1.15    Does **self-esteem** change during the life span?

        1.16    Are some domains more salient than others to the adolescent's **self-esteem**?

        1.17    How important is perceived physical appearance to an adolescent's **self-esteem**?

        1.18    What role does peer acceptance play in the **self-esteem** of adolescents?

        1.19    What parental influences and behaviors are associated with boys' **self-esteem**?

        1.20    What role do peer judgments play in **self-esteem**?

        1.21    Is classmate support more strongly linked to **self-esteem** than close-friend support?

        1.22    What is the consequence of low **self-esteem** for most adolescents?

        1.23    What are the ramifications for some adolescents when low **self-esteem** persists?

        1.24    What can happen if **self-esteem** is compounded by difficult school transitions?

        1.25    What are four ways that adolescents' **self-esteem** can be improved?

        1.26    Why should adolescents be taught to value competence?

**2.0   EXPLAIN THE MANY FACETS OF IDENTITY DEVELOPMENT**

    **A.   Erikson's Ideas on Identity**

        2.1      What is the meaning and significance of Erikson's fifth stage, **identity versus identity confusion**?

        2.2      What is **psychosocial moratorium** as it relates to identity development?

        2.3      What is revealed by Erikson's insights?

        2.4      According to Erikson, what do personality and role exploration have to do with identity development?

        2.5      What are some contemporary views of identity development?

        2.6      How long does identity development take?

2.7      Is identity development complex?

**B.**      **The Four Statuses of Identity**

2.8      What is Marcia's view of identity?

2.9      What are the four statuses of identity?

2.10      What are the characteristics of **identity diffusion** and **identity foreclosure**?

2.11      How is **crisis** identified?

2.12      How is **commitment** identified?

2.13      What is **identity moratorium**?

2.14      What does Marcia mean by **identity achievement**?

2.15      What is the role of crisis and **commitment** in Marcia's theory of identity statuses?

2.16      What are the criticisms of Marcia's identity statuses?

**C.**      **Developmental Changes in Identity**

2.17      What three aspects of the young adolescent's development are important in identity formation?

2.18      What are "MAMA" cycles?

**D.**      **Identity and Social Contexts**

2.19      How do parents influence adolescents' identity development?

2.20      What is **individuality**?

2.21      What is **connectedness**?

2.22      What family processes promote adolescent identity development?

2.23      What do adolescent **individuality** and **connectedness** have to do with identity development?

2.24      What emphasis did Erikson place on the role of culture in identity development?

2.25      What is meant by **ethnic identity**?

2.26      Why is adolescence a special juncture in the identity development of ethnic minority individuals?

2.27      How does identity change across generations?

2.28      Do ethnic minority individuals have bicultural gender identities?

2.29      Do adolescent males have a stronger vocational identity than females?

2.30      Do female adolescents have a stronger social identity than males?

**3.0**      **DISCUSS THE EMOTIONAL DEVELOPMENT OF ADOLESCENTS**

**A.**      **The Emotions of Adolescence**

3.1      What is **emotion?**

3.2      Why is it important for adults to realize that moodiness is normal in adolescence?

**B.**      **Hormones, Experience, and Emotions**

3.3      What is the relationship between puberty and emotionality?

**C.**      **Emotional Competence**

3.4      What role does awareness of emotional cycles play in adolescence?

3.5      Which emotional competencies are important for adolescents to develop?

**4.0**      **CHARACTERIZE THE PERSONALITY DEVELOPMENT OF ADOLESCENTS**

**A.**      **Personality Traits**

4.1      What are the **big five factors of personality**?

4.2      Why is it good to view personality not only in terms of traits, but also in terms of contexts and situations?

**B.**      **Temperament**

4.3      How is **temperament** defined?

4.4      What are the three basic types of temperament?

4.5      How did Mary Rothbart and John Bates revise Thomas and Chess's framework for classifying temperament?

4.6    Is temperament in childhood linked to adjustment in adolescence and adulthood?

4.7    What is meant by **goodness of fit?**

# Exercises

## KEY TERMS COMPLETION EXERCISE

This exercise presents each key term in the form of an incomplete sentence. Complete each sentence by either defining the term or giving an example. Compare your definitions with those given at the end of the study guide chapter.

1.    **Self-understanding** is seen in the

     _____

     _____

2.    Jacob is pondering his **possible self.** This means he is

     _____

     _____

3.    **Self-esteem** is presented as a measure of

     _____

     _____

4.    A person's **self-concept** is

     _____

     _____

5.    In proposing **identity versus identity confusion,** Erikson was suggesting

     _____

     _____

6.    **Psychosocial moratorium** is Erikson's term for

     _____

     _____

7.    **Crisis** is represented by

     _____

     _____

8.     Fred is showing **commitment** to his schoolwork as evidenced by

_____

_____

9.     According to James Marcia, **identity diffusion** is when

_____

_____

10.    Marcia uses to term **identity foreclosure** to describe the state when an adolescent

_____

_____

11.    While a person is in **identity moratorium,** he or she is likely

_____

_____

12.    **Identity achievement** suggests

_____

_____

13.    Evidence of expressing **individuality** is seen in

_____

_____

14.    **Connectedness** consists of what two dimensions:

_____

_____

15.    A sense of **ethnic identity** is seen

_____

_____

16.    **Emotion** is defined as

_____

_____

17.    The **big five factors of personality** are

_____

_____

18. **Temperament** is defined as

_____

_____

19. An **easy child** generally is

_____

_____

20. A **difficult child**'s traits include

_____

_____

21. A **slow-to-warm-up child** has

_____

_____

22. **Goodness of fit** means

_____

_____

## KEY PEOPLE IN THE STUDY OF ADOLESCENCE

Match the person with the concept of adolescent development with which they are associated.

____ 1. Susan Harter      A. Most famous for his theory of identity development

____ 2. Reed Larson and Maryse Richards      B. Developed an assessment for adolescent self-esteem

____ 3. Erik Erikson      C. Expanded on Erikson's identity development theory

____ 4. James Marcia      D. Proposed three basic types or clusters of temperament

____ 5. Alan Waterman      E. Found that adolescents reported more extreme emotions than did their parents

____ 6. Catherine Cooper      F. Conducted research on ethnic identity

____ 7. Stuart Hauser      G. Believes that ethnic minority youth must bridge multiple worlds in constructing identity

____ 8. Jean Phinney      H. Argued that personality varies according to the situation

____ 9. Alexander Thomas and Stella Chess      I. Illuminated family processes that promote adolescent identity development

____ 10. Walter Mischel      J. Conducted research on timing of identity achievement

## "DR. DETAIL'S" IDENTITY STATUS EXERCISE

What is your identity status? Think about your exploration and commitment in the areas listed below. For each area, check whether your identity status is diffused, foreclosed, moratorium, or achieved. If you check "diffused" or "foreclosed" for any areas, take some time to think about what you need to do to move into a moratorium identity status in those areas.

| Identity Component | Diffused | Foreclosed | Moratorium | Achieved |
|---|---|---|---|---|
| Vocational (career) | | | | |
| Political | | | | |
| Religious | | | | |
| Relationship | | | | |
| Achievement | | | | |
| Sexual | | | | |
| Gender | | | | |
| Ethnic/Cultural | | | | |
| Interests | | | | |
| Personality | | | | |
| Physical | | | | |

## ADOLESCENT MYTH AND FACT

Which of the following statements regarding adolescents are true (T) and which are false (F)?

1. Children, when describing themselves, are more likely than adolescents to use abstract and idealistic ways of explaining.  T or F

2. Adolescents cannot distinguish between their true and false selves.  T or F

3. Girls have a higher level of public self-consciousness than boys.  T or F

4. Adolescents are prone to deny their negative characteristics in an effort to try to protect the self.  T or F

5. Research has indicated that self-esteem decreases when children make the transition from elementary to middle school.  T or F

6. Adolescents with high self-esteem perform better in school.  T or F

7. Adolescents with high self-esteem are prone to exclusively prosocial behaviors.  T or F

8. Support from close friends is most strongly related to self-worth in adolescence.  T or F

9. Contemporary views of identity development suggest that it is a lengthy process, and in many instances, more cataclysmic than Erickson's term 'crisis' implies.  T or F

10. Marcia's approach to identity development has been sharply criticized by some researchers who believe it distorts and trivializes Erikson's concepts of crisis and commitment.  T or F

11. Higher levels of ethnic identity are linked to more positive attitudes towards members of other ethnic groups.  T or F

12. Minority students with a stronger ethnic identity are more likely to take radical viewpoints and become aggressive.  T or F

13. Moodiness is a "normal" aspect of early adolescence.  T or F

14. Personality becomes most stable after 50 years of age.  T or F

15. Today, most psychologists are interactionists and believe that both traits and situations go into formulating personality.  T or F

# THE SELF
## SECTION REVIEW

1. List and give an example or explanation for each of Harter's five ways that an adolescent's sense of self differs from that of a child.

   a. _____

   _____

   b. _____

   _____

   c. _____

   _____

   d. _____

   _____

   e. _____

   _____

2. What forms an adolescents' self-understanding?

   _____

   _____

3. How is an adolescent's self-understanding different than that of children?

   _____

   _____

4. What is meant by possible self?

   _____

   _____

5. Why are adolescents more likely than children to use social comparison in evaluating themselves?

   _____

   _____

6. What is social comparison?

   _____

   _____

7.      What is an adolescent culture broker?

_____

_____

8.      Complete the chart by filling in the positive and negative behavioral indicators of self-esteem.

| Positive Indicators | Negative Indicators |
|---|---|
|  |  |
|  |  |
|  |  |
|  |  |
|  |  |
|  |  |
|  |  |
|  |  |
|  |  |
|  |  |

9.      What is self-esteem?

_____

_____

10.     How do we measure adolescent self-esteem and self-concept?

_____

_____

11.     What is Harter's Self-Perception Profile for adolescents?

_____

_____

12      How important is perceived physical appearance to an adolescent's self-esteem?

_____

_____

13.     What role does peer judgments play in self-esteem?

_____

_____

14.     What are four ways that adolescents' self-esteem can be improved?

_____

_____

# IDENTITY
## SECTION REVIEW

1. What is the meaning and significance of Erikson's fifth stage, identity versus identity confusion?

   _____

   _____

2. Define psychosocial moratorium as it relates to identity development.

   _____

   _____

3. How long does identity development take?

   _____

   _____

4. What are the four statuses of identity?

   _____

   _____

5. What are some characteristics of identity diffusion and identity foreclosure?

   _____

   _____

6. Differentiate between crisis and commitment.

   _____

   _____

7. Identify three aspects of the young adolescent's development that are important in identity formation.

   _____

   _____

8. What is identity consolidation?

   _____

   _____

9. Define individuality.

   _____

   _____

10. Identify the two dimensions of connectedness?

_____

_____

11. According to Stuart Hauser, which family processes promote adolescent identity development?

_____

_____

12. How did Jean Phinney define ethnic identity?

_____

_____

13. What problems face inner-city ethnically diverse youth, according to Heath and McLaughlin (1993)?

_____

_____

14. Contrast the vocational identity and social identity of males versus females.

_____

_____

## EMOTIONAL DEVELOPMENT
## SECTION REVIEW

1. What is emotion?

_____

_____

2. Why is it important for adults to realize that moodiness is normal in adolescence?

_____

_____

3. What is the relationship between puberty and emotionality?

_____

_____

4. What role does awareness of emotional cycles play in adolescence?

_____

_____

5.     Which emotional competencies are important for adolescents to develop?

_____

_____


## PERSONALITY DEVELOPMENT
## SECTION REVIEW

1.     Identify the big five factors of personality?

_____

_____


2.     How stable are personality traits in adolescence?

_____

_____


3.     How is temperament defined?

_____

_____


4.     What are the three basic types of temperament?

_____

_____


5.     How did Rothbart and Bates classify temperament?

_____

_____


## COGNITIVE CHALLENGE

1.     Think about what your future selves might be. Which of your prospective selves do you think will make you the happiest? Which of your prospective selves might have negative possibilities?

_____

_____


## ADOLESCENCE IN RESEARCH

Concerning Daphna Oyserman and her colleagues' (2002) research on promoting adolescents feeling connected and involved with school, state the hypothesis, the research methods (if known), the research conclusions, and the implications and applications for adolescent development.

_____

_____

1. Bernie describes himself as in control, masculine, and intelligent when he is with his girlfriend, but when he is with his buddies, he describes himself as fun loving and spontaneous. Bernie is
   a. two-faced.
   c. schizophrenic.
   b. differentiated.
   d. lacking an identity.

2. _____ believed that when the real and ideal selves are too discrepant; it is a sign of maladjustment.
   a. Susan Harter
   c. Carl Rogers
   b. Erik Erikson
   d. Jean Phinney

3. Rosenberg's (1970) term for the fluctuating adolescent sense of self is the
   a. hypothermic self.
   c. hyperbolic self.
   b. hyperthermic self.
   d. barometric self.

4. Adolescents are more likely than children to
   a. use social comparison.
   c. be preoccupied with understanding.
   b. be self-conscious.
   d. All the above are correct.

5. The _____ represents what individuals might become, what they would like to become, and what they are afraid of becoming.
   a. real self
   c. ideal self
   b. possible self
   d. barometric self

6. _____ is NOT one of Marcia's phases describing changes in adolescence?
   a. Reconstruction
   c. Self-understanding
   b. Deconstruction
   d. Consolidation

7. Joyce is on a date with someone she wants to impress. She uses large words that she does not normally use and exaggerates her intellectual ability. She is exhibiting her
   a. negative possible self.
   c. ideal self.
   b. positive possible self.
   d. false self.

8. _____ involves domain-specific evaluations of the self.
   a. Self-esteem
   c. Positive possible self
   b. Self-concept
   d. Negative possible self

9. _____ is the global evaluative dimension of the self.
   a. Self-esteem
   c. Positive possible self
   b. Self-concept
   d. Negative possible self

10. _____ refers to an individuals' beliefs that they can master a situation and produce positive outcomes.
    a. Self-esteem
    c. Self-efficacy
    b. Self-concept
    d. Self-reference

11. According to a study by Robins and others (2002), the ages when we see declines in self-esteem are
    a. in the twenties and thirties.
    b. in adolescence and the seventies and eighties.

c. in the fifty and sixties.
d. in the twenties and fifties.

12. An adolescent who starts to admit inconsistencies in his or her behavior is achieving
    a. his ideal self.
    c. self-reference.
    b. egocentrism.
    d. self-integration.

13. Which of the following is NOT an explanation for the decline in self-esteem among females during early adolescence?
    a. Girls have more negative body images during pubertal change than boys.
    b. School performance and self-esteem are highly correlated, and girls do worse in school than boys.
    c. Adolescent girls take greater interest in social relationships.
    d. Society fails to reward girls greater interest in social relationships.

14. Which of the following parental characteristics is associated with self-esteem in children?
    a. expression of affection
    c. conflicted family environments
    b. setting permissive rules
    d. parental intelligence

15. Rodney's parents don't set any limits on his behavior. The family seems to always be in a state of chaos. Research indicates that Rodney's self-esteem will likely be
    a. low.
    c. unconscious.
    b. high.
    d. differentiated.

16. In a recent study of family cohesiveness (Baldwin & Hoffman, 2002), which of the following factors was NOT noted as positively influencing adolescent self-esteem?
    a. amount of time spent together as a family
    b. the extent to which the adolescent was involved in family decision-making
    c. the quality of family communication
    d. the amount of money that parents would spend on their children

17. Erik Erikson called the gap between childhood security and adult autonomy
    a. identity confusion.
    c. self-efficacy.
    b. psychosocial moratorium.
    d. generation gap.

18. According to James Marcia and others, identity formation
    a. is a lifetime activity.
    b. should occur after intimacy.
    c. is much easier than Erikson made it out to be.
    d. does not require advanced thinking skills.

19. Karyn, who is in a state of identity foreclosure,
    a. has not experienced any crisis or made any commitment.
    b. has made a commitment but has not experienced a crisis.
    c. is in the midst of a crisis.
    d. has undergone a crisis and made a commitment.

20. Jackson came home with green spiked hair. Of the following explanations for his behavior, _____ is the LEAST adequate.
    a. identity moratorium
    c. identity confusion
    b. negative identity
    d. identity foreclosure

21. The two core ingredients in Erikson's theory of identity development are
    a.    trust and confidence.
    b.    personality and role experimentation.
    c.    self-efficacy and self-confidence.
    d.    temperament and self-esteem.

22. According to Erikson, identity development ends with
    a.    the development of a sense of self.
    b.    the emergence of independence.
    c.    the resolution of the identity issue in adolescence.
    d.    a life review and integration in old age.

23. According to Cooper and her colleagues, the two dimensions of connectedness are
    a.    bonding and respect.
    b.    mutuality and sensitivity.
    c.    self- and other-connectedness.
    d.    mutuality and permeability.

24. Adolescence may be a particularly difficult time for minority individuals because this is the time they
    a.    are subject to the most intense discrimination.
    b.    also confront its ethnicity.
    c.    have the fewest resources to achieve identity.
    d.    become aware of other people's resources.

25. Gender differences in identity formation
    a.    are a backlash against the women's movement.
    b.    are greater now because of the New Age movement.
    c.    have decreased in the last twenty years.
    d.    are the same as they have always been.

26. According to Alan Waterman (1985, 1989, 1992, 1999), the _____ is MOST likely to be identity achieved?
    a.    high school freshman        c.    college freshman
    b.    high school senior          d.    college senior

27. Jacob Orlofsky discovered that college students who had a stable sense of identity were more likely to achieve _____ status.
    a.    stereotyped                 c.    pseudointimacy
    b.    preintimacy                 d.    intimacy

28. Which of the following has the weaker ethnic identity?
    a.    a member of a minority group
    b.    an older person who belongs to an ethnic group
    c.    a member of a mainstream group
    d.    an ethnic minority college student

29. Robert Weiss distinguished between
    a.    emotional and social isolation.
    b.    individuation and connectedness.
    c.    intimate and isolated relationships.
    d.    situational and chronic loneliness.

30. Between 5th and 9th grades, both boys and girls experience a ____ decrease in the state of being "very happy."
    a. 100 %                    c. 50 %
    b. 75 %                     d. 25 %

31. _____ arises when a person lacks an intimate relationship.
    a. Social isolation         c. Immersion/emersion
    b. Emotional isolation      d. Laconic malaise

32. Which of the following is NOT one of the big five factors of personality?
    a. neuroticism              c. agreeableness
    b. conscientiousness        d. externalization

33. Five-year-old Teddy seems to be always in a good mood and is considered happy-go-lucky. Which of Chess and Thomas's basic types of temperament does he best fit?
    a. difficult child          c. easy child
    b. positive affect and approach   d. fast-to-warm-up child


## ADOLESCENCE ON THE SCREEN

■ *The Cider House Rules* Follows a young boy born and raised in an orphanage as he charts his own course in life and breaks away from his surrogate father who runs the orphanage.

■ *King Gimp* Two University of Maryland professors won the Academy Award in 2000 for best documentary short subject with this film spanning the adolescence and young adulthood of Dan Keplinger, a young man suffering from a highly disabling form of cerebral palsy, as he searches for identity in a world that shuns him.

■ *Shine* Based on the true story of Australian pianist David Helfgott, the movie chronicles Helfgott's search for an identity. He has to overcome an abusive childhood, the loss of his family in concentration camps, and mental illness before he finds himself and achieves success as a concert pianist.

■ *Simon Birch* Relates the story of Simon Birch, age 12, who believes God made him for a special purpose. The movie presents his quest to fulfill the destiny he believes God gave him.


## ADOLESCENCE IN BOOKS

■ *Gandhi*, by Erik Erikson (Norton: NY, 1966), the Pulitzer Prize-winning biography of Mahatma Gandhi, emphasizes Gandhi's identity crisis.

■ *Identity's Architect: A Biography of Erik H. Erikson*, by Lawrence J. Friedman (Scribner: NY, 1999), traces Erik Erikson's own identity crises, which contributed to the development of his psychosocial theory.

■ *Intimate Connections*, by David D. Burns (William Morrow: NY, 1985), presents a program for overcoming loneliness.

# Answer Key

## KEY TERMS

1. **self-understanding** The adolescent's cognitive representation of the self, the substance and content of the adolescent's self-conceptions.

2. **possible self** What individuals might become, what they would like to become, and what they are afraid of becoming.

3. **self-esteem** The global evaluative dimension of the self. Self-esteem is also referred to as self-worth or self-image.

4. **self-concept** Domain-specific evaluations of the self.

5. **identity versus identity confusion** Erikson's fifth developmental stage, which individuals experience during the adolescent years. At this time, individuals face finding out who they are, what they are all about, and where they are going in life.

6. **psychosocial moratorium** Erikson's term for the gap between childhood security and adult autonomy that adolescents experience as part of their identity exploration.

7. **crisis** A period of identity development when the adolescent is choosing among meaningful alternatives.

8. **commitment** The part of identity development when adolescents show a personal investment in what they are going to do.

9. **identity diffusion** Marcia's term for the state adolescents are in when they have not yet experienced a crisis or made any commitments.

10. **identity foreclosure** Marcia's term for the state adolescents are in when they have made a commitment but have not experienced a crisis.

11. **identity moratorium** Marcia's term for the state of adolescents who are in the midst of a crisis, but whose commitments are either absent or are only vaguely defined.

12. **identity achievement** Marcia's term for having undergone a crisis and made a commitment.

13. **individuality** An important element in adolescent identity development. It consists of two dimensions: self-assertion, the ability to have and communicate a point of view; and separateness, the use of communication patterns to express how one is different from others.

14. **connectedness** An important element in adolescent identity development. It consists of two dimensions: mutuality, sensitivity to and respect for others' views; and permeability, openness to others' views.

15. **ethnic identity** An enduring, basic aspect of the self that includes a sense of membership in an ethnic group and the attitudes and feelings related to that membership.

16. **emotion** Feeling or affect that involves physiological arousal, behavioral expression, and sometimes conscious experience.

17. **big five factors of personality** Five core traits of personality: openness to experience, conscientiousness, extraversion, agreeableness, and neuroticism.

18. **temperament** An individual's behavioral style and characteristic way of responding.

19. **easy child** Generally in a positive mood, quickly establishes regular routines, and adapts easily to new experiences.

20. **difficult child** This child reacts negatively to many situations and is slow to accept new experiences.

21. **slow-to-warm-up child** This child has a low activity level, is somewhat negative, and displays a low intensity of mood.

22. **goodness of fit** The match between an individual's temperament style and the environmental demands the individual must cope with.

## KEY PEOPLE IN THE STUDY OF ADOLESCENCE

| | | | | |
|---|---|---|---|---|
| 1. B | 2. E | 3. A | 4. C | 5. J |
| 6. G | 7. I | 8. F | 9. D | 10. H |

## "DR. DETAIL'S" IDENTITY STATUS EXERCISE

Individual answers may vary.

## ADOLENCENT MYTH AND FACT

| | | | | |
|---|---|---|---|---|
| 1. F | 2. F | 3. T | 4. T | 5. T |
| 6. F | 7. F | 8. F | 9. F | 10. T |
| 11. T | 12. F | 13. T | 14. T | 15. T |

## THE SELF
## SECTION REVIEW

1. Individual answers may vary.
   a. **Abstraction and idealism**: A teenager is more apt to describe himself/herself in abstract terms, such as saying that he/she is compassionate and caring.
   b. **Differentiation**: An adolescent is likely to describe himself/herself as having one set of characteristics in relationship to his/her families and another in relationship to his/her peers and friends.
   c. **The fluctuating self**: Adolescents' sense of themselves changes over short periods. They can be self-confident one moment and anxious the next.
   d. **Contradictions within the self**: Adolescents' self-descriptions show contradictions. They may think of themselves as both attractive and unattractive.
   e. **Real versus ideal, true versus false selves**: Depression and self-doubt can arise when an adolescent feels that they are not living up to their ideal sense of self.

2. (a) abstract and idealistic, (b) differentiated, (c) the fluctuating self, (d) contradictions within the self, (e) real and ideal, true and false selves.

3. Over time an adolescent's self-understanding becomes increasingly differentiated. Adolescents are more likely than children to note contextual or situational variations in describing themselves.

4. What individuals might become, what they would like to become, and what they are afraid of becoming.

5. Developmentalists believe that adolescents are more likely than children to use social comparison in evaluating themselves; however, during adolescence their willingness to admit using it declines.

6. They ways in which adolescents evaluate themselves.

7. Culture brokers are youth who can navigate effectively between different worlds and develop bicultural or multicultural selves.

8.

| Positive Indicators | Negative Indicators |
| --- | --- |
| Gives others directives or commands | Puts down others by teasing, name-calling, or gossiping |
| Uses voice quality appropriate for situation | Uses gestures that are dramatic or out of context |
| Expresses opinions | Engages in inappropriate touching or avoids physical contact |
| Sits with others during social activities | Gives excuses for failures |
| Works cooperatively in a group | Glances around to monitor others |
| Faces others when speaking or being spoken to | Brags excessively about achievements, skills, appearance |
| Maintains eye contact during conversation | Verbally puts self down; self-deprecation |
| Initiates friendly contact with others | Speaks too loudly, abruptly, or in a dogmatic tone |
| Maintains comfortable space between self and others | Does not express views or opinions, especially when asked |
| Little hesitation in speech, speaks fluently | Assumes a submissive stance |

9. Self-esteem is the global evaluative dimension of the self.

10. Susan Harter developed a separate measure for adolescents called the Self-Perception Profile for Adolescents. It assesses scholastic competence, athletic competence, social acceptance, physical appearance, behavioral conduct, close friendship, romantic appeal, and job competence.

11. Scholastic competence, athletic competence, social acceptance, physical appearance, behavioral conduct, close friendship, romantic appeal, and job competence.

12. Very important. It's the foundation of adolescent self-perception.

13. Peer judgments gain greater importance among older children and adolescents.

14. (a) identifying the causes of low esteem and the domains of competence important to the self, (b) emotional support and social approval, (c) achievement, and (d) coping.

# IDENTITY
## SECTION REVIEW

1. It is Erikson's fifth developmental stage that individuals experience during the adolescent years. Adolescents examine who they are, what they are all about, and where they are going in life.

2. Erikson's term for the gap between childhood security and adult autonomy that adolescents experience as part of their identity exploration.

3. It is a lengthy process that neither begins nor ends in adolescence.

4. (a) identity diffusion, (b) identity foreclosure, (c) identity moratorium, and (d) identity achievement.

5.      Identity diffusion is Marcia's term for the state adolescents are in when they have not yet experienced a crisis or made any commitments. Identity foreclosure is Marcia's term for the state adolescents are in when they have made a commitment but have not experienced a crisis.

6.      Crisis is defined as a period of identity development during which the adolescent is choosing among meaningful alternatives. Commitment is a part of identity development in which adolescents show a personal investment in what they are going to do.

7.      Young adolescents must be confident that they have parental support, must have an established sense of industry, and must be able to adopt a self-reflective stance toward the future.

8.      The process of refining and enhancing the identity choices that are made in emerging adulthood.

9.      Individuality consists of two dimensions: self-assertion, the ability to have and communicate a point of view; and separateness, the use of communication patterns to express how one is different from others.

10.     Connectedness consists of mutuality, or sensitivity to and respect for others' views; and permeability, openness to others' views.

11.     Parents who enable (i.e., explain, accept, and give empathy) foster development. Those who constrain (i.e., judge or devalue) do not.

12.     An enduring, basic aspect of the self that includes a sense of membership in an ethnic group and the attitudes and feelings related to that membership.

13.     According to Heath and McLaughlin, inner-city youth have too much time on their hands, too little to do, and too few places to go. They want to participate in programs that nurture their needs, but these are often unavailable.

14.     In recent decades, differences that once existed have now begun to disappear as females close the gap.

## EMOTIONAL DEVELOPMENT
## SECTION REVIEW

1.      Emotion is feeling or affect that involves physiological arousal, behavioral expression, and sometimes conscious experience.

2.      It is normal for adolescents to behave this way, and eventually they emerge from it.

3.      Puberty is associated with an increase in negative emotions.

4.      Awareness of emotional cycles will allow an adolescent to better control his/her ability to cope with those emotions.

5.      Being aware that the expression of emotions plays a major role in relationships; adaptively coping with negative emotions by using self-regulatory strategies that reduce the intensity and duration of such emotional states. Understanding that inner emotional states do not have to correspond to outer expressions. Being aware of one's emotional states without becoming overwhelmed by them.

## PERSONALITY DEVELOPMENT
## SECTION REVIEW

1.      Openness to experience, conscientiousness, extraversion, agreeableness, and neuroticism.

2.      Some researchers have found that personality is not as stable in adolescence as in adulthood. It appears that personality becomes much more stable after the age of 50.

3.  An individual's behavioral style and characteristic way of responding.

4.  According to Thomas and Chess, they are: easy child, difficult child, and slow-to-warm-up child.

5.  Their framework focuses more on: positive affect and approach; negative affectivity; effortful control.


## COGNITIVE CHALLENGE

1.  No answers provided. Individual activity


## ADOLESCENCE IN RESEARCH

Oyserman's project, called "school-to-jobs," was designed to promote the development of academically focused possible selves that could help adolescents feel connected and involved with school. The hypothesis was that the program could help kids, even from economically challenged backgrounds. They used both an experimental and control group to measure the effectiveness of the intervention. The intervention showed positive results by the end of the year, including better school attendance and performance and fewer troubles at school. A 2-year follow-up showed continued improvement.

## ⊠ COMPREHENSIVE REVIEW

| 1 | b | 9. | a | 17. | b | 25. | c |
|---|---|---|---|---|---|---|---|
| 2. | c | 10. | c | 18. | a | 26. | d |
| 3. | d | 11. | b | 19. | b | 27. | d |
| 4. | d | 12. | d | 20. | d | 28. | c |
| 5. | d | 13. | b | 21. | b | 29. | a |
| 6. | c | 14. | a | 22. | d | 30. | c |
| 7. | d | 15. | a | 23. | d | 31. | b |
| 8. | b | 16. | d | 24. | b | 32. | d |
| | | | | | | 33. | c |

# ✧ Chapter 6    Gender

**Learning Goals with Key Terms and Key People in Boldface**

**1.0    DESCRIBE THE BIOLOGICAL, SOCIAL, AND COGNITIVE INFLUENCES ON GENDER**

    **A.    Biological Influences on Gender**

        1.1    What is the nature of gender?

        1.2    What is meant by one's **gender role**?

        1.3    How strong are the biological influences on gender?

        1.4    What is the role of sexuality in adolescent gender development?

        1.5    How do Freud and Erikson's ideas promote the premise that anatomy is destiny?

        1.6    How do today's developmentalists believe that biological and environmental influences affect gender?

        1.7    What are some criticisms of the anatomy-is-destiny view?

        1.8    What is the evolutionary psychology view of gender development?

    **C.    Social Influences on Gender**

        1.9    What is **social role theory**?

        1.10    What roles do gender hierarchy and sexual division of labor play in sex-differentiated behavior?

        1.11    According to the **social cognitive theory of gender**, what role do parents play in the development of gender-appropriate behavior?

        1.12    How do peers reward gender-appropriate behavior?

        1.13    How has the increase in the number of working mothers in recent years influenced adolescents?

        1.14    What evidence suggests that gender inequity still exists in education?

        1.15    Does evidence exist that the classroom is biased against boys?

        1.16    How does television program to specifically male and females audiences, and what impact does it have?

        1.17    How are men portrayed on television?

    **D.    Cognitive Influences on Gender**

        1.18    What was **Kohlberg's** theory of gender development?

        1.19    What is a **schema**?

        1.20    What does the **gender schema theory** state about individual gender development?

        1.21    According to the **cognitive development theory of gender,** when does gender typing occur?

**2.0    DISCUSS GENDER STEREOTYPES, SIMILARITIES, AND DIFFERENCES**

    **A.    Gender Stereotyping**

        2.1    What is the nature of **gender stereotypes** today?

        2.2    How common is stereotyping?

        2.3    How widespread is feminine and masculine stereotyping?

        2.4    What is **sexism?**

    **B.    Gender Similarities and Differences**

        2.5    What are the physical and biological differences that characterize male and female comparisons?

        2.6    Have male/female differences been exaggerated?

2.7     How is modern **sexism** different from that in the past?

2.8     What distinguishes **rapport talk** from **report talk**?

2.9     What is the current nature of the controversy over the differences between males and females?

**C.    Gender in Context**

2.10    Why is context an important factor in understanding gender?

**3.0    CHARACTERIZE THE VARIATIONS IN GENDER-ROLE CLASSIFICATION**

**A.    Masculinity, Femininity, and Androgyny**

3.1     According to past tradition, what were the characteristics of a well-adjusted male?

3.2     According to past tradition, what were the characteristics of a well-adjusted female?

3.3     When did alternatives to traditional masculinity and femininity begin to be explored?

3.4     What is meant by **androgyny**?

3.5     How do androgynous individuals compare with either masculine or feminine individuals?

**B.  Context, Culture, and Gender Roles**

3.6     Do gender roles vary around the world?

3.7     How do males and females differ on how they show anger?

**C.    Androgyny and Education**

3.8     Should **androgyny** be taught to students?

**D.    Traditional Masculinity and Problem Behaviors in Adolescent Males**

3.9     Explain what Pollack meant by "boy code".

**E.    Gender-Role Transcendence**

3.10    What do critics of androgyny suggest as an alternative?

3.11    What are some concerns regarding teaching children and adolescents to depart from socially approved behavior patterns?

**4.0    SUMMARIZE DEVELOPMENTAL CHANGES IN GENDER**

**A.    Early Adolescence and Gender Intensification**

4.1     What is the **gender intensification hypothesis**?

4.2     Do all researchers consider the **gender intensification hypothesis** valid?

**B.    Is Early Adolescence a Critical Juncture for Females?**

4.3     Is early adolescence a critical juncture for females?

4.4     What is Gillian's belief about the critical juncture for adolescent females?

4.5     What are some criticisms about Gillian's beliefs about male and female differences in intimacy and connectedness?

# Exercises

KEY TERMS COMPLETION EXERCISE

This exercise presents each key term in the form of an incomplete sentence. Complete each sentence by either defining the term or giving an example. Compare your definitions with those given at the end of the study guide chapter.

1.     Simply put, **gender** refers to

_____

_____

2.    **Gender role** refers to one's

_____

_____

3.    **Cognitive developmental theory of gender** states

_____

_____

4.    **Social role theory** is based on

_____

_____

5.    **Social cognitive theory of gender** states

_____

_____

6.    A good example of a **schema** is

_____

_____

7.    A **gender schema** is a

_____

_____

8.    **Gender schema theory** suggests that

_____

_____

9.    **Gender stereotypes** can be seen in

_____

_____

10.   **Sexism** is seen in situations where

_____

_____

11.   Jill uses **rapport talk** when she is

_____

_____

12.    Bart uses **report talk** because

_____

_____

13.    A sure sign of **androgyny** is when

_____

_____

14.    **Gender-role transcendence** is a belief that

_____

_____

15.    The **gender intensification hypothesis** states that

_____

_____


## KEY PEOPLE IN THE STUDY OF ADOLESCENCE

Match the person with the concept of adolescent development with which they are associated.

____    1.  Sigmund Freud          A. An evolutionary psychologist
____    2.  Erik Erikson           B. Proposed the cognitive developmental theory of gender
____    3.  Alice Eagly            C. Developed an assessment instrument for androgyny
____    4.  Eleanor Maccoby        D. Finds that males and females have different styles of "talk"
____    5.  Carol Gilligan         E. Worked with Eleanor Maccoby and concluded that males have better
                                       math and visuospatial abilities
____    6.  Lawrence Kohlberg      F. Proposes that women have a different "voice"
____    7.  Carol Jacklin          G. Argued that male and female psychological differences are related to
                                       genital structure
____    8.  Janet Shibley Hyde     H. Argued that gender and sexual behavior are unlearned and instinctual
____    9.  Deborah Tannen         I. Proponent of the male role-strain perspective
____   10.  David Buss             J. Proposes that differences in male and female verbal ability have now
                                       virtually disappeared
____   11.  Sandra Bem             K. Says that psychological sex differences arise from social roles of men
                                       and women
____   12.  Joseph Pleck           L. Argues that cognitive differences between females and males have
                                       been exaggerated


## ADOLESCENT MYTH AND FACT

Which of the following statements regarding adolescents are true (T) and which are false (F)?

1.    According to Udry, hormone increases in puberty are strongly related to gender behaviors.  T or F

2.    Many parents believe that math is more important to their sons' futures than their daughters.  T or F

3.   Studies have suggested that intelligent girls are often portrayed as unattractive on television.  T or F

4.   Research evidence clearly suggests a school classroom bias against boys and in favor of girls.  T or F

5.   Studies by Jhally (1990) show that MTV is clearly slanted towards a female audience.  T or F

6.   Researchers have found that children do NOT develop gender constancy until they are about 6 or 7 years old.  T or F

7.   Women have twice the body fat of men.  T or F

8.   On average, men grow to be 20 percent taller than women.  T or F

9.   Men are less likely than women to develop physical or mental disorders.  T or F

10.  Boys in all cultures are consistently more physically aggressive than girls.  T or F

11.  Girls usually show less self-regulation of emotions and behavior than men.  T or F

12.  According to Bem, androgynous women and men are more flexible and mentally healthy then either masculine or feminine individuals.  T or F

13.  Latinas experience far greater restrictions within families than do Latinos.  T or F

14.  It is easier to teach androgyny to boys than girls.  T or F

15.  Studies show that males and females nearing the end of high school show less masculinity than eighth graders.  T or F


## BIOLOGICAL, SOCIAL, AND COGNITIVE INFLUENCES ON GENDER SECTION REVIEW

1.   What is gender?

_____

_____

2.   What is meant by one's gender role?

_____

_____

3.   How strong are biological influences on gender?

_____

_____

4.   Compare Freud's and Erikson's theories related to gender, and explain how they promote the notion that anatomy is destiny.

_____

_____

5.   To what extent do hormones play a role in the sexual activities of boys and girls?

_____

6.      What is the evolutionary view of gender development?

_____

_____

7.      What roles do gender hierarchy and sexual division of labor play in sex-differentiated behavior?

_____

_____

8.      According to the social cognitive theory of gender, what role do parents play in the development of gender-appropriate behavior?

_____

_____

9.      What did Luria and Herzog (1985) mean when they referred to play settings as "gender school?"

_____

_____

10.     How does television programming appeal specifically to male and female audiences, and what impact does it have?

_____

_____

11.     How are men typically portrayed on television?

_____

_____

12.     What was Kohlberg's theory of gender development?

_____

_____

13.     What is a schema?

_____

_____

14.     What does gender schema theory state about individual gender development?

_____

_____

# GENDER STEREOTYPES, SIMILARITIES, AND DIFFERENCES
## SECTION REVIEW

1.  What is the nature of gender stereotypes today?

    _____

    _____

2.  How common is gender stereotyping?

    _____

    _____

3.  How widespread is feminine and masculine stereotyping?

    _____

    _____

4.  What is sexism?

    _____

    _____

5.  What are some identifiable brain differences between men and women?

    _____

    _____

6.  Differentiate between "old fashioned" and "modern" sexism.

    _____

    _____

7.  Using Tannen's model, distinguish between rapport talk and report talk.

    _____

    _____

8.  What is David Buss's hypothesis regarding how gender differences develop?

    _____

    _____

9.  Why is context an important factor in understanding gender?

    _____

    _____

## GENDER-ROLE CLASSIFICATION
## SECTION REVIEW

1.      Do gender roles vary around the world? If so, give an example of how they vary.

        _____

        _____

2.      When did alternatives to traditional masculinity and femininity begin to develop?

        _____

        _____

3.      How do androgynous individuals compare with either masculine or feminine individuals?

        _____

        _____

4.      Should androgyny be actively taught to students?

        _____

        _____

5.      What are some concerns associated with teaching children and adolescents to depart from socially
        approved behavior patterns?

        _____

        _____

6.      Explain what Pollack meant by "boy code."

        _____

        _____

## SUMMARIZE DEVELOPMENTAL CHANGES AND JUNCTURES
## SECTION REVIEW

1.      What is the gender intensification hypothesis?

        _____

        _____

2.      Is early adolescence a critical juncture for females?

        _____

        _____

3. What is Gillian's belief about the critical juncture for adolescent females?

_____

_____

4. What are some criticisms of Gillian's beliefs and theories?

_____

_____

## EXPLORATIONS IN ADOLESCENCE DEVELOPMENT

How widespread is gender stereotyping today? Generate two lists, one for males and one for females, of current gender stereotypes you can identify.

_____

_____

## COGNITIVE CHALLENGE

1. Make a list of words that you associate with masculinity and femininity. Identify those words that have negative connotations for males and/or females. Then replace them with words that have more positive connotations.

_____

_____

2. Suppose you have children: How will you attempt to raise them in terms of gender roles? Will you try to raise gender-neutral children, or will you encourage more traditional gender distinctions?

_____

_____

3. What factors during your childhood led you to develop your gender role?

_____

_____

## ADOLESCENCE IN RESEARCH

Describe the attitudes towards masculinity as given by Pleck and colleagues. State hypotheses and other research relevant observations you have regarding their research and outcomes.

1.  _____ refers to a set of expectations about sex-appropriate behavior.
    a.  Stereotype            c.  Gender intensification .
    b.  Gender role           d.  Sexism

2.  According to Robert Udry, boys' increased sexual activity is strongly influenced by _____, whereas girls sexual behavior is most influenced by _____.
    a.  androgen levels; estrogen levels
    b.  estrogen levels; androgen levels
    c.  androgen levels; type of friends they have
    d.  alcohol consumption; religious background

3.  According to Freud and Erikson, _____ is the largest single factor regarding gender behavior of adolescents.
    a.  temperament           c.  attitudes of the parents
    b.  religion              d.  genitals they are born with

4.  Erik Erikson and Sigmund Freud believed that the differences between males and females
    a.  were the result of females' ability and males' inability to articulate their feelings.
    b.  resulted from prenatal hormonal influences.
    c.  resulted from anatomical differences.
    d.  were gender stereotypes rather than gender differences.

5.  _____ argued that because of genital structure, males are more intrusive and aggressive and that females are more inclusive and passive.
    a.  Erik Erikson          c.  Robert Udry
    b.  Sigmund Freud         d.  David Buss

6.  An adolescent mother can reduce the sex-role stereotypes of her children by
    a.  dressing them all the same.
    b.  withholding praise for their physical appearance.
    c.  holding a job outside the home.
    d.  divorcing their father.

7.  Which of the following is TRUE regarding families with young boys?
    a.  They are more likely to have curfews.
    b.  They experience intense concerns about choice of friends.
    c.  They allow boys more independence than girls.
    d.  They experience more intense conflict about sex.

8.  According to contemporary views of evolutionary psychology, which of the following is NOT an evolved disposition of men?
    a.  violence               c.  risk taking
    b.  competition            d.  compassion

9. On the playground, girls teach girls and boys teach boys about their gender behaviors. This is known as
   a. gender socialization.                c. peer socialization.
   b. gender intensification.              d. peer generalization.

10. DeZolt and Hull (2001) noted that in some ways boys might not receive a fair education. Which is NOT one of their listed concerns?
    a. Boys are more likely than girls to be identified as having learning problems.
    b. Boys are more likely than girls to be criticized.
    c. School personnel tend to stereotype boys' behavior as problematic.
    d. A large majority of teachers are males who inherently distrust boys, based on experiences.

11. Sadker and Sadker (2003) noted that in some ways both boys and girls might not receive a fair education. Which is NOT one of their listed concerns?
    a. Girls' learning problems are not identified as often as boys' learning problems.
    b. Boys are given the lion's share of attention in school.
    c. Pressure to achieve is more likely to be heaped on boys than on girls.
    d. More girls than boys come from families living in poverty.

12. Which of the following is NOT a mechanism by which gender develops, according to social cognitive theory?
    a. observation                          c. imitation
    b. negative reinforcement               d. punishment

13. Adolescent females watching television are likely to find
    a. fewer role models than their brothers will.
    b. accurate representations of women's roles.
    c. important lessons on managing relationships.
    d. little to identify with in terms of sexual intimacy.

14. A boy recognizes that he is a male and then starts doing "male" things. This description is consistent with the _____ theory of gender.
    a. socialization                        c. cognitive-developmental
    b. genderization                        d. intensification

15. Frank asks Suzy when "…she is going to quit her job at the corporation to 'go have babies'". Frank's suggestion that Suzy's corporate goals are misplaced is an example of:
    a. modern sexism                        c. old-fashioned sexism
    b. sexual bias                          d. gender reference

16. According to Kohlberg, the main changes in gender development occur
    a. in infancy.                          c. in childhood.
    b. in adolescence.                      d. as young adults.

17. Pointing to the considerable overlap in the distribution of female and male scores on math and visuospatial tasks, _____ suggests that the cognitive differences between females and males have been exaggerated.
    a. Janet Shibley Hyde                   c. Carol Jacklin
    b. Eleanor Maccoby                      d. Carol Gilligan

18. Which of the following is NOT part of Pollack's "boy code"?
   a. Boys are taught to express their anxieties.
   b. Boys should show little if any emotion.
   c. Bottling emotions is a way to regulate aggression.
   d. Boys adopt a masculine role in adolescence.

19. Of the following, which type of aggression is most often seen in boys?
   a. relational aggression
   b. spreading malicious rumors
   c. physical aggression
   d. verbal aggression

20. Pat gets embarrassed when making a mistake in public and experiences episodes of jealousy and passion. What gender is Pat likely to be?
   a. male
   b. female
   c. equally likely to be male or female
   d. There is no research on which to base an answer.

21. Which of the following is most characteristic of how girls play games?
   a. They play in large groups.
   b. Their games focus on taking turns.
   c. They have a leader who tells them what to do.
   d. Their groups are hierarchically structured.

22. According to the Bem Sex-Role Inventory, an adolescent is androgynous if she scores
   a. high on masculinity and high on femininity.
   b. high on masculinity and low on femininity.
   c. low on femininity and low on masculinity.
   d. half way between masculinity and femininity.

23. In the past, which of the following was NOT a characteristic of a well-adjusted boy?
   a. independent          c. aggressive
   b. nurturant            d. powerful

24. In the past, which of the following was NOT a characteristic of a well-adjusted girl?
   a. independent          c. uninterested in power
   b. nurturant            d. dependent

25. The concept of _____ involves the notion that an individual's competence should not be conceptualized along the lines of gender orientation, but rather, the emphasis should be on the individual.
   a. gender-neutrality    c. gender-role transcendence
   b. humanism             d. critical feminism

26. The greatest change in attitudes towards traditional roles for women in the U.S. occurred in
   a. the 1990's           c. the 1960's and early 1970's
   b. the 1980's           d. the World War II Era (1940's)

27. The gender intensification hypothesis indicates that behavioral differences between males and females become greater during adolescence because of
    a. hormones.
    b. pressures to conform to stereotypes.
    c. television commercials.
    d. the development of a new schema.

28. The concept of _____ refers to the fact that the amount, timing, and intensity of gender socialization are different for girls and boys.
    a. gender intensification
    b. asymmetric gender socialization
    c. gender role transcendence
    d. sex difference

29. According to Tannen, which of the following is NOT an example of "report talk"?
    a. joking                          c. lecturing
    b. storytelling                    d. relationship oriented conversation

30. According to Tannen, _____ is an example of "rapport talk"?
    a. joking                          c. lecturing
    b. story telling                   d. relationship oriented conversation

31. Carol Gilligan has suggested that girls
    a. are better than boys.           c. are different from boys.
    b. are equal to boys.              d. None of the above is correct.

32. Gender-role critics, or those who favor gender-role transcendence, would most likely suggest that
    a. parents raise their children to be competent boys and girls.
    b. parents raise their children to take on a masculine role.
    c. parents raise their children to take on feminine roles.
    d. parents raise their children to take on androgynous roles.

## ADOLESCENCE IN RESEARCH

Concerning Pleck and colleagues' 1994 National Survey of Adolescent Males, state the hypothesis, the research methods (if known), the research conclusions, and the implications and applications for adolescent development.

_____

_____

## ADOLESCENCE ON THE SCREEN

- *Boys Don't Cry* Hilary Swank won an academy award for her portrayal of the true story of a boy with gender identity disorder who was murdered when his biological sex was revealed.

- *The Crying Game* A shocking ending reveals that one of the main characters is a transsexual.

- *Mr. and Mrs. Bridges* Joanne Woodward and Paul Newman portray an upper-class couple in the American Midwest of the 1940s who embody the male and female stereotypical roles of the time.

- *Ma Vie En Rose (My Life in Pink)* A French movie (with English subtitles) about a boy with gender identity disorder who dresses and lives as a girl.

- *Antonia's Line* A longitudinal portrayal of the transformation from adolescence to womanhood and the life decisions involved.

- *The Body Beautiful* Provides a generative example of how our various bodily and social identities are built and given meaning concurrently.

- *Whale Rider* Offers a contemporary look at the hazards of being born the wrong gender in certain cultures.

- *Daughters of the Dust* Life and development on a barrier island amongst the Gullah Subculture. An isolated African-American culture off the coast of South Carolina.

## ADOLESCENCE IN BOOKS

- *A New Psychology of Men*, by Ronald Levant and William Pollack (Basic Books, 1995), is a collection of essays on men's issues and male gender roles.

- *As Nature Made Him*, by John Colapinto (HarperCollins: NY, 2000), tells the true story of one of identical twins whose penis was accidentally severed during circumcision and who was given female hormones and raised as a girl until his parents revealed the accident. He then had penile reconstructive surgery and hormone treatments and resumed life as a man.

- *Stiffed: The Betrayal of the American Man*, by Susan Faludi (William Morrow: NY, 1999), examines the problems of men in modern life, emphasizing the stress of male sex roles.

- *You Just Don't Understand*, by Deborah Tannen (Ballantine: NY, 1990), explores the differences in male and female communication styles.

# Answer Key

## KEY TERMS

1. **gender** The sociocultural dimension of being male or female.

2. **gender role** A set of expectations that prescribes how females and males should think, act, and feel.

3. **cognitive developmental theory of gender** In this view, children's gender-typing occurs after they have developed a concept of gender. Once they begin to consistently conceive of themselves as male or female, children often organize their world based on gender.

4. **social role theory** States that gender differences result from the contrasting roles of females and males.

5. **social cognitive theory of gender** Emphasizes that children's and adolescents' gender development occurs through observation and imitation of gender behavior, and through rewards and punishments they experience for gender-appropriate and -inappropriate behavior.

6. **schema** A cognitive structure of network of associations that organizes and guides an individual's perception.

7. **gender schema** A cognitive structure that organizes the world in terms of male and female.

8. **gender schema theory** According to this theory, an individual's attention and behavior are guided by an internal motivation to conform to gender-based sociocultural standards and stereotypes.

9. **gender stereotypes** Broad categories that reflect our impressions and beliefs about females and males.

10. **sexism** Prejudice and discrimination against an individual because of his or her sex.

11. **rapport talk** The language of conversation and a way of establishing connections and negotiating relationships.

12. **report talk** Conversation that gives information. Public speaking would be an example.

13. **androgyny** The presence of a high degree of desirable feminine and masculine characteristics in the same individual.

14. **gender-role transcendence** The belief that, when an individual's competence is at issue, it should be conceptualized not on the basis of masculinity, femininity, or androgyny; rather it should be determined on a person basis.

15. **gender intensification hypothesis** This hypothesis states that psychological and behavioral differences between boys and girls become greater during early adolescence because of increased socialization pressures to conform to masculine and feminine gender roles.

## KEY PEOPLE IN THE STUDY OF ADOLESCENCE

| | | | | | | | |
|---|---|---|---|---|---|---|---|
| 1. | H | 4. | J | 7. | E | 10. | A |
| 2. | G | 5. | F | 8. | L | 11. | C |
| 3. | K | 6. | B | 9. | D | 12. | I |

## ADOLESCENT MYTH AND FACT

| | | | | | |
|---|---|---|---|---|---|
| 1. | F | 6. | T | 11. | F |
| 2. | T | 7. | T | 12. | T |
| 3. | T | 8. | F | 13. | T |
| 4. | F | 9. | F | 14. | F |
| 5. | F | 10. | T | 15. | T |

## BIOLOGICAL, SOCIAL, AND COGNITIVE INFLUENCES ON GENDER SECTION REVIEW

1. Gender refers to the psychological and sociocultural dimensions of being male or female.

2. Gender role is a set of expectations that prescribes how females or males should think, act, and feel.

3. Hormones and pubertal change contribute to an increased incorporation of sexuality in the gender attitudes and behavior of adolescents.

4. Both felt that genitals were the primary source of influence on gender behavior.

5. Androgen levels are related to sexual activity in boys, but girls were more likely to be influenced by the kinds of friends they hung out with.

6.    Evolutionary psychologists argue that men and women faced different evolutionary pressures in primeval environments, and adapted to these.

7.    From the perspective of social influences, gender hierarchy and sexual division of labor are important causes of sex-differentiated behavior.

8.    Emphasizes that childrens' and adolescents' gender development occurs through observation and imitation of gender behavior, and through rewards and punishments they experience for gender-appropriate and -inappropriate behavior.

9.    After extensive observations, they labeled play settings as "gender school" pointing out that boys teach one another the required masculine behavior and reinforce it, and girls also teach one another the required feminine behavior and reinforce it.

10.   Television targets teens, in particular teenage girls in its depiction of females on TV.

11.   Males are more often seen in work roles, cars, or in sports. Females receive much less TV time and are more likely to be seen in the home.

12.   Children's gender typing occurs after they have developed a concept of gender. Once they begin to consistently conceive of themselves as male or female, children often organize their world based on gender.

13.   A schema is a cognitive structure, a network of associations that organizes and guides an individual's perceptions.

14.   Gender Schema Theory states that an individual's attention and behavior are guided by an internal motivation to conform to gender-based sociocultural standards and stereotypes.

## GENDER STEREOTYPES, SIMILARITIES, AND DIFFERENCES
## SECTION REVIEW

1.    These are broad categories that reflect our impressions and beliefs about females and males.

2.    They are so general that they are often ambiguous.

3.    According to college students in 30 countries, it is very common.

4.    Sexism is prejudice and discrimination against an individual because of her or his sex.

5.    Researchers have found some differences. One part of the hypothalamus involved in sexual behavior tends to be larger in men than women. Portions of the corpus callosum appears to be larger in women. The areas of the brain involved in emotional expression tend to show more metabolic activity in females than in men.

6.    Old-fashioned is characterized by endorsement of traditional gender roles, differential treatment for men and women with the assumption that women are less competent then men. Modern sexism is characterized by the denial that there is still discrimination and lack of support for policies designed to help women.

7.    Rapport talk is the language of conversation and a way of establishing connections and negotiating relationships. Report talk is talk that gives information (e.g., public speaking).

8.    Buss argues that men and women differ psychologically in those domains in which they have faced different adaptive problems across their evolutionary history.

## GENDER-ROLE CLASSIFICATION
## SECTION REVIEW

1.      Yes. Many cultures have quite different views regarding the roles of men and women.

2.      Alternatives were introduced in the 1960s and 1970s.

3.      Androgynous individuals are described as more flexible and more mentally healthy.

4.      In general, it is easier to teach androgyny to girls than to boys, and it is easier to teach before the middle school years. With girls, in particular, it is probably a good idea in today's changing society.

5.      Ethical concerns are raised when the program involves teaching children and adolescents to depart from socially approved behavior patterns.

6.      The boy code, according to Pollack, is essentially how they are raised and taught not to show their feelings and to act tough. They are taught by parents, teachers, coaches, friends in the sandboxes, schools, playgrounds, etc.

## SUMMARIZE DEVELOPMENTAL CHANGES AND JUNCTURES
## SECTION REVIEW

1.      This states that psychological and behavioral differences between boys and girls become greater during early adolescence because of increased socialization pressures to conform to traditional masculine and feminine gender roles.

2.      Yes. Much is learned from the age of 6 through 18.

3.      Gilligan suggests that the critical juncture for the development of little girls is around 11–12 years of age.

4.      Critics argue that Gilligan overemphasized differences in gender.

## EXPLORATIONS IN ADOLESCENCE DEVELOPMENT

No answers provided. Individual activity.

## COGNITIVE CHALLENGE

1.      No answers provided. Individual activity.

2.      No answers provided. Individual activity.

3.      No answers provided. Individual activity.

## ADOLESCENCE IN RESEARCH

Pleck and colleagues hypothesized that problem behaviors in adolescent males are associated with their attitudes toward masculinity. They also examined the risk and protective influences for problem behaviors. They studied 1,680 15- to 19-year-old males, and their findings supported their hypothesis. Males who had traditional beliefs about masculinity were more likely to have difficulty in school, use drugs and alcohol, be sexually active, and participate in delinquent activities. Risk factors for problem behaviors included low parental education, being the son of a teenage mother, living in a mother-headed household or having no nonmaterial family member in the home, lenient family rules, and infrequent church attendance. Protective factors included strict family rules and frequent church attendance.

## ☒ COMPREHENSIVE REVIEW

| | | | | | | | |
|---|---|---|---|---|---|---|---|
| 1. | b | 10. | c | 19. | c | 28. | a |
| 2. | c | 11. | c | 20. | c | 29. | d |
| 3. | d | 12. | b | 21. | b | 30. | d |
| 4. | c | 13. | a | 22. | a | 31. | c |
| 5. | a | 14. | c | 23. | b | 32. | a |
| 6. | c | 15. | c | 24. | a | | |
| 7. | c | 16. | c | 25. | a | | |
| 8. | d | 17, | a | 26. | c | | |
| 9. | c | 18. | b | 27. | b | | |

# ✦ Chapter 7    Sexuality

**Learning Goals with Key Terms and Key People in Boldface**

**1.0    DISCUSS SOME BASIC IDEAS ABOUT THE NATURE OF ADOLESCENT SEXUALITY**

A.    **A Normal Aspect of Development**

1.1    Do cultures differ in how they view adolescent sexuality?

1.2    What other chapters in the text serve as a backdrop for understanding adolescent sexuality?

B.    **The Sexual Culture**

1.3    What is the nature of adolescent sexuality in today's culture?

1.4    Describe the level of discomfort in discussing sexuality between adolescents and parents in the United States when compared to other cultures?

C.    **Developing a Sexual Identity**

1.5    What is involved in forming a sexual identity?

1.6    What is an adolescent's sexual preference?

D.    **Obtaining Information about Adolescent Sexuality**

1.7    Who is most likely to respond to a sex survey?

1.8    Why is it difficult to obtain valid information about adolescent sexuality?

**2.0    SUMMARIZE SEXUAL ATTITUDES AND BEHAVIOR IN ADOLESCENCE**

A.    **Heterosexual Attitudes and Behavior**

2.1    What is the progression of sexual behaviors?

2.2    Are some adolescents more vulnerable to irresponsible sexual behavior than others?

2.3    Have the number of females engaging in intercourse increased more rapidly than that of males?

2.4    Are there ethnic and racial differences in sexual activity?

2.5    What is the current profile of sexual activity of adolescents?

2.6    What are the common male and female adolescent **sexual scripts**?

2.7    What are some of the risks faced by sexually active adolescents?

2.8    What are specific risk factors for sexual problems in adolescence?

2.9    What is the importance of self-regulation?

B.    **Sexual Minority Attitudes and Behaviors**

2.10    How is the attitude regarding homosexuality changed in the U.S. since the 20th century?

2.11    Explain what is meant by **bisexual** behavior.

2.12    What do we know about adolescents' same-sex attractions?

2.13    What is the continuum of sexual orientation?

2.14    What conclusions can be reached about adolescents who disclose their gay or lesbian identity?

2.15    What is meant by homophobia?

2.16    What is a harmful aspect of the stigmatization of homosexuality?

C.    **Self-stimulation**

2.17    What is the nature of sexual self-stimulation?

2.18    What role does masturbation play in sexual development?

D.    **Contraceptive Use**

2.19    How many adolescents are using contraceptives?

2.20     Which adolescents are least likely to use contraceptives?

**3.0     DESCRIBE THE MAIN SEXUAL PROBLEMS THAT CAN EMERGE IN ADOLESCENCE**

    **A.     Adolescent Pregnancy**

        3.1     How many adolescent females have children before their eighteenth birthday?

        3.2     Is adolescent pregnancy increasing or decreasing?

        3.3     What cultural changes have taken place in the last forty years regarding adolescent sexuality and pregnancy?

        3.4     What are the health risks for mother and offspring?

        3.5     How does adolescent pregnancy affect a mother's school and work opportunities?

        3.6     How does the personal fable impact on pregnancy prevention efforts?

        3.7     What infant risks are associated with being born to an adolescent mother?

        3.8     What kind of mothers do adolescents make?

        3.9     What is the nature of adolescent fatherhood?

        3.10     What are Congers four recommendations for reducing adolescent pregnancy?

        3.11     What programs have reduced adolescent pregnancy?

        3.12     What is the Teen Outreach Program?

        3.13     Describe the 4 programs associated with Girls, Inc.

    **B.     Sexually Transmitted Infections**

        3.14     What are **sexually transmitted infections** (STIs)?

        3.15     How are **STIs** contracted?

        3.16     What is **AIDS**?

        3.17     What is the rate of **AIDS** in adolescence?

        3.18     How does the long incubation period affect adolescents who may have been infected with the **AIDS** virus as teenagers?

        3.19     Where is the region of most concern regarding the spread of HIV/AIDS?

        3.20     How is **AIDS** transmitted?

        3.21     How is **AIDS** prevented?

        3.22     What is **genital herpes**?

        3.23     What are **genital warts**?

        3.24     What is **gonorrhea**?

        3.25     What is **syphilis**?

        3.26     What is **chlamydia**?

        3.27     What is the most common **STI** in the adolescent age group?

    **C.     Forcible Sexual Behavior and Sexual Harassment**

        3.28     What is the nature and incidence of **rape**?

        3.29     What is **date, or acquaintance, rape**?

        3.30     Who are the victims of acquaintance rape?

        3.31     What is sexual harassment?

        3.32     How prevalent is adolescent sexual harassment?

        3.33     What is **quid pro quo sexual harassment**?

        3.34     What is the nature of **hostile environment sexual harassment**?

**4.0     CHARACTERIZE THE SEXUAL LITERACY OF ADOLESCENTS AND SEX EDUCATION**

    **A.     Sexual Literacy**

        4.1     How much do American adolescents and adults know about sex?

    **B.     Sources of Sex Information**

        4.2     What is the nature or source of most sex information?

        4.3     What are the sources of sex information?

    **C.     Sex Education in the Schools**

        4.4     What is the incidence and nature of sex education in the schools?

# Exercises

## KEY TERMS COMPLETION EXERCISE

This exercise presents each key term in the form of an incomplete sentence. Complete each sentence by either defining the term or giving an example. Compare your definitions with those given at the end of the study guide chapter.

1.     A **sexual script** is

_____

_____

2.     James is **bisexual,** which means he

_____

_____

3.     People must learn about **sexually transmitted infections (STIs)** because

_____

_____

4.     The symptoms of **gonorrhea** are

_____

_____

5.     The symptoms of **syphilis** are

_____

_____

6.     The symptoms of **Chlamydia** are

_____

_____

7.     The symptoms of **genital herpes** are

_____

_____

8.   The symptoms of **genital warts** are

_____

_____

9.   **AIDS** is an acronym standing for

_____

_____

10.  The description of **rape** is

_____

_____

11.  **Date, or acquaintance, rape** occurs when

_____

_____

12.  **Quid pro quo sexual harassment** occurs when

_____

_____

13.  **Hostile environment sexual harassment** occurs when

_____

_____

## KEY PEOPLE IN THE STUDY OF ADOLESCENCE

Match the person with the concept of adolescent development with which they are associated.

____   1. Jeanne Brooks-Gunn       A. Director of Kinsey Institute for Sex, Gender, and Reproduction
____   2. Alfred Kinsey            B. Researched the pattern of gay and lesbian adolescents' disclosure
                                      of sexual orientation
____   3. Richard Savin-Williams   C. Studies developmental issues in adolescent sexuality
____   4. Simon LeVay              D. Early and famous sex researcher
____   5. June Reinisch            E. Studied the brains of gay men for clues to causes of
                                      homosexuality

## "DR. DETAIL'S" MATCHING EXERCISE

Match the STI with the associated features.

____   1. Syphilis         A. Colloquially called "the drip" or "clap"
____   2. Chlamydia        B. Caused by a large family of viruses with many different strains
____   3. Genital herpes   C. Destroys the body's immune system

| ___ | 4. Gonorrhea | D. Is caused by the bacterium *Treponema pallidum* |
| ___ | 5. AIDS | E. Common sexually transmitted infection that infects genital organs of both sexes |
| ___ | 6. Genital Warts | F. Is the most common of all sexually transmitted diseases in the U.S. |

## ADOLESCENT MYTH AND FACT

Which of the following statements regarding adolescents are true (T) and which are false (F)?

1. Sexuality is a normal part of adolescence.  T or F

2. Watching sexually explicit TV shows makes an adolescent more likely to engage in sex.  T or F

3. Early maturation is related to early sexual activity.  T or F

4. Sexual orientation tends to be either exclusively heterosexual or exclusively homosexual.  T or F

5. The American Psychological Association considers homosexuality to be a form of mental illness.  T or F

6. Twins studies on homosexual individuals suggests a clear biological interpretation of the cause of homosexuality.  T or F

7. College-aged males are twice as likely as females to engage in  masturbation.  T or F

8. Very few adolescents who become pregnant now marry before their baby is born.  T or F

9. Research suggests that adolescents who have abortions are psychologically harmed by their abortion experience.  T or F

10. Adolescents are more likely than adults to become infected with the AIDS virus through homosexual contact.  T or F

## EXPLORING ADOLESCENT SEXUALITY
## SECTION REVIEW

1. Do cultures differ in how they view adolescent sexuality?

   _____

   _____

2. Identify other chapters in the text that can serve as a backdrop for understanding adolescent sexuality?

| Chapter | Concept |
|---|---|
| Biological Differences | |
| Cognitive Differences | |
| Families | |
| Peers | |
| Schools | |
| Culture | |
| The Self and Identity | |
| Gender | |

3. What is the nature of adolescent sexuality in today's culture?

_____

_____

4. What is involved in forming a sexual identity?

_____

_____

5. Who is most likely to respond to a sex survey?

_____

_____

6. What is the typical progression of sexual behaviors?

_____

_____

7. Have the number of females engaging is intercourse increased more rapidly than males?

_____

_____

## SEXUAL ATTITUDES AND BEHAVIOR
## SECTION REVIEW

1. Are there ethnic and racial differences in sexual activity?

_____

_____

2. What is the current profile of sexual activity of adolescents?

_____

_____

3. What are the common male and female adolescent sexual scripts?

_____

_____

4. What are some of the risk factors faced by sexually active adolescents?

_____

_____

5. What is the attitude today about sexual orientation?

_____

_____

6. What is meant by homophobia?

_____

_____

7. What is a harmful aspect of the stigmatization of homosexuality?

_____

_____

8. What five conclusions did Savin-Williams (1998, 2000) make about adolescents who disclose their gay or lesbian identity?

_____

_____

9. What is the nature of sexual self-stimulation?

_____

_____

10. Which adolescents are least likely to use contraceptives?

_____

_____

11. Why is the issue of contraception more difficult for adolescents than adults?

_____

_____

**KEY PEOPLE IN SECTION** (describe the contributions of this individual to the study and understanding of adolescence).

**Alfred Kinsey —** _____

_____

**Simon LeVay —**

_____

_____

ADOLESCENT SEXUAL PROBLEMS
SECTION REVIEW

1.  How many adolescent births are unintended?

    _____

    _____

2.  What cultural changes have taken place in the last forty years regarding adolescent sexuality and
    pregnancy?

    _____

    _____

3.  What are the health risks for mother and child of adolescent pregnancy?

    _____

    _____

4.  What are some reason that teens in the United States have a higher pregnancy rate than adolescents in
    other countries?

    _____

    _____

5.  How does adolescent pregnancy affect a mother's school and work opportunities?

    _____

    _____

6.  How does the *personal fable* affect pregnancy prevention efforts?

    _____

    _____

7.  What infant risks are associated with teenage pregnancy?

    _____

    _____

8.  What are some of the dilemmas and problems faced by adolescent fathers in the United States?

    _____

    _____

9.  What are Conger's four recommendations for reducing adolescent pregnancy?

    _____

    _____

10. What is the Teen Outreach Program?

_____

_____

11. What are sexually transmitted infections?

_____

_____

12. What is AIDS?

_____

_____

13. Where is the region of most concern regarding the spread of HIV/AIDS?

_____

_____

14. How is AIDS transmitted?

_____

_____

15. How is AIDS prevented?

_____

_____

16. What is the nature and incidence of rape?

_____

_____

17. What is acquaintance rape?

_____

_____

18. What is sexual harassment?

_____

_____

19. What is quid pro quo sexual harassment?

_____

_____

20.     What is the nature of hostile environment sexual harassment?

_____

_____


**KEY PEOPLE IN SECTION** (describe the contributions of this individual to the study and understanding of adolescence).

**John Conger —** _____

_____

## SEXUAL LITERACY AND SEX EDUCATION
## SECTION REVIEW

1.      How much do American adolescents and adults know about sex?

_____

_____


2.      What are the sources of most sex information?

_____

_____


3.      Why do some experts believe that school-linked sex education tied to community health centers is a promising strategy?

_____

_____


4.      What are some criticisms of school-linked sex education?

_____

_____


**KEY PEOPLE IN SECTION** (describe the contributions of this individual to the study and understanding of adolescence).

**June Reinisch —** _____

## COGNITIVE CHALLENGE

1.      Caroline contracted genital herpes from an old boyfriend. When she started dating Charles, she told him she had the herpes infection and he broke up with her. Now she is dating Jeff, and she is afraid to tell him about the herpes because she thinks he will also break up with her. She thought maybe she should just

tell him to use a condom so she won't get pregnant, and then she won't need to mention the herpes. What do you think Caroline should do?

_____

_____

2.    Based upon how you learned about sexuality, how do you expect to teach your children about sex? How do you want the schools to be involved in sex education for your children? Who other than parents and schools do you think should be involved in sex education?

_____

_____

## ADOLESCENCE IN RESEARCH

Buzwell and Rosenthal (1996) conducted an investigation of an adolescent's sexual identity; state the hypothesis, the research methods (if known), the research conclusions, and the implications and applications for adolescent development.

_____

_____

## COMPREHENSIVE REVIEW

1.    Sexual behaviors usually progress in the following order:
      a.    kissing, oral sex, necking.
      b.    petting, necking, kissing.
      c.    intercourse, sexual adventure, oral sex.
      d.    necking, petting, intercourse.

2.    Which of the following is NOT a context where a sexual identity emerges?
      a.    In the context of physical factors.
      b.    In the context of social factors.
      c.    In the context of cultural factors.
      d.    In the context of religious factors.

3.    A _____ is a pattern involving stereotyped role prescriptions for how individuals should behave sexually.
      a.    sexual bias          c.    sexual role
      b.    sexual schema        d.    sexual script

4.    Which of the following is NOT an adolescent sexual orientation?
      a.    androgynous          c.    heterosexual
      b.    homosexual           d.    bisexual

5.    An individual sexually attracted to both females and males is
      a.    bisexual.            c.    heterosexual.
      b.    homosexual.          d.    transsexual.

6. According to a National Survey, the most common "reason" for girls to have sex is
   a. they think they are ready.
   b. they are being pressured by a boy.
   c. they want to be loved.
   d. they don't want to be teased for being a virgin.

7. The most frequent sexual outlet for an adolescent is
   a. oral sex.                    c. masturbation.
   b. sexual fantasy.              d. sexual intercourse.

8. Which of the following is NOT linked with early sexual involvement by girls in early adolescence?
   a. schizophrenia               c. depression
   b. lower self-esteem           d. lower grades

9. Which of the following is NOT one of the stages of "coming out" in gay male adolescents?
   a. declaration
   b. sensitization
   c. awareness with confusion, denial, guilt, and shame
   d. acceptance

10. Compared to those who wait to have children until they are in their mid- to late twenties, adolescent parents
    a. have a better chance of staying married.
    b. are less lonely.
    c. have fewer children throughout their adult lives.
    d. have lower incomes.

11. Infants born to adolescent mothers are more likely to
    a. be overweight.                  c. bond with their mothers.
    b. have an average survival rate.  d. have low birth weights.

12. Sexually transmitted infections are defined as those contracted through
    a. vaginal intercourse.
    b. vaginal intercourse and oral-genital contact.
    c. oral-genital and anal-genital contact.
    d. oral-genital and anal-genital contact and vaginal intercourse.

13. The most fatal sexually transmitted infection caused by a bacterium is
    a. syphilis.                   c. AIDS.
    b. herpes.                     d. gonorrhea.

14. _____ is the first person that a homosexual adolescent is likely to disclose their orientation to
    a. The mother                  c. The father
    b. A friend                    d. A sibling

15. The most common sexually transmitted disease among adolescents is
    a. genital warts.              c. syphilis.
    b. herpes.                     d. gonorrhea.

16. If you come into intimate sexual contact with an infected person, your risk of contracting the disease is greatest for
    a. gonorrhea.                  c. herpes.
    b. syphilis.                   d. AIDS.

17. Most boys have an ejaculation for the first time at about the age of
    a. 8 to 9 years of age          c. 12 to 13 years of age
    b. 10 to 11 years of age        d. 14 to 15 years of age

18. Which of the following STIs is NOT a virus?
    a. genital warts                c. syphilis
    b. HIV                          d. genital herpes

19. Sexually active adolescent girls are most likely to choose which form of contraception?
    a. condoms                      c. the pill
    b. withdrawal                   d. an injectable contraceptive

20. _____ are usually the main source of an adolescent's sexual information.
    a. Parents                      c. Peers
    b. Schools                      d. Literature

21. Which of the following statements concerning sex education in the schools is accurate?
    a. The majority of adults in the United States do not approve of sex education in the schools.
    b. Sex education programs are more likely to appear in high schools and junior high schools than elementary schools.
    c. The emphasis in sex education classes is on contraception and variations in sexual behavior.
    d. Most sex education programs consist of full-semester courses on human sexuality.

22. Belinda's boyfriend used a variety of psychological and physical ploys to coerce her into having sex, even though she had said no to him. Her boyfriend's behavior is referred to as _____ rape.
    a. power
    b. sexual
    c. controlling
    d. acquaintance

23. Fourteen-year-old Mandy has decided to become sexually active with her boyfriend. Despite knowing several young girls who have become pregnant, Mandy believes 'it won't happen to me.' Mandy's behavior suggests she is being impacted by
    a. adolescent depersonalization.
    b. adolescent idealism.
    c. the imaginary audience.
    d. the personal fable.

24. The factor that is most important in facilitating the recovery from rape is
    a. physical health.
    b. retaliation against the rapist.
    c. resumption of consensual sexual relations.
    d. social support.

25. Which of the following is most indicative of sex education today in the U.S.?
    a. discussion about abstinence
    b. discussion about abortion
    c. discussion about birth control
    d. discussion about sexual orientation

26. The purpose of sex education programs in such countries as Holland and Sweden is to _____ the experience of adolescent sexuality.
    a. promote          c. demystify
    b. discourage       d. simplify

## ADOLESCENCE ON THE SCREEN

- *Chasing Amy* A young man is attracted to a girl who tells him that she is a lesbian. Actually, she has had a wild heterosexual past and is manipulating the boy's attraction for her.

- *Taxi Driver* A New York City taxi driver tries to save a child prostitute.

- *The Summer of '42* A young boy has his first sexual experience with a kind, older woman on whom he has a crush.

- *The Middle School Chronicles* [HBO] Offers a startling view of sexuality and sex as well as other problem behaviors of youth.

- *The Lost Kids of Rockdale County* [PBS Frontline] Chilling details regarding an epidemic of syphilis that raged through the school in this quiet town. There is also discussion on school-related violence.

- *Rain* A 13-year-girl becomes increasingly aware of problems in her parents' marriage while at the same time starting to discover her own sexuality.

## ADOLESCENCE IN BOOKS

- *Boys and Sex*, by Wardell Pomery (Delacorte Press: NY, 1991), was written for adolescent boys and stresses the responsibility that comes with sexual maturity.

- *Girls and Sex*, by Wardell Pomery (Delacorte Press: NY, 1991), poses a number of questions that young girls often ask about sex and then answers them. Many myths that young girls hear about sex are also demystified.

# Answer Key

## KEY TERMS

1. **sexual script** A stereotypical pattern of role prescriptions for how individuals should behave sexually. Females and males have been socialized to follow different sexual scripts.

2. **bisexual** A person who is attracted to people of both sexes.

3. **sexually transmitted infections (STIs)** Infections that are contracted primarily through sexual contact. This contact is not limited to vaginal intercourse but includes oral-genital contact and anal-genital contact as well.

4.      **gonorrhea** Reported to be one of the more common STIs in the United States, this sexually transmitted infection is caused by a bacterium called *gonococcus,* which thrives in the moist mucous membrane lining the mouth, throat, vagina, cervix, urethra, and anal tract. This infection is commonly called the "drip" or the "clap."

5.      **syphilis** A sexually transmitted infection caused by the bacterium *Treponema pallidum,* a spirochete.

6.      **Chlamydia** A common sexually transmitted infection, is named for Chlamydia trachomatis, an organism that infects both sexual partners.

7.      **genital herpes** A sexually transmitted infection caused by a large family of viruses of different strains. These strains produce other, nonsexually transmitted diseases such as chicken pox and mononucleosis.

8.      **genital warts** The most common STI in the United States, it is caused by the Human Papilloma Virus and is highly contagious.

9.      **AIDS** Acquired immune deficiency syndrome, primarily a sexually transmitted infection caused by the HIV virus, which destroys the body's immune system.

10.     **rape** Forcible nonconsensual sexual intercourse.

11.     **date or acquaintance rape** Coercive sexual activity directed at someone with whom the perpetrator is at least casually acquainted.

12.     **quid pro quo sexual harassment** Occurs when a school employee threatens to base an educational decision (such as a grade) on a student's submission to unwelcome conduct

13.     **hostile environment sexual harassment** Occurs when students are subjected to unwelcome sexual conduct that is so severe, persistent, or pervasive that it limits the students' ability to benefit from their education.

## KEY PEOPLE IN THE STUDY OF ADOLESCENCE

**1.** c

**2.** d

**3.** b

**4.** e

**5.** a

## "DR. DETAIL'S" MATCHING EXERCISE

**1.** D

**2.** E

**3.** B

**4.** A

**5.** C

**6.** F

## ADOLENCENT MYTH AND FACT

1.  T
2.  T
3.  T
4.  F
5.  F

6.  T
7.  T
8.  T
9.  F
10. F

# EXPLORING ADOLESCENT SEXUALITY
## SECTION REVIEW

1. Yes. In some societies women are escorted or get married before any sexual activity. Other societies are less concerned regarding sexual exploration.

2.

| Prompt | Chapter | Concept |
|---|---|---|
| Biological Differences | 3: Puberty and Biological Foundations | Early pubertal maturation in girls may lead to early dating and sexual activity. |
| Cognitive Differences | 4: Cognitive Development | Adolescent egocentrism may lead to sexual risk-taking. |
| Families | 9: Families | Prolonged family conflict and lack of parental monitoring can lead to problems in sexuality |
| Peers | 10: Peers | Peers and friends influence learning about and discussing sexual behavior. |
| Schools | 11. Schools | Schools have a big role in sex education. |
| Culture | 8: Moral Development, Values, and Religion | Sexuality in the media is often presented to adolescents in an unrealistic way. |
| The Self and Identity | 5: The Self, Identity, Emotions, and Personality | Sexual identity is one dimension of identity. |
| Gender | 6: Gender | Pubertal changes may lead to boys and girls conforming to traditional masculine and feminine behaviors. |

3. Many Americans are ambivalent about sex. It is used to sell just about everything.

4. An adolescent's sexual identity involves an indication of sexual preference (homosexual, heterosexual, bisexual).

5. The most likely people to respond would be those least inhibited. So surveys may measure an extreme.

6. Kissing preceded petting, which preceded sexual intercourse and oral sex.

7. The proportion of female college students who report that they have had sexual intercourse has increased more rapidly than that of males.

# SEXUAL ATTITUDES AND BEHAVIOR
## SECTION REVIEW

1. Male African Americans are more likely to have a less restrictive timetable for sexual behaviors than other groups, whereas Asian Americans are more likely to have a more restrictive one. Male African Americans and inner-city adolescents report being the most sexually active.

2. Eight in 10 girls and seven in 10 boys are virgins at age 15. The probability that adolescents will have sexual intercourse increases steadily with age, but 1 in 5 individuals have not had intercourse by age 19. Initial sexual intercourse occurs in the mid- to late-adolescent years for a majority of teenagers. The majority of females' first sexual partners are similar in age.

3. A sexual script is a stereotyped pattern of role prescriptions for how individuals should sexually behave. Females and males have been socialized to follow different sexual scripts.

4. Pregnancy and sexually transmitted infections.

5. Exclusively heterosexual behavior; largely heterosexual; equal amounts of heterosexual and homosexual behavior; largely homosexual; exclusively homosexual behavior.

6. Having irrational negative feelings against homosexuals.

7. Self-devaluation.

8. Parents are seldom the first to hear about the same-sex attraction. Mothers are usually told before fathers, and mothers are more likely than fathers to find out about a son's or a daughter's same-sex attraction. Approximately 50 to 60 percent of gay adolescents have told a sibling. The first person told about same-sex attraction is usually a friend.

9. It's a way to deal with arousal.

10. Sexually active younger adolescents.

11. The issue of contraception is more difficult for adolescents than adults because of differing patterns of sexual activity. Adults very often plan to have sex, whereas it is generally intermittent and unplanned for adolescents.

## KEY PEOPLE IN SECTION (describe the contributions of this individual to the study and understanding of adolescence).

**Alfred Kinsey**—described sexual orientation as a continuum on a six-point scale.

**Simon LeVay**—found that an area of the hypothalamus that governs sexual behavior is twice as large in heterosexual men as in homosexual men.

## ADOLESCENT SEXUAL PROBLEMS
## SECTION REVIEW

1. More than 200,000 females in the U.S. have a child before their 18th birthday.

2. More acceptance of sexual practice, contraception, and abortion.

3. Adolescent mothers often drop out of school. Children are often of low birth weight, which is associated with a variety of problems later in life.

4. European countries give a strong consensus that childbearing belongs in adulthood. In other countries, they are more accepting of teen sex than in the U.S. Many countries make it easier to access family planning services.

5. She is more likely to drop out of school and have a low skilled job.

6. "It won't happen to me."

7. Low birth weight, neurological problems and illness.

8. Most are uninvolved with their children.

9. (a) Sex education and family planning, (b) access to contraceptives, (c) the life options approach, and (d) broad community involvement and support.

10.     It focuses on engaging adolescents in volunteer community service and stimulates enlightening discussions.

11.     Diseases that are contracted primarily through sexual contact.

12.     Is a sexually transmitted infection that is caused by a virus, the human immunodeficiency virus, which destroys the body's immune system.

13.     Sub-Saharan Africa.

14.     Heterosexual sex, homosexual sex, blood transfusion, shared needles.

15.     Using condoms, not sharing needles, and screening blood donations.

16.     Forcible sexual intercourse with a person who does not give consent.

17.     Coercive sexual activity directed at someone with whom the perpetrator is at least casually acquainted.

18.     Unwanted touch or harassing remarks.

19.     A school employee threatens to base an educational decision, such as a grade, on a student's submission to sex.

20.     Students are subjected to unwelcomed sexual conduct that is so severe, persistent, or pervasive that it limits the student's ability to benefit from their education.


KEY PEOPLE IN SECTION (describe the contributions of this individual to the study and understanding of adolescence).

**John Conger** — offered four recommendations for attacking the high rate of adolescent pregnancy.


## SEXUAL LITERACY AND SEX EDUCATION
## SECTION REVIEW

1.     According to June Reinisch, they know more about their cars than how their bodies function sexually.

2.     Peers.

3.     The attitude is that this can be more informative and reach more children in an unintrusive environment.

4.     Some feel that the knowledge is used to experiment with sexual behaviors, as opposed to abstaining.


KEY PEOPLE IN SECTION (describe the contributions of this individual to the study and understanding of adolescence).

**June Reinisch** — feels that U.S. citizens know more about how their automobiles function than about how their bodies function sexually.

## COGNITIVE CHALLENGE

1.     Individual activity. No answer provided.

2.     Individual activity. No answer provided.

# ADOLESCENCE IN RESEARCH

The reasearchers' hypothesis proposed that adolescents, in choosing their sexual identity, adopt different styles. They studied 470 tenth- to twelfth-grade Australian youth. Their results showed five different styles: sexually naïve; sexually unassured; sexually competent; sexually adventurous; sexually driven.

## ☒ COMPREHENSIVE REVIEW

| | | | | | | | |
|---|---|---|---|---|---|---|---|
| 1. | d | 8. | a | 15. | a | 21. | b |
| 2. | d | 9. | a | 16. | c | 22. | d |
| 3. | d | 10. | d | 17. | c | 23. | d |
| 4. | a | 11. | d | 18. | c | 24. | d |
| 5. | a | 12. | d | 19. | c | 25. | a |
| 6. | b | 13. | a | 20. | c | 26. | c |
| 7. | c | 14. | b | | | | |

# Chapter 8   Moral Development, Values, and Religion

**Learning Goals with Key Terms and Key People in Boldface**

**1.0   DISCUSS THE DOMAINS OF MORAL DEVELOPMENT**

**A.   Domains of Moral Development**

1.1   What is involved in **moral development**?

1.2   What are the dimensions of **moral development**?

**B.   Moral Thought**

1.3   What is the difference between **Piaget's heteronomous morality** and his **autonomous morality**?

1.4   What is the concept of **immanent justice**?

1.5   What does the development of formal operational thought have to do with adolescent moral reasoning?

1.6   What is **Hoffman's** proposed **cognitive disequilibrium theory** of moral development?

1.7   What is **internalization**?

1.8   What are **Kohlberg's** three levels of moral development?

1.9   What are the differences between **preconventional reasoning, conventional reasoning, and postconventional reasoning**?

1.10   What stage of moral reasoning is characterized by **heteronomous morality**?

1.11   What stage of moral reasoning is characterized by individualism, instrumental purpose and exchange?

1.12   What stage of moral reasoning is characterized by mutual interpersonal expectations, relationships, and interpersonal conformity?

1.13   What is the meaning of the social contract or utility and individual rights?

1.14   What are universal ethical principles?

1.15   What are some major criticisms of Kohlberg's theories?

1.16   What is the Defining Issues Test?

1.17   According to Richard Shweder, there are three ethical orientations or world views, what are they?

1.18   What was the basis for **Gilligan's** criticism of **Kohlberg**?

1.19   What are the **justice perspective** and **care perspective**?

1.20   Why is it important to make distinctions regarding different domains when considering adolescent's sociocognitive reasoning?

1.21   What are social-conventional concepts?

1.22   What three domains have been given the most attention?

1.23   Why do some theorists argue it is important to distinguish between moral reasoning and **social conventional reasoning**?

**C.   Moral Behavior**

1.24   How is moral behavior determined by the processes of reinforcement, punishment, and imitation?

1.25   What situational variations are involved in moral behavior?

1.26   What did **Hartshorne** and **May** find about situational variation in moral behavior?

1.27   What is the nature of the **social cognitive theory of moral development**?

1.28     What is the difference between moral competence and moral performance?

1.29     Explain Kohlberg's conceptualization of "extra-moral" factors.

1.30     What are the social cognitive theorists' criticisms of Kohlberg's theory of moral development?

1.31     What is the nature of **altruism**?

1.32     How are reciprocity and exchange involved in altruism?

1.33     What is the role of **forgiveness** in prosocial behavior?

**D.**     **Moral Feeling**

1.34     According to **Freud,** what is the moral part of personality?

1.35     How does the process of identification affect moral development?

1.36     Why do children conform to moral standards, according to **Freud**?

1.37     What did **Freud** mean by the **ego ideal** and the **conscience**?

1.38     What were **Erikson's** views regarding three stages of moral development?

1.39     What is **empathy** and how does it contribute to moral development?

1.40     How are emotions interwoven with moral development?

**E.**     **The Moral Exemplar Approach**

1.41     What does the **moral exemplar approach** emphasize?

**2.0**     **DESCRIBE HOW THE CONTEXTS OF PARENTING AND SCHOOLS CAN INFLUENCE MORAL DEVELOPMENT**

**A.**     **Parenting**

2.1     What do child-rearing techniques have to do with moral development?

2.2     How do **love withdrawal, power assertion,** and **induction** affect a child's moral development?

2.3     According to **Eisenberg,** what qualities do parents of moral children and adolescents have?

**B.**     **Schools**

2.4     What is meant by the **hidden curriculum**?

2.5     Who was **John Dewey**?

2.6     What is **character education**?

2.7     What is the nature of moral literacy?

2.8     What is the nature of **values clarification**?

2.9     What is **cognitive moral education**?

2.10     Whose theory of moral development is the basis for many **cognitive moral education** programs?

2.11     What is **service learning**?

**3.0**     **EXPLAIN THE ROLES OF VALUES, RELIGION, AND CULTS IN ADOLESCENTS' LIVES**

**A.**     **Values**

3.1     How are **values** defined?

3.2     How are adolescent values changing?

3.3     What is some evidence that today's college students are shifting toward a stronger interest in the welfare of society?

**B.**     **Religion**

3.4     What is the scope of religion interest in children and adolescents?

3.5     Is adolescence a special juncture in religious development?

3.6     What is Piaget's theory about the role of religion in development?

3.7     What is Fowler's life-span development view of the six stages of finding meaning in life?

3.8     Are there links between religiousness and sexuality?

# Exercises

## KEY TERMS COMPLETION EXERCISE

This exercise presents each key term in the form of an incomplete sentence. Complete each sentence by either defining the term or giving an example. Compare your definitions with those given at the end of the study guide chapter.

1.      **Moral development** influences an adolescent's

_____

_____

2.      You can tell that Mick is in the stage of **heteronomous morality** because

_____

_____

3.      As Justin passes age 10, he enters the stage of **autonomous morality,** which means

_____

_____

4.      **Immanent justice** should be used when

_____

_____

5.      **Cognitive disequilibrium theory** suggests that

_____

_____

6.      **Internalization** refers to

_____

_____

7.  In **preconventional reasoning** children

_____

_____

8.  In **conventional reasoning** children begin to

_____

_____

9.  During **postconventional reasoning** morality

_____

_____

10. From the **justice perspective** individuals

_____

_____

11. According to Carol Gilligan, **care perspective** is

_____

_____

12. In contrast with moral reasoning, **social conventional reasoning**

_____

_____

13. According to the **social cognitive theory of moral development**

_____

_____

14. Characteristics of an act of **altruism** are

_____

_____

15. **Forgiveness** is when

_____

_____

16. Shoshana's behavior is consistent with her parent's **ego ideal** because

_____

_____

17. You can tell Peggy has a **conscience** because

_____

_____

18. Parents practicing **love withdrawal** are likely to

_____

_____

19. **Power assertion** suggests a parenting style that uses

_____

_____

20. According to Hoffman, **induction** is when parents

_____

_____

21. A good example of **empathy** is

_____

_____

22. The **moral exemplar approach** emphasizes

_____

_____

23. **Hidden curriculum** in schools is

_____

_____

24. Good **character education** begins with

_____

_____

25. An example of **values clarification** is

_____

_____

26. **Cognitive moral education** is based on the belief that

_____

_____

27.    **Service learning** is a form of education that

_____

_____

28.    **Values** are

_____

_____

_____


## KEY PEOPLE IN THE STUDY OF ADOLESCENCE

Match the person with the concept of adolescent moral development with which they are associated.

| | | |
|---|---|---|
| ___ | 1. Jean Piaget | A. Associated with social-cognitive perspective of moral development |
| ___ | 2. Martin Hoffman | B. Finds that parents play a role in moral development |
| ___ | 3. Lawrence Kohlberg | C. Developed a six-stage model of moral development, with three levels of moral reasoning |
| ___ | 4. James Rest | D. Proposed that there were two types of morality, depending upon the age of the child |
| ___ | 5. Robert Shweder | E. Believed that moral education was the schools' hidden curriculum |
| ___ | 6. Carol Gilligan | F. Proposed that adolescents develop an ideology as part of their identity |
| ___ | 7. Hugh Hartshorne and Mark May | G. Developed the cognitive disequilibrium theory |
| ___ | 8. Albert Bandura | H. Thought that resolution of the Oedipus complex was associated with moral development |
| ___ | 9. Sigmund Freud | I. Developed the Defining Issues Test to measure morality |
| ___ | 10. Erik Erikson | J. Proposes that there are three types of ethical orientation |
| ___ | 11. Nancy Eisenberg | K. Insists that girls' need for relationships is significant factor in their sense of morality |
| ___ | 12. John Dewey | L. Involved in large study of situational morality |
| ___ | 13. James Fowler | M. Proposed a theory of religious development that focuses on the motivation to discover meaning in life |
| ___ | 14. Lawrence Walker | N. A leading advocate of the moral exemplar approach |


## "DR. DETAIL'S" STAGE MASTERY EXERCISE

Complete the table by listing the main characteristics of each of Kohlberg's stages of moral development.

| Stage | Characteristic |
|---|---|
| **Preconventional Reasoning** | |
| Heteronomous morality | |
| Individualism, instrumental purpose, and exchange | |

| Conventional Reasoning | |
|---|---|
| Mutual interpersonal expectations, relationships, and interpersonal conformity | |
| Social systems morality | |
| **Postconventional Reasoning** | |
| Social contract or utility and individual rights | |
| Universal ethical principles | |

## ADOLENCENT MYTH AND FACT

Which of the following statements regarding adolescents are true (T) and which are false (F)?

1.  According to the 6th and highest stage in Kolberg's theory, when faced with a conflict between law and conscience, a person will follow conscience – even if there is some personal risk involved.  T or F

2.  The change in moral reasoning between late adolescence and early adulthood appears to be quite sudden.  T or F

3.  Kohlberg believed that peer interaction is a critical part of the social stimulation that challenges individuals to change their moral orientation.  T or F

4.  Researchers have found that the hypothetical moral dilemmas posed in Kohlberg's stories are very similar to those actually faced by adolescents.  T or F

5.  Researchers have found that females generate more interpersonal conflicts than males do.  T or F

6.  Prosocial behavior occurs more often in adolescence than in childhood.  T or F

7.  Across childhood and adolescence, females engage in more prosocial behavior than males.  T or F

8.  All adolescents show remarkably similar patterns of empathetic behavior.  T or F

9.  According to Hoffman, power assertions is the most effective form of parental discipline.  T or F

10.  Induction works better with preschool children than with adolescents.  T or F

11.  Toward the end of his career, Kohlberg recognized that the moral atmosphere of the school was more important than he had initially thought.  T or F

12.  Over the past two decades, adolescents have shown an increased concern for personal well-being and a decreased concern for the well-being of disadvantaged people.  T or F

13.  In general, adults tend to adopt the religious teachings of their upbringing.  T or F

14.  Research has shown that personal conservatism, as an orientation, is linked with having unprotected sex.  T or F

# DOMAINS OF MORAL DEVELOPMENT
## SECTION REVIEW

1.  What is moral development?

    _____

    _____

2.  What are the dimensions of moral development?

    _____

    _____

3.  What is the difference between Piaget's heteronomous morality and his autonomous morality?

    _____

    _____

4.  What is immanent justice?

    _____

    _____

5.  What is Hoffman's proposed cognitive disequilibrium theory of moral development?

    _____

    _____

6.  What is internalization?

    _____

    _____

7.  What are Kohlberg's three levels of moral development?

    _____

    _____

8.  What are the justice perspective and care perspective?

    _____

    _____

9.  What are some major criticisms of Kohlberg's theories?

    _____

    _____

10. According to Bandura, engaging in harmful conduct requires that a person justify the morality of their actions to themselves. What does this mean?

_____

_____

11. What is the Defining Issues Test?

_____

_____

12. According to Shweder, there are three ethical orientations or world views, what are they?

_____

_____

13. What did Hartshorne and May find about situational variation in moral behavior?

_____

_____

14. What is the nature of the social cognitive theory of moral development?

_____

_____

15. What is the difference between moral competence and moral performance?

_____

_____

16. What is the nature of altruism?

_____

_____

17. What is the role of forgiveness in altruism?

_____

_____

18. Explain Kohlberg's conceptualization of "extra-moral" factors.

_____

_____

19. What is the best way for parents to help children develop moral maturity, other than setting a good behavioral example?

_____

_____

20. Why is an adolescent more likely to forgive someone if his friends encourage him to do so?

_____

_____

21. What did Freud mean by the ego ideal and the conscience?

_____

_____

22. What were Erikson's views regarding three stages of moral development?

_____

_____

## MORAL DEVELOPMENT
## SECTION REVIEW

1. How do love withdrawal, power assertion, and induction affect a child's moral development?

_____

_____

2. According to Eisenberg, what qualities do parents of moral children and adolescents have?

_____

_____

3. Name two books that promote character education.

_____

_____

4. What is meant by the hidden curriculum?

_____

_____

5. How does values clarification differ from character education?

_____

_____

6. What is cognitive moral education?

_____

_____

7.    What is service learning?

_____

_____


## VALUES, RELIGION, AND CULTS
## SECTION REVIEW

1.    How are values defined?

_____

_____


2.    How are adolescent values changing?

_____

_____


3.    Complete the table by filling in the name of Fowler's stage of religious development, the period of development in which it occurs, and brief descriptions of the characteristics of the stage.

| Name of Stage | Developmental Period | Characteristics |
|---|---|---|
| 1. | | |
| 2. | | |
| 3. | | |
| 4. | | |
| 5. | | |
| 6. | | |


4.    What is Piaget's theory about the role of religion in development?

_____

_____


5.    What is the nature of cults?

_____

_____


6.    Why do people join cults?

_____

_____

## COGNITIVE CHALLENGE

1.  A man who had been sentenced to serve 10 years for selling a small amount of marijuana walked away from a prison camp after serving six months there. Twenty-five years later he was caught. He is now in his 50s and has been a model citizen. Should he be sent back to prison? Why or why not? At what Kohlberg stage is your response? Would you feel differently if he were your sibling?

    _____

    _____

2.  What are your five most important values? How did you get these? Did they come from your parents, friends, teachers, or some event or experience? How carefully do you stick to society's ethical standards.

    _____

    _____

3.  As you progressed through the first four stages of Fowler's stages of religious development, how were your experiences different from or similar to his characterizations? Are you resolved about your choice of religious practice, or do you have some doubts?

    _____

    _____

## ADOLESCENCE IN RESEARCH

Concerning Hartshorne and May's research (1928–1930), state the hypothesis, the research methods (if known), the research conclusions, and the implications and applications for adolescent development.

_____

_____

## ⊠ COMPREHENSIVE REVIEW

1.  The three major aspects of moral development include
    a.  stimulus, response, and consequences.
    b.  thought, feeling, and behaving.
    c.  individual, family, and society.
    d.  id, ego, and superego.

2.  Moral development has a(n) _____ dimension and a(n) _____ dimension.
    a.  cognition; developmental      c.  intrapersonal; interpersonal
    b.  religious; idealistic         d.  social; temperament

3.   Jean Piaget indicates that the heteronomous thinker
     a.   believes that rules can be changed because they are merely conventions.
     b.   recognizes that punishment for wrongdoing is not inevitable.
     c.   judges the goodness of behavior by focusing on the consequences of the behavior.
     d.   is usually a child between the ages of 10 and 12.

4.   _____ is the idea that, if a rule is broken, punishment will be meted out immediately.
     a.   Autonomous morality          c.   Response cost
     b.   Immanent justice             d.   Love withdrawal

5.   Bobby trips and spills a bowl of chili on his Mom's new carpet. Bobby's 5-year-old sister tells him that
     he is going to be in "big trouble" when Mom gets home. Bobby's sister is demonstrating
     a.   rigid thinking.              c.   autonomous thinking.
     b.   heteronomous thinking.       d.   younger sister nerdism.

6.   Six stages of moral development were proposed by
     a.   Martin Hoffman.              c.   Sigmund Freud.
     b.   Jean Piaget.                 d.   Lawrence Kohlberg.

7.   The notion that young children have that punishment will be swift and immediate when rules are broken
     is an example of
     a.   autonomous thinking.         c.   cognitive disequilibrium.
     b.   believing in immanent justice. d.   rigid thinking.

8.   Which of the following was NOT a criticism of Kohlberg's theory of moral development?
     a.   He placed too little emphasis on moral behavior.
     b.   The research was of poor quality.
     c.   He placed too much emphasis on the development of the Superego.
     d.   He did not fully consider cultural or gender variables.

9.   Which of the following is NOT indicative of formal operational thinking?
     a.   Rules are not to be questioned, just followed.
     b.   We should contrast the read with the ideal.
     c.   Things from the past can be applied to the present.
     d.   We must understand our role in society and in the universe.

10.  Martin Hoffman indicates that going to high school is associated with a dramatic change in moral
     reasoning because
     a.   there is more opportunity for sexual exploitation.
     b.   parental supervision is nullified.
     c.   peer pressure to violate community standards is high.
     d.   discussions reveal the variety of moral beliefs.

11.  Which of the following is NOT a social cognitive domain noted in the chapter?
     a.   moral domain                 c.   social-conventional domain
     b.   human domain                 d.   personal domain

12.  _____ developed cognitive disequilibrium theory.
     a.   Lawrence Kohlberg            c.   Jean Piaget
     b.   Martin Hoffman               d.   Albert Bandura

13. _____ is an unselfish interest in helping another person.
   a. Forgiveness      c. Induction
   b. Conscience      d. Altruism

14. Lawrence Kohlberg argues that the distinctions between the three levels of moral reasoning have to do with
   a. the degree of internalization.
   b. the immediacy of the consequences for moral actions.
   c. the severity of punishments experienced.
   d. the social pressure of peers.

15. According to Kohlberg, as children and adolescents develop, their moral thoughts become
   a. more internalized.      c. more externalized.
   b. more unpredictable.      d. more fantasy prone.

16. Of Kohlberg's six stages of moral development, which two tend to vary the most across cultures?
   a. 1 and 2      c. 3 and 4
   b. 5 and 6      d. 1 and 6

17. Who is most likely to join a cult?
   a. someone who is psychologically unstable
   b. a person just recently released from prison
   c. a normal, average person
   d. someone with strong religious beliefs

18. James Rest developed the Defining Issues Test because
   a. there were no available measures of moral reasoning.
   b. he found Piaget's tests too hard for adolescents.
   c. Kohlberg's stories were too difficult to score.
   d. he didn't know that several other tests were available.

19. The most common moral dilemmas generated by 7$^{th}$ graders deal with
   a. sexual relations.      c. interpersonal relations.
   b. physical safety.      d. stealing.

20. There is general agreement that Lawrence Kohlberg's theory
   a. is correct for adolescents, but not for adults.
   b. confused autonomy with autonomous morality.
   c. confused moral reasoning with moral behavior.
   d. underestimates the importance of culture.

21. In contrast to India, where socialization actively instills in children a great respect for their culture's traditional codes and practices, Western moral doctrine tends to elevate such abstract principles as _____ and _____.
   a. material possessions; money      c. law; order
   b. justice; welfare      d. justice; morality

22. Carol Gilligan has criticized Kohlberg's theory for
   a. overemphasizing people's connectedness and communication with other people.
   b. emphasizing moral behavior and ignoring moral reasoning.

c. relying on a single method to assess individual's moral reasoning.

d. understating the importance of interpersonal relationships in moral development.

23. Adolescents' moral performance is influenced by
   a. skills.
   b. awareness of moral rules.
   c. cognitive-sensory processes.
   d. motivation.

24. _____ theory distinguishes between moral competence and moral performance?
   a. Psychosocial
   b. Moral development
   c. Cognitive social learning
   d. Behavioral moral reasoning

25 _____ is NOT one of Shweder's three ethical orientations or worldviews?
   a. Ethic of autonomy
   b. Ethic of divinity
   c. Ethic of morality
   d. Ethic of community

26. _____ is an defined as an unselfish interest in helping someone else.
   a. Charity
   b. Ingratiation
   c. Altruism
   d. Reciprocity

27. _____ is an aspect of prosocial behavior that occurs when the injured person releases the injurer from possible behavioral retaliation.
   a. Clarity
   b. Forgiveness
   c. Altruism
   d. Reciprocity

28. Martin Hoffman believes that parents promote the moral development of their children and adolescents through
   a. love withdrawal.
   b. power assertion.
   c. induction.
   d. altruism.

29. Children, whose feelings of empathy are generally directed towards specific people, expand their concerns to the general problems of people between the ages of
   a. 7 to 9.
   b. 10 to 12.
   c. 13 to 15.
   d. 16 to 18.

30. The failure to develop empathy, if not altruism, is associated with
   a. excessive achievement orientation.
   b. vulnerability to cults.
   c. antisocial behaviors.
   d. chronic depression.

31. Although schools generally do not have specific programs in moral education, children tend to get a moral education being part of this structured system. This is called
   a. academic generalization.
   b. the hidden curriculum.
   c. the covert.
   d. the secret classroom.

32. Service learning in adolescence is an important goal because it helps adolescents
   a. become less self-centered.
   b. develop work skills.
   c. develop a sense of self.
   d. become better at managing their time.

33. _____ is used to describe when a person "releases the injurer from possible behavioral retaliation"?
   a. altruism.
   c. sympathy.
   b. empathy.
   d. forgiveness.

34. Research suggests that only _____ adolescents report having ever done any volunteer work.
   a. 1 in 10
   c. 1 in 3
   b. 1 in 5
   d. 1 in 20

35. According to a poll, _____ percent of the adolescents said that they prayed.
   a. 10
   c. 50
   b. 35
   d. 75

36. Which of the following is NOT one of Piaget's religious development stages?
   a. sensorimotor religious thought
   b. preoperational intuitive religious thought
   c. concrete operational religious thought
   d. formal operational religious thought

37. An adolescent refused to attend church, telling his parents that he would believe what he wants to believe, not what they tell him to believe. This adolescent demonstrated
   a. reflective faith.
   c. catastrophic conversion.
   b. individuative-reflective faith.
   d. moral fundamentalism.

## ADOLESCENCE ON THE SCREEN

■ *A Clockwork Orange* An immoral and violent young man becomes the subject of an experiment to eradicate his violent tendencies.

■ *Saving Private Ryan* Examines morality and the need for personal sacrifice in the context of war and military duty.

■ *A Walk to Remember* A young man, who has drifted into trouble following the divorce of his parents, finds himself infatuated by a young girl with a strong sense of right and wrong.

■ *Stand by Me* Four 12-year-old boys trek into the wilderness to find the body of a missing boy.

■ *Lost and Delirious* Tracks the moral development of a young girl at an all-girls boarding school before and after young love goes sour.

## ADOLESCENCE IN BOOKS

■ *Meeting at the Crossroads*, by Lyn Mikel Brown and Carol Gilligan (Harvard University Press: MA, 1992), provides a vivid portrayal of how adolescent girls are often ignored and misunderstood.

■ *The Lost Boys*, by James Garbarino (the Free Press: NY, 1999). Outstanding compilation of theories and facts related to why children "go bad" and what can be done to stop this.

- *She Said Yes: The Unlikely Martyrdom of Cassie Bernall,* by Misty Bernall (the Plough Publishing House: UK, 1999). A wrenching and honest portrayal of a troubled teenage girl who, just after turning her life around, ends up being a victim in the Columbine massacre.

- *Postconventional Thinking,* by James Rest, Darcia Naraez, Muriel Bebeau, and Stephen Thoma (Erlbaum: NJ, 1999), presents a neo-Kolhbergian analysis of moral development.

# Answer Key

## KEY TERMS

1. **moral development** Thoughts, feelings, and behaviors regarding standards of right and wrong.
2. **heteronomous morality** The first stage of moral development in Piaget's theory, occurring at 4 to 7 years of age. Justice and rules are conceived of as unchangeable properties of the world, removed from the control of people.
3. **autonomous morality** The second stage of moral development in Piaget's theory, displayed by older children (about 10 years of age and older). The child becomes aware that people create rules and laws and that, in judging an action, one should consider the actor's intentions as well as the consequences.
4. **immanent justice** Piaget's concept that if a rule is broken, punishment will be meted out immediately.
5. **cognitive disequilibrium theory** Hoffman's theory that adolescence is an important period in moral development, in which, because of broader experiences associated with the move to high school or college, individuals recognize that their set of beliefs is but one of many and that there is considerable debate about what is right and wrong.
6. **internalization** The developmental change from behavior that is externally controlled to behavior that is controlled by internal standards and principles.
7. **preconventional reasoning** The lowest level in Kohlberg's theory of moral development. The individual shows no internalization of moral values—moral reasoning is controlled by external rewards and punishment.
8. **conventional reasoning** The second, or intermediate, level in Kohlberg's theory of moral development. Internalization is intermediate. Individuals abide by certain standards (internal), but they are the standards of others (external), such as parents or the laws of society.
9. **postconventional reasoning** The highest level in Kohlberg's theory of moral development. Morality is completely internalized.
10. **justice perspective** A moral perspective that focuses on the rights of the individual; individuals independently make moral decisions.
11. **care perspective** The moral perspective of Carol Gilligan, that views people in terms of their connectedness with others and emphasizes interpersonal communication, relationships with others, and concern for others.
12. **social conventional reasoning** Focuses on thoughts about social consensus and convention.
13. **social cognitive theory of moral development** The theory that distinguishes between moral competence—the ability to produce moral behaviors—and moral performance—those behaviors in specific situations.
14. **altruism** Unselfish interest in helping another person.
15. **forgiveness** An aspect of altruism that occurs when an injured person releases the injured from possible behavioral retaliation.
16. **ego ideal** The component of the superego that involves ideal standards approved by parents.

17. **conscience** The component of the superego that involves behaviors disapproved of by parents.
18. **love withdrawal** A discipline technique in which a parent removes attention or love from the child.
19. **power assertion** A discipline technique in which a parent attempts to gain control over a child or a child's resources.
20. **induction** A discipline technique in which a parent uses reason and explanation of the consequences for others of a child's actions.
21. **empathy** Reacting to another's feelings with an emotional response that is similar to the other's response.
22. **moral exemplar approach** Emphasizes the development of personality, character, and virtue in terms of moral excellence.
23. **hidden curriculum** The pervasive moral atmosphere that characterizes schools.
24. **character education** A direct moral education approach that involves teaching students a basic moral literacy to prevent them from engaging in immoral behavior or doing harm to themselves or others.
25. **values clarification** Helping people to clarify what their lives are for and what is worth working for. Students are encouraged to define their own values and understand others' values.
26. **cognitive moral education** Is based on the belief that students should learn to value things like democracy and justice as their moral reasoning develops; Kohlberg's theory has been the basis for many of the cognitive moral education approaches.
27. **service learning** A form of education that promotes social responsibility and service to the community.
28. **values** Beliefs and attitudes about the way people think things should be.


## KEY PEOPLE IN THE STUDY OF ADOLESCENCE

| | | | | | | | |
|---|---|---|---|---|---|---|---|
| 1. | D | 5. | J | 9. | H | 13. | M |
| 2. | G | 6. | K | 10. | F | 14. | N |
| 3. | C | 7. | L | 11. | B | | |
| 4. | I | 8. | A | 12. | E | | |


## "DR. DETAIL'S" STAGE MASTERY EXERCISE

| Stage | Characteristic |
|---|---|
| **Preconventional Reasoning** | Individual shows no internalization of moral values; moral reasoning is controlled by external rewards and punishment. |
| Heteronomous morality | Moral thinking is tied to punishment. |
| Individualism, instrumental purpose, and exchange | Individuals pursue their own interests but let others do the same. |
| **Conventional Reasoning** | Internalization is intermediate. Individuals abide by certain internal standards, but they are the standards of others, such as parents or the laws of society. |
| Mutual interpersonal expectations, relationships, and interpersonal conformity | Individuals value trust, caring, and loyalty to others as a basis of moral judgment. |
| Social systems morality | Moral judgments are based on understanding the social order, law, justice, and duty. |
| **Postconventional Reasoning** | Morality is completely internalized and is not based on others' standards. The individual recognizes alternative moral courses, explores the options, and then decides on a |

| | personal moral code. |
|---|---|
| Social contract or utility and individual rights | Individuals reason that values, rights, and principles underscore or transcend the law. |
| Universal ethical principles | The person has developed a moral standard based on universal human rights. |

## ADOLENCENT MYTH AND FACT

| | | | |
|---|---|---|---|
| 1. | T | 8. | F |
| 2. | F | 9. | F |
| 3. | T | 10. | F |
| 4. | F | 11. | T |
| 5. | T | 12. | T |
| 6. | T | 13. | T |
| 7. | T | 14. | T |

## DOMAINS OF MORAL DEVELOPMENT
## SECTION REVIEW

1.　　It involves thoughts, feelings, and behaviors regarding standards of right and wrong.

2.　　(a) How do adolescents think about rules for ethical conduct? (b) How do adolescents actually behave in moral circumstances? (c) How do adolescents feel about moral matters?

3.　　Heteronomous morality is the first stage of moral development. Justice and rules are conceived of as unchangeable properties of the world, removed from the control of people. Autonomous morality is the second stage. Here the child becomes aware that rules and laws are created by people and that in judging an action one should consider the actor's intentions as well as the consequences.

4.　　Piaget's concept that if a rule is broken, punishment will be meted out immediately.

5.　　This states that adolescence is an important period in moral development, especially as individuals move from the relatively homogeneous grade school to the more heterogeneous high school.

6.　　This is the developmental change from behavior that is externally controlled to behavior that is controlled by internal standards and principles.

7.　　According to Kohlberg, there are three levels of moral development: Preconventional—moral reasoning is controlled by external rewards and punishments. Conventional reasoning—individuals abide by others standards, such as the laws of society. Postconventional reasoning—morality is completely internalized and is not based on other's standards. The individual recognizes alternative moral courses, explores options, and then decides on a personal moral code.

8.　　Justice perspective is a moral perspective that focuses on the rights of the individual; individuals who stand alone and independently make moral decisions. The care perspective is a moral perspective that views people in terms of their connectedness with others and emphasizes interpersonal communication, relationships with others, and concern for others.

9.　　Some of the major criticisms of Kohlberg's theories are that they are culturally and gender biased.

10. Bandura argues that people usually don't engage in harmful conduct until they have justified the morality of the actions to themselves. This process of moral justification makes things socially acceptable.

11. The DIT attempts to determine which moral issues individuals feel are more critical in a given situation by presenting them with a series of dilemmas.

12. (a) an ethic of autonomy, (b) an ethic of community, and (c) an ethic of diversity.

13. Adolescents were more likely to cheat when their friends pressured them to do so and when the chances of being caught were slim.

14. The theory distinguishes between moral competence and moral performance.

15. Moral competence—the ability to produce moral behaviors. Moral performance—those behaviors in specific situations.

16. Altruism is an unselfish interest in helping another person.

17. Forgiveness is an aspect of altruism that occurs when the injured person releases the injurer from possible behavioral retaliation.

18. "Extra-moral" factors are things such as the desire to avoid embarrassment, which may cause children to fail to do what they believe to be morally right.

19. Trying to probe and elicit their child's opinions, instead of giving too much information that may come across as preaching or lecturing.

20. It is often difficult for the victim of harm to try to take steps toward forgiveness. His friends can encourage him to consider why that might be the better response.

21. Ego ideal is the component of the superego that involves ideal standards approved by parents, whereas conscience is the component of the superego that involves behaviors not approved of by parents.

22. Specific moral learning in childhood, ideological concerns in adolescence, and ethical consolidation in adulthood.

## MORAL DEVELOPMENT
## SECTION REVIEW

1. Love withdrawal is a discipline technique in which a parent withholds attention or love from the adolescent. This leads to insecurity in the adolescent. Power assertion is a discipline technique in which a parent attempts to gain control over the adolescent or his/her resources. Spanking is an example. Induction is where parents explain consequences of actions and likely outcomes. These adolescents are the most well-rounded emotionally.

2. They are warm and supportive. They provide opportunities for their children to learn about others' feelings. They use inductive discipline. They involve children in decision making. They stimulate adolescents to question and expand their moral reasoning. They model moral behaviors and thinking for their children.

3. William Bennett's *Book of Virtues* (1993) and William Damon's *Greater Expectations* (1995).

4. Hidden curriculum is conveyed by the moral atmosphere that is a part of every school.

5. Values clarification differs from character education in that it does not tell students what their values should be.

6.     It is an educational approach based on the belief that students should learn to value things like democracy and justice.

7.     Service learning is a form of education that promotes social responsibility and service to the community.

## VALUES, RELIGION, AND CULTS
## SECTION REVIEW

1.     Values are beliefs and attitudes about the way things should be.

2.     Over the past two decades, adolescents have shown increased concern for personal well-being and less concern for the well-being of others.

3.

| Name of Stage | Developmental Period | Characteristics |
|---|---|---|
| 1. Intuitive-Projective Faith | Early Childhood | Intuitive images of good and evil; fantasy and reality are the same. |
| 2. Mythical-Literal Faith | Middle/Late Childhood | More logical, concrete thought; literal interpretation of religious stories. |
| 3. Synthetic-Conventional Faith | Early Adolescence | More abstract thought; conformity to religious beliefs of others. |
| 4. Individuative-Reflective Faith | Late Adolescence, Early Adulthood | Capable of taking full responsibility for religious beliefs; In-depth exploration of one's own values and beliefs. |
| 5. Conjunctive Faith | Middle Adulthood | More open to opposing viewpoints; awareness of one's finiteness and limitations. |
| 6. Universalizing Faith | Middle and Late Adulthood | Transcending belief systems to achieve a sense of oneness with all. |

4.     Piaget felt that they progressed through three stages: preoperational intuitive religious thought; concrete operational religious thought; and formal operational religious thought.

5.     They are usually controlled by a charismatic leader, and their energies and focus are turned inward, as opposed to outward. The more isolated the cult is, the greater likelihood of abuse or dangerous practices.

6.     They are usually normal, regular people who are in a transitional phase of life. Only about 5 percent are disturbed.

## COGNITIVE CHALLENGE

1.     Individual activity. No answers provided.

2.     Individual activity. No answers provided.

3.     Individual activity. No answers provided.

## ADOLESCENCE IN RESEARCH

The hypothesis was that moral behavior is situationally dependent. The researchers observed the moral responses of 11,000 children and adolescents who were given the opportunity to lie, cheat, and steal in a variety of circumstances—at home, school, social events, and in athletics. Situation-specific moral behavior was the rule.

Adolescents were more likely to cheat when their friends pressured them to do so and when the chances of getting caught were slim.

 COMPREHENSIVE REVIEW

| | | | | | | | |
|---|---|---|---|---|---|---|---|
| 1. | b | 11. | b | 21. | b | 31. | b |
| 2. | c | 12. | b | 22. | d | 32. | a |
| 3. | c | 13. | d | 23. | d | 33. | d |
| 4. | b | 14. | a | 24. | c | 34. | c |
| 5. | b | 15. | a | 25. | c | 35. | d |
| 6. | d | 16. | b | 26. | c | 36. | a |
| 7. | b | 17. | c | 27. | b | 37. | b |
| 8. | c | 18. | c | 28. | c | | |
| 9. | a | 19. | c | 29. | b | | |
| 10. | d | 20. | d | 30. | c | | |

# Chapter 9    Families

**Learning Goals with Key Terms and Key People in Boldface**

**1.0    DISCUSS THE NATURE OF FAMILY PROCESSES IN ADOLESCENCE**

**A.    Reciprocal Socialization and the Family As A System**
1.1    What is **reciprocal socialization,** and how does it affect adolescent development?
1.2    What is meant by parent-adolescent synchrony?
1.3    What defines a family's social system?
1.4    Why is marriage satisfaction often related to good parenting?

**B.    The Developmental Construction of Relationships**
1.5    What is the **developmental construction** of relationships?
1.6    Why are close relationships with parents important for adolescent's development?
1.7    What are the two main variations of the **developmental construction** views?
1.8    What is the difference between the **continuity view** and the **discontinuity view**?
1.9    What research evidence exists in support of each view?

**C.    Maturation**
1.10    What parental and adolescent maturation processes affect parent-adolescent interaction?
1.11    What are the major changes in adolescence that influence parent-adolescent relationships?
1.12    What dimensions of the adolescent's cognitive world contribute to parent-adolescent relationships?
1.13    What parental changes contribute to parent-adolescent relationships?
1.14    How does the timing of parenthood affect parent-adolescent interaction?
1.15    What sociocultural and historical changes affect family processes?
1.16    What impact did the Great Depression have on families?
1.17    What sociocultural changes have made families different than they were 50 years ago?
1.18    What roles have television and computers played in the changing family.

**2.0    DESCRIBE PARENT-ADOLESCENT RELATIONSHIPS**

**A.    Parents as Managers**
2.1    What do we mean when we say that parents should manage their adolescent's lives?
2.2    How can parents effectively monitor their adolescent?

**B.    Parenting Styles**
2.3    What are the four main parenting categories according to **Baumrind,** and which one is most closely associated with socially competent behavior?
2.4    What is the nature of **authoritarian, authoritative, neglectful,** and **indulgent** parenting styles?
2.5    Which is the most effective parenting style?
2.6    Do the benefits of authoritative parenting transcend the boundaries of ethnicity, socioeconomic status, and household composition?

**C.    Gender, Parenting, and Coparenting**
2.7    What is the mother's role in raising adolescents?
2.8    What major changes have the roles of fathers in families undergone over time?
2.9    How involved are today's fathers in the lives of their adolescents?

2.10     What does the recent research on coparenting suggest?

**D.    Parent-Adolescent Conflict**

2.11     What is the nature and extent of parent-adolescent conflict?

2.12     How are adolescent-parent conflicts usually resolved?

2.13     What is the subject of most parental-adolescent conflict?

2.14     Who do adolescents most often have disagreements with?

2.15     What is the generation gap?

2.16     How much empirical support is there for the existence of a generation gap?

2.17     What percentage of families is parent-adolescent conflict high?

2.18     What problems are associated with intense, prolonged conflict?

2.19     Do patterns of adolescent conflict differ across cultures?

**E.    Autonomy and Attachment**

2.20     How important are autonomy and attachment in an adolescent's successful adaptation to adulthood?

2.21     What is the difference between autonomy and **emotional autonomy**?

2.22     What are the four distinct patterns of adolescent autonomy that typically emerge from an analysis of high school students?

2.23     What problems do parents have with their adolescent's achieving autonomy?

2.24     Are there gender differences seen concerning adolescent autonomy?

2.25     What developmental transition signals autonomy?

2.26     Why do some adolescents run away from home, and what problems might they be susceptible to as a result?

2.27     What recommendation might one give a parent regarding their adolescent's need for autonomy?

2.28     Why is it important that adolescents be both autonomous and attached to their parents?

2.29     What is the difference between **secure attachment** and **insecure attachment**?

2.30     Why is secure attachment related social competence and successful adaptation to the world?

2.31     What is the Adult Attachment Interview (AAI)?

2.32     What is the difference between **dismissing/avoidant attachment, preoccupied/ambivalent attachment,** and **unresolved/disorganized attachment**?

**3.0    CHARACTERIZE SIBLING RELATIONSHIPS IN ADOLESCENCE**

**A.    Sibling Roles**

3.1     What is the nature and extent of conflict in many sibling relationships?

3.2     How much does conflict characterize adolescent relationships?

3.3     How do sibling relationships change over time?

**B.    Birth Order**

3.4     How does birth order affect sibling and parent relationships?

3.5     Is an only child likely to be a "spoiled brat"?

3.6     What is the most reasonable conclusion to be gained from research about the effects of birth order on adolescent behavior and achievement?

**4.0    DESCRIBE THE CHANGING FAMILY IN A CHANGING SOCIETY**

**A.    Divorced Families**

4.1     How do adolescents adjust to divorce in their families?

4.2     Should parents stay together for the sake of their children and adolescents?

4.3     How much do parenting skills matter in divorced families?

4.4     How much do post-divorce family processes affect adolescent adjustment to divorce?

4.5     What factors contribute to adolescent risk and vulnerability to divorce?

4.6      What role does socioeconomic status play in the lives of adolescents in divorced families?

**B.      Stepfamilies**

4.7      How is the make-up of step families different than other families?

4.8      What are the three common types of stepfamily structures?

4.9      Over time stepfamilies fall into three types based on their relationships. What are these?

4.10      What adjustment problems are associated with adolescents who live in stepfamilies?

4.11      What is the most difficult time for adolescents to experience their parents' remarriage?

4.12      What is **boundary ambiguity?**

4.13      How do you compare adolescent's relationships with their biological and stepparents?

**C.      Working Parents**

4.14      What is the effect of parental work on the development of children and adolescents?

4.15      What effect do working mothers have on adolescent development?

4.16      What are the special adjustment problems of latchkey adolescents?

4.17      What is the effect of relocation on adolescent development?

4.18      How does parental unemployment affect adolescents?

**D.      Adoption**

4.19      Define the role of adoption within our society.

4.20      What changes have occurred in the adopted process in recent decades?

4.21      What are some of the complexities faces by adopted children in their teen years?

**E.      Gay and Lesbian Parents**

4.22      How common are gay or lesbian parents?

4.23      Are children raised by gay or lesbian parents different than other children?

**F.      Culture and Ethnicity**

4.24      What roles do culture and ethnicity play in families?

4.25      What is the effect of culture on parental roles, discipline styles and family support systems?

4.26      In what ways do ethnic minority families differ from White American families?

4.27      What are the main differences between White-American families and African-American and Latino families?

**5.0      EXPLAIN WHAT IS NEEDED FOR IMPROVED SOCIAL POLICY INVOLVING ADOLESCENTS AND THEIR FAMILIES**

5.1      What are the recommendations of the Carnegie Council on Adolescent Development regarding social policies for families with adolescents?

# Exercises

## KEY TERMS COMPLETION EXERCISE

This exercise presents each key in the form of an incomplete sentence. Complete each sentence by either defining the term or giving an example. Compare your definitions with those given at the end of the study guide chapter.

1.      By using **reciprocal socialization,** SuLin has changed her parents

_____

_____

2. According to the **developmental construction view**

_____

_____

3. The **continuity view** holds that

_____

_____

4. The **discontinuity view** holds that

_____

_____

5. Bailey's mom uses **authoritarian parenting** in that

_____

_____

6. **Authoritative parenting** allows a child to

_____

_____

7. **Neglectful parenting** can result in

_____

_____

8. **Indulgent parenting** over time can lead to

_____

_____

9. **Emotional autonomy** is the capacity to

_____

_____

10. **Insecure attachment** is a maladaptive pattern that is seen in

_____

_____

11. **Secure attachment** is very important because

_____

_____

12. **Dismissing/avoidant attachment** can result in

_____

_____

13. **Preoccupied/ambivalent attachment** can result in

_____

_____

14. **Unresolved/disorganized attachment** can lead to

_____

_____

15. **Boundary ambiguity** can be a problem in stepfamilies because

_____

_____

## KEY PEOPLE IN THE STUDY OF ADOLESCENCE

Match the person with the event or concept in adolescent development with which they are associated.

| ___ | 1. Andrew Collins | A. Parenting styles |
| ___ | 2. Diana Baumrind | B. Infant attachment research |
| ___ | 3. John Bowlby and Mary Ainsworth | C. Adolescent adjustment to parental divorce |
| ___ | 4. Joseph Allen | D. Adolescent-parental attachment |
| ___ | 5. E. Mavis Hetherington | E. Adolescent cognitive changes |
| ___ | 6. Lois Hoffman | F. Studied effects of maternal employment |

## "DR. DETAIL'S" LIBRARY EXERCISE

Go to the library at your institution and look up archival materials that describer what family life was in the year 1900 in some detail. Then, using that information, compare families then with families now. How are they similar, and how are they different?

_____

_____

_____

_____

## ADOLESCENT MYTH AND FACT

Which of the following statements regarding adolescents are true (T) and which are false (F)?

1. In studies of family interaction (Gjerde, 1986), it was found that the presence of the mother increased the quality of father-son relations.  T or F

2. Parents who communicate better also tend to be more affectionate to their children and adolescents. T or F

3. Although motherhood has been associated with mostly positive qualities, it has been accorded relatively low prestige in our society. T or F

4. According to research, it appears that parent-adolescent conflict decreases from early adolescence through late adolescence. T or F

5. Adolescents raised in the United States seek autonomy from parents earlier than adolescents in Japan. T or F

6. Both one-time runaways and repeat runaways are likely to be school dropouts. T or F

7. Peggy, a 'later-born' child, likely has more friends than her 'first-born' sister Shirley. T or F

8. Compared with virtually all other countries, the United States has the highest percentage of single-parent families. T or F

9. The divorce rate in the United States has increased since the 1980's. T or F

10. The 'complex' or blended (Brady Bunch kind) of stepfamily, shows the best results for child adjustment. T or F

11. In Bray's assessment, the "Romantic" stepfamily has the best long-term chance for success. T or F

12. Researchers have shown that adopted children and adolescents often show more psychological and school-related problems than nonadopted children. T or F

13. Most children growing up in a gay family will choose that lifestyle for themselves once they are adults. T or F

14. Single-parent families are less common among African Americans than among non-Latino Whites. T or F

15. Compared with families with small children, families with adolescents have been neglected in community programs and public policies. T or F

## FAMILY PROCESSES
## SECTION REVIEW

1. Describe how a child might use the process of reciprocal socialization to his/her advantage.

_____

_____

2. Compare and contrast the continuity and discontinuity views.

_____

_____

3. In Mark Twain's view, what transforms as adolescents move from childhood to adulthood?

_____

_____

4. What dimensions of the adolescent's social world contribute to parent-adolescent relationships?

_____

_____

5. Is parent-child interaction different for families in which parents delay having children until their thirties or forties?

_____

_____

6. What kinds of effects did the Great Depression have on families?

_____

_____

7. What role do cognitive processes play in socialization within families?

_____

_____

KEY PEOPLE IN SECTION (Describe the contributions of this individual to the study and understanding of adolescence.)

**Alan Sroufe** — _____

_____

**Andrew Collins** — _____

_____

**Mark Twain** — _____

_____

**Margaret Mead** — _____

_____

## PARENT-ADOLESCENT RELATIONSHIPS
## SECTION REVIEW

1. Match the terms with the correct definitions or descriptions.

    ____    1. autonomy                  A. Parents are uninvolved

    ____    2. emotional autonomy        B. Highly restrictive, punitive parenting style

    ____    3. authoritarian parenting style    C. Adolescents de-emphasize the importance of attachment

    ____    4. authoritative parenting style    D. Adolescents are hypertuned to attachment issues

190

| | | |
|---|---|---|
| ___ | 5. indulgent parenting style | E. Parenting style associated with social competence |
| ___ | 6. neglectful parenting style | F. Parenting style associated with social incompetence |
| ___ | 7. dismissing/avoidant attachment | G. Relinquishing childlike dependence on parents |
| ___ | 8. preoccupied/ambivalent attachment | H. Adolescent has an unusually high fear |
| ___ | 9. unresolved/disorganized attachment | I. Caregiver (usually mom) is used as a secure base from which to explore the environment |
| ___ | 10. secure attachment | J. Related with independence and self-direction |
| ___ | 11. Insecure attachment | K. Infants avoid caregiver, or show ambivalence toward them |

2. What are the four main parenting categories according to Baumrind?

_____

_____

3. Why is authoritative parenting likely to be the most effective style?

_____

_____

4. What major changes have the roles of fathers in families undergone over time?

_____

_____

5. How involved are today's fathers with their children and adolescents?

_____

_____

6. What are the four distinct patterns of adolescent autonomy that typically emerge form an analysis of high school students?

_____

_____

7. According to Furstenburg and Harris, how are low-income African American families impacted by attachment and identification with their fathers?

_____

_____

8. Why do adolescents run away from their homes?

_____

_____

KEY PEOPLE IN SECTION (Describe the contributions of this individual to the study and understanding of adolescence.)

**Diana Baumrind** — _____

_____

**Judith Smetana** — _____

_____

**Reed Larson** — _____

_____

**John Bowlby** — _____

_____

**Mary Ainsworth** — _____

_____


## SIBLING RELATIONSHIPS
## SECTION REVIEW

1.     How much of a problem is sibling conflict in adolescence?

_____

_____

2.     What are later-born children like as compared to first-born?

_____

_____

3.     Is the "only child" typically a "spoiled brat?"

_____

_____


## THE CHANGING FAMILY IN A CHANGING SOCIETY
## SECTION REVIEW

1.     What factors affect the adolescent's individual risk and vulnerability in a divorced family?

_____

_____

2.     What role does socioeconomic status play in the lives of adolescents in divorced families?

_____

_____

3.     How much do family processes matter in a divorce?

_____

_____

4.     What are the three common types of stepfamily structures?

_____

_____

5.     Do children in stepfamilies have more adjustment problems than other children?

_____

_____

6.     What are some negative experiences faced by "latchkey" adolescents?

_____

_____

7.     What effect does unemployment have on families and on adolescents' development?

_____

_____

8.     Are children raised by gay or lesbian parents different from other children?

_____

_____

9.     In what ways do minority families differ from White American families?

_____

_____

10.     What is the mother's role in the family?

_____

_____

11.     What is the father's role in the family?

_____

_____

12.    How actively are today's fathers involved with their children and adolescents?

_____

_____


KEY PEOPLE IN SECTION (Describe the contributions of this individual to the study and understanding of adolescence.)

**James Bray** — _____

_____

**E.Mavis Hetherington** — _____

_____

**Lois Hoffman** — _____

_____

**Nancy Galambos** —_____

_____

**Thomas and Lynette Long** — _____

_____

**Joan Lipsitz** — _____

_____

**Frank Furstenburg and Kathleen Harris** —

_____

_____


SOCIAL POLICY, ADOLESCENTS, AND FAMILIES
SECTION REVIEW

1.    What must parents do if they wish to see their adolescents develop in a competent manner?

_____

_____

# EXPLORATIONS IN ADOLESCENCE

1.      Compare and contrast the extended family structures in African-American and Mexican-American families. What positive effects do these systems have on adolescent development?

_____

_____


# COGNITIVE CHALLENGE

1.      Write down your ideas for how an adolescent boy or girl (you choose which one you would like to discuss) and his or her parents could engage in collaborative problem solving to set ground rules for dating.

_____

_____


2.      Talk to one of your friends or acquaintances whose parents separated when they were teenagers (or use yourself if your parents did so). When, how, and what did their parents tell them about the separation? Could they have done it in a better way? What suggestions would they give to parents of teenagers who are about to separate?

_____

_____


# ADOLESCENCE IN RESEARCH

Concerning James Bray's study of stepfamilies (1998, 1999), state the hypothesis, the research methods (if known), the research conclusions, and the implications and applications for adolescent development.

_____

_____


# ⊠ COMPREHENSIVE REVIEW

1.      According to Alan Sroufe, social competence is related to
        a.      early academic success.         c.      parental marital satisfaction.
        b.      early secure attachment.        d.      family standard of living.

2.      _____ relationships more likely to consist of participants who relate to each other on equal terms.
        a.      Sibling-child                   c.      Peer-child
        b.      Parent-child                    d.      Teacher-child

3.　　　　＿＿＿＿＿＿＿＿ once remarked that when he was 14 his father was so ignorant he could hardly stand him, but by age 21 he was surprised at how much his father had learned in those 7 years.
a.　　Jean Piaget　　　　　　c.　　Mark Twain
b.　　Charles Darwin　　　　d.　　Sigmund Freud

4.　　Conflict between mothers and sons is most stressful
a.　　during infancy.
b.　　when the son reaches college age.
c.　　during the apex of pubertal growth.
d.　　between the ages of 7 and 10.

5.　　Married individuals with children tend to display a greater amount of marital dissatisfaction when their offspring is
a.　　a newborn.　　　　　　c.　　a child.
b.　　an adolescent.　　　　d.　　an adult.

6.　　These child-bearing couples tend to have more egalitarian relationships, and the men participate in child care and household tasks more often.
a.　　couples with only one child
b.　　late-starting couples in their 30's or 40's
c.　　early-starting teen couples
d.　　couples who began childbearing in their early 20's

7.　　Chad's parents carefully check places Chad plans to go and who he is going with. This type of parenting behavior is called
a.　　monitoring.　　　　　　c.　　eavesdropping.
b.　　regulating.　　　　　　d.　　proctoring.

8.　　Which of the following is NOT one of Baumrind's four types of parenting?
a.　　indulgent　　　　　　　c.　　authoritarian
b.　　power assertion　　　　d.　　neglectful

9.　　A restrictive, punitive style of parenting is
a.　　indulgent.　　　　　　c.　　authoritarian.
b.　　authoritative.　　　　d.　　neglectful.

10.　　Parents who encourage their adolescents to be independent but still place limits on what they can do are
a.　　indulgent.　　　　　　c.　　authoritarian.
b.　　authoritative.　　　　d.　　neglectful.

11.　　A style in which the parent is very uninvolved in the life of the adolescent is
a.　　indulgent.　　　　　　c.　　authoritarian.
b.　　authoritative.　　　　d.　　neglectful.

12.　　Diana Baumrind describes authoritative parents as
a.　　restrictive, punitive, and allowing little verbal guide.
b.　　encouraging independence and placing limits on adolescents' actions.
c.　　power assertive, rejecting, unresponsive, and parent centered.
d.　　undemanding, rejecting, uninvolved, and controlling.

13. Most researchers consider _____ parenting to be the most effective form of parenting.
    a. authoritarian
    c. authoritative
    b. indulgent
    d. neglectful

14. Jeremy's parents have few rules for household conduct or academic expectations. They do not punish Jeremy when he violates rules, but merely accept his behavior. Jeremy is likely to develop
    a. social competence because his parents unconditionally accept him.
    b. anxiety about social comparisons and social inferiority feelings.
    c. self-reliance, social responsibility, and autonomy.
    d. little impulse control and disregard for rules.

15. Chao describes an authoritarian style of parenting that appears effective in some Asian and Asian American families. Chao call this parenting style
    a. synchrony.
    c. hoshini.
    b. training.
    d. proctoring.

16. The increased independence that typifies adolescence is known as
    a. synchrony.
    c. indulgence.
    b. autonomy.
    d. reciprocal socialization.

17. Conflict between adolescents and parents is typically strongest in early adolescence and may be a healthy aspect of the development of
    a. autonomy.
    c. parenting skills.
    b. attachment.
    d. dating skills.

18. Because of the dangerous environments in which they often raise their children, _____ parents are likely to use physical punishment.
    a. Asian
    c. Latino
    b. African American
    d. Arab

19. You are depressed because you argue with your 10-year-old daughter almost daily, and these arguments last for several minutes. Experts on adolescents would tell you that
    a. this high level of conflict will lead to later disturbances.
    b. this type of conflict is normal, and you should not worry about it.
    c. if you are arguing this much now, your arguments will increase in later adolescence.
    d. these arguments will prevent your daughter from developing an autonomous identity.

20. The most crucial transition for the development of adolescent autonomy is from
    a. school to work.
    c. middle school to high school.
    b. high school to college.
    d. virginity to sexual activity.

21. What percent of American adolescents currently have one or more siblings?
    a. 50%     b. 25%     c. 60%     d. 80%

22. Royce, a father of five children, has the role of 'bread winner' in his family. What time period did Royce likely live in?
    a. 1970's
    c. the colonial period
    b. post World War II
    d. the Industrial Revolution through the Great Depression

23. Adolescents who are securely attached to their parents
    a.  cannot adequately develop autonomy.
    b.  show less secure attachment to peers.
    c.  have more difficulty engaging with peers and separating from parents.
    d.  have higher self-esteem than insecurely attached peers.

24. Sibling conflict is often lower in adolescence than in childhood due to changes in
    a.  social development.          c.  the power relationship.
    b.  physical development.        d.  the way parents deal with conflict.

25. Which of the following is rarely a source of parent-adolescent conflict in families?
    a.  keeping one's bedroom clean   c.  drug use
    b.  getting homework done         d.  choice of clothing worn

26. Firstborn children are
    a.  more achievement-oriented than those born later.
    b.  less achievement-oriented than those born later.
    c.  more psychologically well adjusted than those born later.
    d.  on the average, less socially responsible than those born later.

27. Which of the following is NOT one of the three common types of stepfamily structures?
    a.  stepfather                  c.  complex
    b.  compound                    d.  stepmother

28. _____ refers to the confusion in stepfamilies regarding the membership of the family and each individual's responsibility.
    a.  family blending             c.  stepfamily dynamism
    b.  boundary ambiguity          d.  stepfamily individuation

29. According to James Bray, given time stepfamilies fall into three types based on their relationships. Which of the following is NOT one of those types?
    a.  neo-traditional             c.  romantic
    b.  matriarchal                 d.  new breed

30. It has been estimated that in about _____ percent of families, parents and adolescents engage in prolonged, intense, unhealthy conflict.
    a.  10                          c.  40
    b.  20                          d.  75

31. After coming home from school, Juan washes the breakfast dishes, does a load of laundry, and starts dinner before his parents get home at 6 P.M. Juan is a
    a.  hurried child.              c.  neglected child.
    b.  latchkey child.            d.  stepchild.

32. Ethnic families tend to differ from White American families in that the former
    a.  are smaller.
    b.  show more extended networks.
    c.  encourage more autonomy among girls than boys.
    d.  have more employed mothers.

33. According to old sayings, what are the only lasting things we can leave our children?
    a. love and money
    b. our name and our legacy
    c. bills and ashes
    d. roots and wings

34. It is a mistake to attribute the problems of adolescents to their mothers because
    a. fathers spend more time with children and adolescents than ever before.
    b. mothers and fathers are partners in parenting.
    c. behavior is determined by multiple factors.
    d. peers and siblings have more influence on adolescents than parents.

35. This is the capacity to relinquish child-like dependencies on parents.
    a. independence
    b. emotional autonomy
    c. free will
    d. adolescence

36. Which of the following is NOT often seen in families with runaway children?
    a. sexual exploitation
    b. physical abuse
    c. alcoholic parents
    d. strong religious affiliation

37. Which of the following is NOT a common description of 'first-born children'?
    a. more aggressive
    b. comforting
    c. adult oriented
    d. self-controlled

38. An infant that tries to avoid its primary caregiver is showing evidence of
    a. insecure attachment.
    b. secure attachment.
    c. emotional autonomy.
    d. preoccupied attachment.

39. African American and Latino adolescents are most likely to differ from White adolescents in that the former are more likely to
    a. live in extended families.
    b. live in rural areas.
    c. attend church.
    d. use drugs.

40. Bernie is the first born child in his family. Which of the following is LESS likely due to Bernie's ordinal position?
    a. Bernie will end up in prison.
    b. Bernie will appear in *Who's Who*.
    c. Bernie will become a physician.
    d. Bernie will become a Rhode's Scholar.

41. In studies of social relationships, adolescents report more disagreements with their _____ than any other.
    a. best friend
    b. father
    c. mother
    d. younger sibling

42. Which of the following is the MOST LIKELY outcome for a child in a "divorced" family?
    a. he/she will drop out of school
    b. he/she will take drugs
    c. he/she will completely cope with the parent's divorce
    d. he/she will become sexually active at an earlier age

43. This observation came out of the most recent studies on divorce.
   a. Japanese families are now the most likely to divorce.
   b. African-American families are now the least likely to divorce.
   c. Divorce rates in America are now the highest ever.
   d. Divorce rates in America, after decades of increase, are now starting to decline.

## ADOLESCENCE ON THE SCREEN

- *Ordinary People* concerns parents and their teenage son's struggle to deal with the death of a younger sibling. The surviving son feels guilt and blame, leading him to suicidal depression.

- *Tumbleweeds* presents the story of a displaced single mother and her teenage daughter who move from place to place and live on a shoestring, while the mother looks for a man who will give them a better life.

- *Liberty House* depicts the changing sociopolitical climate of the 1950s, including integration, interracial dating, and changing family structure and influence.

## ADOLESCENCE IN BOOKS

- *Between Parent & Teenager*, by Haim Ginott (Avon: NY, 1999), continues to be one of the most widely read and recommended books for parents who want to communicate more effectively with their teenagers.

- *Surviving the Breakup: How Children and Parents Cope with Divorce*, by Judith Wallerstein & Joan B. Kelly (Basic Books: NY, 1996), adds more empirical data to back up theories regarding what happens after divorce.

- *Growing Up with Divorce*, by Neil Kalter (Free Press: NY, 1990), provides divorced parents with information to help their children and youth avoid emotional problems.

- *I'm Not Mad, I Just Hate You!* by R. Cohen-Sandler & M. Silver (Viking: NY, 1999), deals with adolescent mother/daughter conflict.

- *The Shelter of Each Other: Rebuilding Our Families*, by Mary Pipher (Ballantine: NY, 1996), calls for strengthening the family for the benefit of children, parents, and grandparents.

# Answer Key

## KEY TERMS

1. **reciprocal socialization** The process by which children and adolescents socialize parents, just as parents socialize them.

2. **developmental construction views** Views sharing the belief that as individuals grow up, they acquire modes of relating to others. There are two main variations of this view. One emphasizes continuity and

stability in relationships throughout the life span, the other emphasizes discontinuity and changes in relationships throughout the life span.

3. **continuity view** A developmental view that emphasizes the role of early parent-child relationships in constructing a basic way of relating to people throughout the life span.

4. **discontinuity view** A developmental view that emphasizes change and growth in relationships over time.

5. **authoritarian parenting** This is a restrictive, punitive style in which the parent exhorts the adolescent to follow the parent's directions and to respect work and effort. Firm limits and controls are placed on adolescents, and little verbal exchange is allowed. This style is associated with adolescents' socially incompetent behavior.

6. **authoritative parenting** This style encourages adolescents to be independent but still places limits and controls on their actions. Extensive verbal give-and-take is allowed, and parents are warm and nurturing toward the adolescent. This style is associated with adolescents' socially competent behavior.

7. **neglectful parenting** A style in which the parent is very uninvolved in the adolescent's life. It is associated with adolescents' social incompetence, especially a lack of self-control.

8. **indulgent parenting** A style in which parents are highly involved with their adolescents but place few demands or controls on them. This is associated with adolescents' social incompetence, especially a lack of self-control.

9. **emotional autonomy** The capacity to relinquish childlike dependencies on parents.

10. **insecure attachment** In this attachment pattern, infants either avoid the caregiver or show considerable resistance or ambivalence toward the caregiver. This pattern is theorized to be related to difficulties in relationships and problems in later development.

11. **secure attachment** In this attachment pattern infants use their primary caregiver, usually the mother, as a secure base from which to explore the environment. Secure attachment is theorized to be an important foundation for psychological development later in childhood, adolescence, and adulthood.

12. **dismissing/avoidant attachment** An insecure attachment category in which individuals de-emphasize the importance of attachment. This category is associated with consistent experiences of rejection of attachment needs by caregivers.

13. **preoccupied/ambivalent attachment** An insecure attachment category in which adolescents are hypertuned to attachment experiences. This is thought to occur mainly because parents are inconsistently available to the adolescents.

14. **unresolved/disorganized attachment** An insecure category in which the adolescent has an unusually high level of fear and is disoriented. This may result from such traumatic experiences as a parent's death or abuse by parents.

15. **boundary ambiguity** The uncertainty in stepfamilies about who is on or out of the family and who is performing or responsible for certain tasks in the family system.

## KEY PEOPLE IN THE STUDY OF ADOLESCENCE

| | | | |
|---|---|---|---|
| **1.** | E | **4.** | D |
| **2.** | A | **5.** | C |
| **3.** | B | **6.** | F |

## "DR. DETAIL'S" LIBRARY EXERCISE

Individual answers will vary, but most should report changes in the size of the family and mobility of the family. Other issues could be income, divorce rates, etc.


## ADOLESCENT MYTH AND FACT

| | | | | | |
|---|---|---|---|---|---|
| 1. | F | 6. | T | 11. | F |
| 2. | T | 7. | T | 12. | T |
| 3. | T | 8. | T | 13. | F |
| 4. | T | 9. | T | 14. | F |
| 5. | T | 10. | F | 15. | T |


## FAMILY PROCESSES
## SECTION REVIEW

1.   Reciprocal socialization is the process by which children and adolescents socialize parents just as parents socialize them.

2.   The continuity view emphasizes the role that early parent-child relationships play in constructing a basic way of relating to people throughout the life span. The discontinuity view emphasizes change and growth in relationships over time.

3.   Twain felt that as adolescents grow older, they come to understand their parents better.

4.   Adolescents today are required to function in a more anonymous, larger environment with multiple and varying teachers.

5.   The primary difference found is that the fathers are warmer and communicate better with their children.

6.   During its height, the depression produced economic deprivation, adult depression and discontent, marital conflict, inconsistent child-rearing, and unhealthy behaviors (e.g., drinking).

7.   Cognitive processes are increasingly believed to be central to understanding socialization in the family.


## KEY PEOPLE IN SECTION

**Alan Sroufe** — Found in his research support for continuity.

**Andrew Collins** — In his longitudinal study, he found evidence for the discontinuity view of relationships.

**Mark Twain** — Once remarked that when he was 14 his father was so ignorant he could hardly stand to have the man around, but when Twain turned 21, he was astonished at how much his father had learned in those seven years.

**Margaret Mead** — Described subtle changes in a culture that have significant influences on the family.

# PARENT-ADOLESCENT RELATIONSHIPS
## SECTION REVIEW

1. Matching Answers:

   | | |
   |---|---|
   | **1.** J | **7.** C |
   | **2.** G | **8.** D |
   | **3.** B | **9.** H |
   | **4.** E | **10.** I |
   | **5.** F | **11.** K |
   | **6.** A | |

2. Authoritarian parenting, which emphasizes a restrictive punitive style. Authoritative parenting, which encourages adolescents to be independent and active in decision making. Neglectful parenting, where parents are not actively involved in their child's lives. Indulgent parenting, where parents allow too many freedoms to their children.

3. Authoritative parents establish an appropriate balance between control and autonomy. They are more likely to engage children in verbal give-and-take. They are warmer and the children are more receptive to them.

4. The current role of father in the family presents a shift from breadwinner and moral guardian to a role that incorporates far more nurturing and involvement in day-to-day living.

5. Fathers spend only a small portion of their time with adolescents. About 1/3 to 3/4s as much time as mothers do.

6. Permissiveness in outside activities; permissiveness in age-related activities; parent regard for judgment; activities with status implications.

7. According to Furstenberg and Harris, children who reported close attachment and identification with their fathers during adolescence were twice as likely as young adults to have a stable job and enter college, and they are much less likely to be unwed parents or in jail.

8. The reasons are numerous. Some escape poverty, abuse, overcontrolling parents and still others are just simply adventure-seeking.

## KEY PEOPLE IN SECTION

**Diana Baumrind** — believes that parents should be neither punitive nor aloof from their adolescents, but rather should develop rules and be affectionate with them.

**Judith Smetana** — believes that parent-adolescent conflict can be better understood by considering the adolescent's changing social cognitive abilities.

**Reed Larson** — spent six months in India studying middle-SES adolescents and their families; he observed that in India there is little parent-adolescent conflict and many would fit Baumrind's model of "authoritarian."

**John Bowlby** — argued that secure attachment in infancy is central to the development of social competence.

**Mary Ainsworth** — argued that secure attachment in infancy is central to the development of social competence.

## SIBLING RELATIONSHIPS
## SECTION REVIEW

1.  Sibling relationships show a higher degree of conflict than with relationships with other social agents (parents, peers, teachers, and romantic partners).

2.  Later-borns usually enjoy better relations with peers than first-born children.

3.  Contrary to public opinion of "spoiled brat," most research suggests goal orientation and many positive personality traits.


## THE CHANGING FAMILY IN A CHANGING SOCIETY
## SECTION REVIEW

1.  Most research suggests that adolescents from divorced families show poorer adjustment, such as externalizing disorders.

2.  One of the biggest adjustments following divorce is lower SES. There is a greater decline if the child lives with the mother.

3.  They matter a lot. When divorced parents have a harmonious relationship, the children do much better.

4.  a. stepfather, b. stepmother, and c. blended or complex families

5.  Yes. Their adjustment problems are very similar to those of kids in divorced families.

6.  Abusing siblings, stealing, vandalizing, using substances, etc.

7.  Deprived adolescents show less positive peer interaction.

8.  Researchers have found no discernable differences between adolescents raised by gay and/or lesbian parents as opposed to heterosexual parents.

9.  Ethnic minority families differ from White American families in their size, structure, reliance on kinship networks, level of income, and education.

10. Mothers tend to get little of the credit for their children's successes and much of the blame for their failures.

11. During the Industrial Revolution, fathers gained the role of breadwinner, although moral role model has also been a historic part of the father's role as well.

12. Today's fathers spend only a small portion of their time with their children. As little as 1/3 what mothers do. They have adapted a more nurturing role as opposed to primarily bread winner.


## KEY PEOPLE IN SECTION

**James Bray** — found that over time stepfamilies often fall into three types based on their relationships: neo-traditional, matriarchal, and romantic.

**E. Mavis Hetherington** — prominent researcher regarding the effects of divorce on children.

**Lois Hoffman** — a leading authority on maternal employment; she says it's a fact of life.

**Nancy Galambos** — studied the effects of parents' work overload on their relationships with their adolescent on the adolescent's development.

**Thomas and Lynette Long** — concluded that a slight majority of latchkey children had negative experiences.

**Joan Lipsitz** — called the lack of adult supervision of children and adolescents in the after-school hours one of the nation's major problems.

**Frank Furstenburg and Kathleen Harris** — documented how nurturant fathering can overcome children's difficult life circumstances.

## SOCIAL POLICY, ADOLESCENTS, AND FAMILIES
## SECTION REVIEW

1.  Show them warmth and respect; demonstrate sustained interest in their lives; recognize and adapt to their changing cognitive and socioemotional development; communicate expectations for high standards of conduct and achievement; display authoritative, constructive ways of dealing with problems and conflict.

## EXPLORATIONS IN ADOLESCENCE

Both ethnic groups tend to "stick together." African-American grandmothers are a great resource for mothers and infants. Mothers of adolescents who have good relationships with their mothers pass that on to their children. Family support has been directly related to adolescent school success and self-reliance. In Mexican-American families the father is the undisputed authority but the mother is the main source of affection and care. These families exist more for each other, rather than for themselves. Self-reliance is not valued as highly as it is in African-American (and White) families.

## COGNITIVE CHALLENGE

1.  Example: Parents and adolescent should set aside a time when the teen first indicates an interest in dating to discuss only this issue. Each come to the "meeting" with a list of what they feel they "must" have and what they would "like" to have. Beginning with the "must" have list, they should discuss and negotiate, then move on to the "like" to have list. They should come up with a written agreement that both are comfortable with signing. The agreement could have a method for resolving disputes that arise about dating, such as submitting the issue to a respected and neutral party (such as an aunt or uncle).

2.  Example: Parents should tell their child as soon as the separation is decided upon. Both parents should be present and should make it clear that they respect each other and love their child, and that the separation is no fault of the child's. The teenager should be consulted about which parent he or she wishes to live with and the arrangements for visiting the other parent. The teen should be given the opportunity to ask questions and express his or her feelings.

# ADOLESCENCE IN RESEARCH

Bray hypothesized that there would be consistent and identifiable patterns in relationships within stepfamilies. He studied 200 stepfamilies (probably through survey and observations – although not stated) and found that over time stepfamilies fall into three types based on their relationships: nontraditional, matriarchal, and romantic.

---

☒ **COMPREHENSIVE REVIEW**

| | | | | | | | |
|---|---|---|---|---|---|---|---|
| 1. | b | 12. | b | 23. | d | 34. | c |
| 2. | c | 13. | c | 24. | c | 35. | b |
| 3. | c | 14. | d | 25. | c | 36. | d |
| 4. | c | 15. | b | 26. | a | 37. | a |
| 5. | b | 16. | b | 27. | b | 38. | a |
| 6. | b | 17. | a | 28. | b | 39. | a |
| 7. | a | 18. | b | 29. | d | 40. | a |
| 8. | b | 19. | c | 30. | b | 41. | c |
| 9. | c | 20. | b | 31. | b | 42. | c |
| 10. | b | 21. | d | 32. | b | 43. | d |
| 11. | d | 22. | d | 33. | d | | |

# ✧ Chapter 10  Peers

**Learning Goals with Key Terms and Key People in Boldface**

**1.0**　**DISCUSS THE ROLE OF PEER RELATIONS IN ADOLESCENT DEVELOPMENT**
- **A.**　**Peer Group Functions**
  - 1.1　What are **peers,** and how are they important to adolescent social development?
  - 1.2　How do **peers** provide a basis for social comparison and a source of information about the world outside the family?
  - 1.3　Why are good peer relations necessary for normal social development?
  - 1.4　What do adolescents do when they are with their peers?
  - 1.5　How can peer relations be either positive or negative?
  - 1.6　What did Jean Piaget and Harry Stack Sullivan stress about peer relations?
  - 1.7　According to Hartup, in what ways do peer relations vary?
- **B.**　**Family-Peer Linkages**
  - 1.8　How do healthy family relations promote healthy peer relations?
  - 1.9　What are some of the ways in which the worlds of parents and peers are connected?
  - 1.10　What is the main difference between the quality of adolescent's relations with their peers and parents?
- **C.**　**Peer Conformity**
  - 1.11　What is **conformity?**
  - 1.12　How can **conformity** to peer pressure in adolescence be positive or negative?
  - 1.13　At what point does conformity to antisocial standards of peers peak?
  - 1.14　How can the effects of peer pressure be observed?
- **D.**　**Peer Statuses**
  - 1.15　How would you describe **popular children**?
  - 1.16　How would you describe **average children**?
  - 1.17　What is the peer status of **neglected children**?
  - 1.18　How well do **rejected children** fare among their peers?
  - 1.19　Where do **controversial children** fit in with their peer group?
- **E.**　**Social Cognition and Emotion**
  - 1.20　How is social knowledge associated with improved peer relations?
  - 1.21　How do good information processing skills improve peer relations?
  - 1.22　What are the five steps children go through in processing information about their social world?
  - 1.23　What part does the ability to regulate emotion play in successful peer relations?
- **F.**　**Strategies for Improving Social Skills**
  - 1.24　How do **conglomerate strategies** improve social skills?
  - 1.25　How can neglected children and adolescents be trained to interact more effectively with their peers?

**2.0**　**EXPLAIN HOW FRIENDSHIP CONTRIBUTES TO ADOLESCENT DEVELOPMENT**
- **A.**　**It's Importance**
  - 2.1　What is a **friend**?
  - 2.2　What are the six functions that friendship plays in adolescence?

B. **Sullivan's Idea**

    2.3    How does research support or refute **Sullivan's** ideas?

C. **Intimacy and Similarity**

    2.4    What are the key characteristics of friendship?

    2.5    What similarities do friends share?

    2.6    How would you define **intimacy in friendship**?

D. **Mixed-Age Friendships**

    2.7    What happens to adolescents who become close friends with older individuals?

## 3.0 SUMMARIZE WHAT TAKES PLACE IN ADOLESCENT GROUPS

A. **Group Function and Formation**

    3.1    How do groups satisfy adolescents' personal needs, reward them, provide information, raise their self-esteem, and give them an identity?

    3.2    How do **norms** and **roles** play a part in any group?

    3.3    What are group **norms**?

    3.4    What are group **roles**?

B. **Groups in childhood and Adolescence**

    3.5    In what ways do children's groups differ from those of adolescents?

    3.6    What did Dexter Dunphy learn about adolescent groups?

C. **Cliques and Crowds**

    3.7    What is the difference between a **clique** and a **crowd**?

    3.8    What different cliques are found in most secondary schools?

    3.9    With what type of cliques is membership associated with high self-esteem?

    3.10    What is the main feature distinguishing a **crowd**?

    3.11    What are Brown's conclusions about adolescent crowds?

D. **Youth Organizations**

    3.12    In what way do youth organizations influence adolescent development?

    3.13    What is the mission of boys' clubs and girls' clubs?

## 4.0 DESCRIBE THE ROLES OF GENDER AND CULTURE IN ADOLESCENT PEER GROUPS AND FRIENDSHIPS

A. **Gender**

    4.1    How do boys and girls differ when interacting with various groups?

    4.2    What are some features of lower-socioeconomic status groups?

    4.3    Why do ethnic minority adolescents often have two sets of peers?

    4.4    Why do ethnic minority adolescents turn to peer groups more than White adolescents?

B. **Socioeconomic Status and Ethnicity**

    4.5    Why has athletic team participation become an important group function for lowered SES and minority families?

C. **Culture**

    4.6    Why is access to peers restricted in some countries?

    4.7    Explain the role of the dormitory in the Murian culture.

## 5.0 CHARACTERIZE ADOLESCENT DATING AND ROMANTIC RELATIONSHIPS

A. **Functions of Dating**

    5.1    What is dating and what are its functions?

    5.2    What eight functions can be served by dating?

B. **Types of Dating and Developmental Changes**

    5.3    At what age do adolescents start to hang out together in heterosexual groups?

    5.4    What is cyberdating?

    5.5    How much time do young adolescents spend thinking about the opposite sex as opposed to actually being with them?

5.6    What are common myths associated with dating among sexual minority youth?

5.7    What special problems do immigrant adolescents face with their families in relationship to dating?

**C.    Emotion and Romantic Relationships**

5.8    How do romantic relationships affect an adolescent's life?

5.9    What emotions are associated with adolescent romantic relationships?

**D.    Romantic Love and Its Construction**

5.10    What is the difference between **romantic love** and **affectionate love**?

5.11    How does the relationship of the adolescent's parents influence their own dating relationships?

5.12    What role does secure attachment play in adolescent relationships?

5.13    What is the developmental construction view of romantic love?

5.14    According to Mavis Hetherington, how are the relationships of girls and boys impacted by the divorce of their parents?

5.15    What is Sullivan's conceptualization of collaboration in dating?

5.16    How important are peers and friends in adolescent romantic relationships?

5.17    What is the relationship between group leadership and dating?

**E.    Gender and Culture**

5.18    Do male and female adolescents bring different motivations to the dating experience?

5.19    What are the differences between male and female **dating scripts**?

5.20    How is adolescent dating different for Latinos than traditional American dating styles?

5.21

# Exercises

## KEY TERMS COMPLETION EXERCISE

This exercise presents each key term in the form of an incomplete sentence. Compare each sentence by either defining the term or giving an example. Compare your definitions with those given at the end of the study guide chapter.

1.    To adolescents, **peers** are

_____

_____

2.    **Conformity** means to

_____

_____

3.    **Popular children** are those who

_____

_____

4.      **Average children** are those who

_____

_____

5.      **Neglected children** are very likely to

_____

_____

6.      **Rejected children** often

_____

_____

7.      **Controversial children** are those who

_____

_____

8.      **Conglomerate strategies** are meant to

_____

_____

9.      **Friends** are those who

_____

_____

10.     **Intimacy in friendship** is exemplified by

_____

_____

11.     Examples of **norms** are

_____

_____

12.     The importance of **roles** is

_____

_____

13.     **Cliques** are meant to

_____

_____

14. **Crowds** are seen when

_____

_____

15. **Dating scripts** are used by

_____

_____

16. An example of **romantic love** is

_____

_____

17. An example of **affectionate love** is

_____

_____

## KEY PEOPLE IN THE STUDY OF ADOLESCENCE

| | | | |
|---|---|---|---|
| _____ | 1. Reed Larson | A. | Studied conformity |
| _____ | 2. Thomas Berndt | B. | Studied nature and function of adolescent and children's groups, emphasizing change in sexual make-up |
| _____ | 3. Kenneth Dodge | C. | Studied role of attachment patterns in adolescent romantic relationships |
| _____ | 4. William Hartup | D. | Studied role of peers in romantic involvement |
| _____ | 5. Harry Stack Sullivan | E. | Encouraged structured volunteer activities as a way to develop initiative |
| _____ | 6. Candice Feiring | F. | Studied the impact of insecure attachment on dating relationships |
| _____ | 7. Dexter Dunphy | G. | Psychoanalytical theorist who emphasized importance of friendship for adolescents |
| _____ | 8. Wyndol Furman | H. | Studied nature of child and adolescent friendships |
| _____ | 9. Bradford Brown | I. | Found that aggressive boys are more likely to perceive another child's actions as hostile when the peer's intentions are ambiguous. |
| _____ | 10. Jennifer Connolly | J. | Found that males and females bring different motivations to the dating experience |

## ADOLESCENT MYTH AND FACT

Which of the following statements regarding adolescents are true (T) and which are false (F)?

1. Age grading would occur even if schools were not age graded and adolescents were left alone to determine the composition of their own societies.  T or F

2. In adolescence, team sports accounts for 26 percent of boy's activities with peers; however, it accounts for 45 percent of girl's activities with peers.  T or F

3.      Poor peer relations in childhood might be associated with dropping out of school in adolescence.  T or F

4.      Rejection by one's peers in adolescence has not proven to be rrelated to criminal problems later in life. T or F

5.      Conformity to peer pressure in adolescence can be positive or negative.  T or F

6.      Despite the existence of many outstanding programs, researchers often find it difficult to.improve the social skills of adolescents who are actively disliked and rejected.  T or F

7.      Social skills training programs are much more successful with adolescents over the age of 10, as opposed to those younger than 10 years of age.  T or F

8.      Affiliation with friends who are significantly older does not make an adolescent more prone to deviant behavior.  T or F

9.      Crowds are less personal than cliques.  T or F

10.     Adolescents who join youth organizations have higher self esteem when they are adults.  T or F

11.     Dating, as we now know it, dates back to the middle ages.  T or F

12.     In a study of more than 8,000 adolescents, those who reported that they were in love has a slightly higher risk for depression than those not romantically involved.  T or F

13.     Most typically, adolescents receive more support for dating from their mothers than other members of the family.  T or F

## EXPLORING PEER RELATIONS
## SECTION REVIEW

1.      How they are seen by peers is the most important aspect of many adolescents' lives. Why?

_____

_____

2.      What do adolescents do when they are with their peers?

_____

_____

3.      How important are good peer relationships for normal social development in adolescence?

_____

_____

4.      What are some of the ways the worlds of parents and peers are connected?

_____

_____

5.      What is conformity?

_____

6.  Does research suggest that parents coach their adolescents in ways of relating to peers.

    _____

    _____

7.  Why do some adolescents from strong, supportive families, nonetheless struggle in peer relations?

    _____

    _____

8.  According to developmentalists, what are three types of children who have a different status than popular children?

    _____

    _____

9.  How can the effects of peer pressure be observed?

    _____

    _____

10. In peer relations, what role do appropriate cognitive skills play?

    _____

    _____

11. How can conglomerate strategies be used to improve adolescents' social skills?

    _____

    _____

12. How can neglected children and adolescents be trained to interact more effectively with their peers?

    _____

    _____

## KEY PEOPLE IN SECTION (Describe the contributions of this individual to the study and understanding of adolescence.)

**Anna Freud —** _____

_____

**Jean Piaget and Harry Stack Sullivan —** _____

_____

**Thomas Berndt —** _____

_____

**James Coleman —** _____

_____

**Kenneth Dodge —** _____

_____

## FRIENDSHIP
## SECTION REVIEW

1.   What is a friend?

_____

_____

2.   What six functions do adolescent friendships serve?

_____

_____

3.   List and give an example of five appropriate strategies for making friends.

_____

_____

4.   List and give examples for three inappropriate strategies for making friends.

_____

_____

5.   How important is similarity in forming friendships?

_____

_____

6.   What happens to adolescents who become close friends with older individuals?

_____

_____

## KEY PEOPLE IN SECTION (Describe the contributions of this individual to the study and understanding of adolescence.)

**Harry Stack Sullivan —** _____

_____

**Willard Hartup —** _____

_____

## ADOLESCENT GROUPS
## SECTION REVIEW

1.  Why does an adolescent join a group?

    _____

    _____

2.  What two things do all groups have in common?

    _____

    _____

3.  Describe what Dunphy found to be the five steps of progression of peer group relations in adolescence.

    _____

    _____

4.  Summarize the conclusions of Bradford Brown and colleagues' most recent research on cliques.

    _____

    _____

5.  Compare and contrast cliques and crowds.

    _____

    _____

6.  What impact can youth organizations have on adolescents?

    _____

    _____

## KEY PEOPLE IN SECTION (Describe the contributions of this individual to the study and understanding of adolescence.)

**Dexter Dunphy —** _____

_____

**Bradford Brown —** _____

_____

**Jane Lohr —** _____

_____

_____

## GENDER AND CULTURE
## SECTION REVIEW

1.    How do boys and girls differ when interacting with various groups?

      _____

      _____

2.    Why is access to peers restricted in some countries?

      _____

      _____

3.    Why has athletic team participation become an important group function for lower SES and minority families?

      _____

      _____

4.    Explain the role of the dormitory in the Murian culture?

      _____

      _____

## DATING AND ROMANTIC RELATIONSHIPS
## SECTION REVIEW

1.    What eight functions are served by dating?

      _____

      _____

2.    a.    Describe the three main activities involved in the male dating script and give an example of each.

            _____

            _____

      b.    Describe the three main activities involved in the female dating script and give an example of each.

            _____

            _____

3.      WHAT is romantic love?

_____

_____

4.      What is affectionate love?

_____

_____

5.      According to Mavis Hetherington, how are the relationships of girls and boys impacted by the divorce of their parents?

_____

_____

6.      How is adolescent dating different for Latinos than traditional American dating styles?

_____

_____


KEY PEOPLE IN SECTION  Describe the contributions of this individual to the study and understanding of adolescence.

**Candice Feiring —** _____

_____

**Wyndol Furman and Elizabeth Wehner —** _____

_____

**Peter Blos —** _____

_____

**Mavis Hetherington —** _____

_____

**Harry Stack Sullivan —** _____

_____

**Jennifer Connolly —** _____

_____

## EXPLORATIONS IN ADOLESCENCE

1.      What did the 1995 Search Institute study find regarding barriers to participation in youth programs?

_____

## COGNITIVE CHALLENGE

1.  How did your relationship with your parents affect your peer relationships and friendships in adolescence? How did your parents influence your choice of peers and friends? How did your parents' marital relationship affect your dating and romantic relationships?

    _____

    _____

2.  Think back over your adolescent dating experiences. How were your experiences different when you were 13, 15, and 17? What would you do differently if you could begin anew today? What advice would you offer today's teenagers of those ages?

    _____

    _____

## ADOLESCENCE IN RESEARCH

Concerning Wentzel, Bary and Caldwell's (2004) research dealing with the prosocial behavior students in grades 6 through 8th, state the hypothesis, the research methods (if known), the research conclusions, and the implications and applications for adolescent development.

_____

_____

## ☒ COMPREHENSIVE REVIEW

1.  Jason is a sixth-grader who spends a lot of time with his peers. Statistically speaking, he is he most likely engaging in
    a.  going to stores.          c.  team sports.
    b.  watching television.      d.  girl-watching.

2.  Beetle is 2 years old. According to Barker and Wright (1951) Beetle spends ____ percent of the day with his peers.
    a.  5                          c.  20
    b.  10                         d.  40

3.  Most cooperative group programs have been conducted in
    a.  children's homes.         c.  academic settings.
    b.  video arcades.            d.  hospitals.

4.  In Anna Freud's observation of children who banded together after their parents died in WWII, she did NOT observe
    a.  the children were a tight knit group.

b.      the children became delinquent.

c.      the children being aloof with outsiders.

d.      the children forming intensive peer attachment.

5.      Participating in a newspaper drive with one's club because the club wants everyone to be involved in this activity is an example of _____ conformity.

      a.     negative             c.     independent

      b.     positive              d.     responsible

6.      In _____ behavioral arenas, parents have the least ability to dictate an adolescent's choices?

      a.     morality              c.     religion

      b.     peer relations       d.     education

7.      Thomas Berndt found that adolescent conformity to antisocial, peer-endorsed behavior _____ in late high school years and _____ agreement between parents and peers begins to occur in some areas.

      a.     decreases; greater      c.     increases; greater

      b.     decreases; lesser      d.     increases; lesser

8.      The adolescent who does not have significant interactions with peers is likely to be

      a.     handicapped.         c.     neglected.

      b.     antisocial.           d.     mature and independent.

9.      Researchers have found that the adolescent's attempt to gain independence meets with more parental opposition around

      a.     $6^{th}$ grade.           c.     $11^{th}$ grade.

      b.     $9^{th}$ grade.           d.     $12^{th}$ grade.

10.      _____ describes the extent to which children are liked or disliked by their peer group.

      a      popularity           c.     leadership index

      b.     Jenkens Likability Scale      d.     sociometric status

11.      _____ is NOT a characteristic of a popular child?

      a.     Enthusiasm          c.     Conceit

      b.     Self-confidence       d.     Concern for others

12.      Children who are frequently nominated as a best friend and are rarely disliked by their peers are

      a.     popular children.      c.     rejected children.

      b.     neglected children.     d.     controversial children.

13.      Children who are infrequently nominated as a best friend but are not disliked by their peers are

      a.     popular children.      c.     rejected children.

      b.     neglected children.     d.     controversial children.

14.      Children who are infrequently nominated as a best friend and are actively disliked by their peers are

      a.     popular children.      c.     rejected children.

      b.     neglected children.     d.     controversial children.

15.      Children who are frequently nominated both as a best friend and as being disliked are

      a.     popular children.      c.     rejected children.

      b.     neglected children.     d.     controversial children.

16. Victor is demonstrating and modeling appropriate social skills to Billy, a rejected child. What Victor is doing might be most appropriately referred to as
    a. guidance.
    c. using conglomerate strategies.
    b. teaching.
    d. enactment strategies.

17. Which of the following is NOT one of the six functions served by friendship?
    a. intimacy/affection
    c. ego support
    b. personal gain
    d. stimulation

18. Which of the following is NOT an example of a formal group?
    a. Panther football team
    c. Boy Scouts
    b. student council
    d. clique

19. _____ are small groups that range from two to about twelve individuals and average about five to six individuals.
    a. Cliques
    c. Crowds
    b. Chumships
    d. Youth organizations

20. Which of the following is NOT one of the myths regarding the romantic relationships of sexual minority youth?
    a. There is a great deal of complexity in the romantic possibilities of sexual minority youth.
    b. Adolescents who sexually desire the same sex always fall in love with the same sex.
    c. All gay and lesbian youth only have same-sex attractions.
    d. All sexual minority youth quietly struggle with same-sex attractions in childhood, shun heterosexual dating, and gradually sense that they are gay in mid- to late-adolescence.

21. _____ stressed the importance of friendship to adolescent development?
    a. Kenneth Dodge
    c. Muzafer Sherif
    b. Erik Erikson
    d. Harry Stack Sullivan

22. As the parent of an adolescent male, you are concerned about his friends who are 3–5 years older than he is. Your concern is
    a. not justified.
    b. not justified, because he will probably not drop out of school.
    c. justified because his friend is probably a drug user.
    d. justified because your son will likely engage in deviant behavior.

23. A subset of peers who engage in mutual companionship, support, and intimacy is called
    a. friends.
    c. cliques.
    b. cohorts.
    d. a gang.

24. Compared to adolescent groups, children's groups
    a. are not as formalized.
    b. include a broader array of members.
    c. have well-defined rules and regulations.
    d. are composed of large cliques.

25. An adolescent who has older friends is LEAST likely to become
    a. pregnant.
    c. involved in underage drinking of alcohol.
    b. involved in drug use.
    d. class valedictorian.

26. Sarah is 16 years old and does not want to belong to any clique. She "does her own thing" and is good at what she does. Her level of self-esteem is likely
    a. the same as that of the "jocks."
    b. lower than that of the "populars."
    c. lower than that of the" normals."
    d. the same as that of the "nobodies."

27. Which of the following is NOT a main function of adolescent dating?
    a. recreation
    b. status
    c. socialization
    d. procreation

28. Small groups that range from two to about twelve individuals and average about five to six individuals are called
    a. cohorts.
    b. cliques.
    c. crowds.
    d. chumships.

29. Affectionate love is also referred to as
    a. *eros.*
    b. *agape.*
    c. passionate love.
    d. companionate love.

30. Cindy is a teenage girl who has been interacting with a teenage boy, Simon, she has only met on the Internet. Simon might be referred to as a
    a. pedophile.
    b. cheap date.
    c. cyber boyfriend.
    d. Web date.

31. In _____ grade, 50 percent of the adolescents report they had a sustained romantic relationship that lasted 2 months or longer.
    a. 4th
    b. 6th
    c. 8th
    d. 10th

32. Boys are more likely than girls to be involved in all of the following EXCEPT
    a. collaborative discourse.
    b. risk taking.
    c. ego displays.
    d. conflict.

## ADOLESCENCE ON THE SCREEN

- *Diner* follows a group of friends during high school and graduation.

- *Breakfast Club* depicts how students who must spend Saturday morning in detention develop into a cohesive group.

- *Trainspotting* involves a group of friends whose lives revolve around using drugs.

- *Romeo and Juliet*, a Shakespearean classic about romantic love, appeals to today's adolescents.

## ADOLESCENCE IN BOOKS

- *Just Friends*, by Lillian Rubin (HarperCollins: NY, 1985), explores the nature of friends and intimacy.

# Answer Key

## KEY TERMS

1. **peers** Children or adolescents who are of about the same age or maturity level.

2. **conformity** This occurs when individuals adopt the attitudes or behaviors of others because of real or imagined pressure from them.

3. **popular children** Children who are frequently nominated as a best friend and are rarely disliked by their peers.

4. **average children** These children receive an average number of both positive and negative nominations from their peers.

5. **neglected children** Children who are infrequently nominated as a best friend but are not disliked by their peers.

6. **rejected children** Children who are infrequently nominated as a best friend and are actively disliked by their peers.

7. **controversial children** Children who are frequently nominated both as being a best friend and as being disliked.

8. **conglomerate strategies** Involves the use of a combination of techniques, rather than a single approach, to improve adolescents' social skills.

9. **friends** A subset of peers who engage in mutual companionship, support, and intimacy.

10. **intimacy in friendship** In most research, this is defined narrowly as self-disclosure or sharing of private thoughts.

11. **norms** Rules that apply to all members of a group.

12. **roles** Certain positions in a group that are governed by rules and expectations. Roles define how adolescents should behave in those positions.

13. **cliques** These units are smaller, involve more intimacy, and are more cohesive than crowds. They are, however, larger and involve less intimacy than friendships.

14. **crowd** The largest, most loosely defined, and least personal unit of adolescent peer society. Crowds often meet because of their mutual interest in an activity.

15. **dating scripts** The cognitive models that adolescents and adults use to guide and evaluate dating interactions.

16. **romantic love** Also called passionate love or Eros, this love has strong sexual and infatuation components, and it often predominates in the early part of a love relationship.

17. **affectionate love** Also called companionate love, this love occurs when an individual wants to have another person near and has a deep, caring affection for that person.

# KEY PEOPLE IN THE STUDY OF ADOLESCENCE

| | | | | | | | | |
|---|---|---|---|---|---|---|---|---|
| **1.** | E | **4.** | H | **7.** | B | **10.** | D |
| **2.** | A | **5.** | G | **8.** | F | | |
| **3.** | I | **6.** | J | **9.** | C | | |

# ADOLENCENT MYTH AND FACT

| | | | | | | | | | |
|---|---|---|---|---|---|---|---|---|---|
| 1. | T | 4. | F | 7. | F | 10. | T | 13. | F |
| 2. | F | 5. | T | 8. | F | 11. | F | | |
| 3. | T | 6. | T | 9. | T | 12. | T | | |

# EXPLORING PEER RELATIONS
# SECTION REVIEW

1. To be excluded means stress, frustration, and sadness. So many will do most anything to be included.

2. For boys (more so than girls) a lot of time was spent doing sports activities. General play and going places was common for both sexes.

3. Good peer relationships might be necessary for normal social development.

4. Parents choose where they will work, live, churches, school districts, etc. All impact the children.

5. When individuals adopt the attitudes or behavior of others because of real or imagined pressure from them.

6. Yes. Research shows that parents discussed with their adolescents ways that disputes could be mediated and how to be less shy. They also discussed peer pressure issues.

7. In this situation other factors contribute, such as unattractiveness, lack of intelligence, late maturation, cultural differences, SES discrepancies.

8. Neglected children, rejected children, and controversial children.

9. Peer pressure is a pervasive theme of adolescents' lives. Its power can be observed in almost every dimension of adolescents' behavior — their choice of dress, music, language, values, leisure activities, and so on.

10. They help generate correct interpretations of situations, which lessens the likelihood of conflict.

11. Refers to coaching to improve an adolescent's social skills.

12 Training programs help them attract attention from their peers in positive ways and to hold their attention by asking questions, by listening in a warm and friendly way, and by saying things about themselves that relate to the peers' interests.

## KEY PEOPLE IN SECTION

**Anna Freud** — studied peer attachment with six children from different families whose parents were killed in WWII.

**Jean Piaget and Harry Stack Sullivan** — were influential theorists who stressed that it is through peer interaction that children and adolescents learn the symmetrical reciprocity mode of relationships.

**Thomas Berndt** — focused on the negative, neutral, and positive aspects of peer conformity.

**James Coleman** — pointed out that for adolescents in the average range, there is little or no relation between physical attractiveness and popularity.

**Kenneth Dodge** — found that aggressive boys are more likely to perceive another child's actions as hostile when the peer's intentions are ambiguous.

## FRIENDSHIP
## SECTION REVIEW

1. A subset of peers who engage in mutual companionship, support, and intimacy.

2. Companionship; stimulation; physical support; ego support; social comparison; intimacy/affection.

3. Initiate interaction; be nice; engage in prosocial behavior; show respect for self and others; provide social support.

4. Using psychological aggression, having a negative self-presentation; engaging in antisocial behavior.

5. Friends are generally similar in terms of age, sex, ethnicity, and other factors.

6. These relationships often lead to delinquency and sexual activities.

## KEY PEOPLE IN SECTION

**Harry Stack Sullivan** — was the most influential theorist to discuss the importance of friendship.

**Willard Hartup** — studied peer relations across four decades, recently concluding that children and adolescents often use friends as cognitive and social resources.

## ADOLESCENT GROUPS
## SECTION REVIEW

1. Groups satisfy adolescents' personal needs, reward them, provide information, raise self-esteem, and give them an identity.

2. Norms and roles.

3.  a.  Precrowd stage of isolated, unisex groups
    b.  Beginning of the crowd; unisex groups start group-group interaction
    c.  Crowd in structural transition; unisex groups are forming mixed-sex groups
    d.  Fully developed crowd; mixed-sex groups are closely associated
    e.  Crowd begins to disintegrate as loosely associated groups of couples pair off

4.  a.   The influence of cliques is not entirely negative
    b.   The influence of cliques is not uniform for all adolescents
    c.   Development changes occur in cliques

5.  Cliques are small groups that range from two to about 12 individuals and average about five. Crowds are a larger group structure than cliques. Adolescents are usually members of a crowd based on reputation.

6.  Youth organizations can have an important influence on the adolescent's development, depending on which they are.

## KEY PEOPLE IN SECTION

**Dexter Dunphy** — indicated that opposite-sex participation in groups increases during adolescence.

**Bradford Brown** — researched the role of crowds in adolescence.

**Jane Lohr** — examined self-esteem of adolescents.

**Reed Larson** — proposed that structured activities, such as selling Girl Scout cookies, are especially well-suited for the development of initiative.

## GENDER AND CULTURE
## SECTION REVIEW

1.  There is increasing evidence that gender plays an important role in the peer group and friendships. The evidence related to the peer group focuses on group size and interaction. Boys are more likely than girls to associate in clusters. Boys are more likely than girls to engage in competition.

2.  In some countries, adults restrict adolescents' access to peers. Examples are India and Arab countries.

3.  Athletic teams are one type of adolescent group in which African American adolescents and adolescents for low SES families can gain popularity and better their status within schools. They tend to get overlooked for most other group and leadership positions.

4.  In the Murian culture of India, male and female children live in a dormitory from the age of 6 until they get married. The dormitory is a religious community.

## DATING AND ROMANTIC RELATIONSHIPS
## SECTION REVIEW

1.  Dating can be a form of recreation. Dating is a source of status and achievement. Dating is part of the socialization process in adolescence. Dating involves learning about intimacy and serves as an opportunity to establish a unique, meaningful relationship with a person of the opposite sex. Dating can be a context for sexual experimentation. Dating can provide companionship through interaction and shared activities. Dating experiences contribute to identity formation and development. Dating can be a means of mate sorting and selection.

2.  a.   (1) Initiating the date; (2) controlling the public domain; and (3) initiating physical contact.
    b.   (1) Concern for the private domain; (2) participating in structure of the date; and (3) responding to sexual gestures.

3.      Also called passionate love or Eros; it has strong sexual and infatuation components and often predominates in the early parts of a relationship.

4.      Also called companionate love; occurs when individuals desire to have another person near and have a deep, caring affection for that person.

5.      According to Hetherington, divorce is associated with a stronger heterosexual orientation in daughters. Girls also had a more negative opinion of males when they came out of a divorced family.

6.      Most Latino youths' parents view U.S. style dating as a violation of traditional courtship styles. As a result, dating for Latinos is often described as full of tension and conflict.

## KEY PEOPLE IN SECTION

**Candice Feiring** — found that male and female adolescents bring different motivations to the dating experience.

**Wyndol Furman and Elizabeth Wehner** — discussed how specific insecure attachment styles might be related to adolescents' romantic relationships.

**Peter Blos** — noted that at the beginning of adolescence, boys and girls try to separate themselves from opposite-sex parents as a love object.

**Mavis Hetherington** — found that divorce was associated with a stronger heterosexual orientation of adolescent daughters.

**Harry Stack Sullivan** — believed that it is through intimate friendships that adolescents learn a mature form of love he referred to as "collaborative."

**Jennifer Connolly** — documented the role of peers in the emergence of romantic involvement in adolescence.

## EXPLORATIONS IN ADOLESCENCE

This study, based in Minneapolis, found that more than 50 percent of the youth said they don't participate in any type of youth program in a typical week. More than 40 percent reported no participation in youth programs during the summer months.

## COGNITIVE CHALLENGE

No answers. Individual activity.

## ADOLESCENCE IN RESEARCH

This was a 2-year longitudinal study that sought to gauge changes in prosocial behaviors as children mature from the 6th grade to the 8th grade. A reasonable hypothesis would be that children would gain prosocial skills and behaviors as they mature; however, the study suggested that the kids who struggled in the 6th grade were still struggling in the 8th grade.

COMPREHENSIVE REVIEW

| | | | | | | | | |
|---|---|---|---|---|---|---|---|
| 1. | c | 10. | d | 19. | a | 28. | b |
| 2. | b | 11. | c | 20. | a | 29. | d |
| 3. | c | 12. | a | 21. | d | 30. | c |
| 4. | b | 13. | b | 22. | d | 31. | d |
| 5. | b | 14. | c | 23. | a | 32. | a |
| 6. | b | 15. | d | 24. | a | | |
| 7. | a | 16. | c | 25. | d | | |
| 8. | c | 17. | b | 26. | a | | |
| 9. | b | 18. | d | 27. | d | | |

# ✧ Chapter 11   Schools

**Learning Goals with Key Terms and Key People in Boldface**

**1.0   DESCRIBE APPROACHES TO EDUCATING STUDENTS**

**A.   Direct Instruction and Constructivist Approaches**

1.1   What is **direct instruction approach** to student learning?

1.2   What are **cognitive constructivist approaches** to student learning?

1.3   What are **social constructivist approaches** to student learning?

1.4   What is the American Psychological Association's learner centered psychological principles?

**B.   Accountability**

1.5   What are some criticisms of No Child Left Behind?

1.6   What is meant by 'teaching to the test?'

**2.0   DISCUSS TRANSITIONS IN SCHOOLING FROM EARLY ADOLESCENCE TO EMERGING ADULTHOOD**

**A.   Transition to Middle or Junior High School**

2.1   What is the origin of junior high schools?

2.2   What is a 6-3-3 system?

2.3   What are some criticisms of junior high and middle schools?

2.4   Why have middle schools become more popular than the junior high model?

2.5   How are middle schools related to pubertal development?

2.6   What are some factors that can make the transition to middle school or junior high stressful?

2.7   Can middle school lessen the numbers of 'bottom dogs?''

2.8   What is the **top-dog phenomenon?**

**B.   What Makes A Successful Middle School?**

2.9   What did the Carnegie Foundation recommend about the redesign of middle schools?

2.10   How did *Turning Points 2000* expand upon the recommendations of *TurningPoints 1989*?

**C.   The American High School**

2.11   According to the National Commission on the High School Senior, what problems do America's high schools need to address for the 21st century?

**D.   High School Dropouts and Non-college Youth**

2.12   Over the past half century, what has been the reason for the drop in the numbers of dropouts?

2.13   What educational deficiencies do students who drop out experience in adulthood?

2.14   What are the extent and characteristics of ethnic minority students who drop out?

2.15   What factors are associated with dropping out?

2.16   What is the optimal size of a high school, with regard to avoiding high numbers of dropouts?

2.17   What approaches can be used to reduce the rate of dropping out and improve student experiences?

**E.   Transition from High School to College**

2.18    What happens to parental interaction during the transition?

2.19    Why does the UCLA survey appear to be showing more stress and depression in college freshmen?

2.20    What are the effects of discontinuity between high school and college?

F.    **Transition from College to Work**

2.21    Why is the transition from college to work a difficult one?

**3.0    EXPLAIN HOW THE SOCIAL CONTEXTS OF SCHOOL INFLUENCE ADOLESCENT DEVELOPMENT**

A.    **Changing Social Developmental Contexts**

3.1    How does the social context change at the different educational levels?

B.    **Size and Climate of Schools**

3.2    What are the most desirable classroom and school sizes?

3.3    What are some benefits of a small school?

3.4    What are some of the drawbacks of large schools?

3.5    What are some benefits of a large school?

3.6    Which class size best benefits student learning?

3.7    What are the components of a positive classroom climate?

3.8    What is the **authoritative strategy of classroom management**?

3.9    What is the **authoritarian strategy of classroom management**?

3.10    What is the **permissive strategy of classroom management**?

3.11    To what variables are classroom climate generally linked?

3.12    What is the effect of school climate on student achievement?

C.    **Person-Environment Fit and Aptitude-Treatment Interaction**

3.13    What happens when the schools do not meet the adolescent's needs?

D.    **Teachers and Parents**

3.14    Can a profile of a competent teacher be compiled?

3.15    How does parental involvement with schools change as students move into adolescence?

3.16    Why do student-teacher relationships often deteriorate after the transition to junior high?

3.17    Why is greater collaboration between schools, families, and communities needed?

3.18    What is Epstein's framework for improving parent involvement in adolescents' schooling?

E.    **Peers**

3.19    How does the structure of the middle school lead to more peer interaction?

3.20    Is popularity related to academic outcomes?

3.21    How significant is the problem of bullying in American schools?

3.22    What are common characteristics of victims of bullies?

F.    **Culture**

3.23    What is the effect of poverty on student learning?

3.24    What are the characteristics of schools in low-income neighborhoods?

3.25    How does ethnicity influence school experiences?

3.26    What is the role of teachers' positive expectations of ethnic students?

3.27    What are some effective teaching strategies for improving relations with ethnically diverse students?

3.28    What is a **jigsaw classroom?**

3.29    How can the concept of the **jigsaw classroom** be used to improve American schools?

3.30    What has been the evaluation of the effectiveness of the Comer schools?

3.31    What are some similarities and dissimilarities between American high schools and those in other countries?

**4.0    CHARACTERIZE ADOLESCENTS WHO ARE EXCEPTIONAL AND THEIR EDUCATION**
   A.    **Who Are Adolescents with Disabilities?**
         4.1      How many U.S. students receive special education services?
         4.2      What percentage of students receiving special education has **learning disabilities**?
   B.    **Learning Disabilities**
         4.3      What are the characteristics of a **learning disability**?
         4.4      Are gender differences observed among those with learning disabilities?
         4.5      How are **learning disabilities** defined?
         4.6      What is the most common problem for students with a learning disability?
   C.    **Attention Deficit/Hyperactivity Disorder (ADHD)**
         4.7      How is **ADHD** defined?
         4.8      What is the controversy related to the diagnosis and treatment of **ADHD**?
         4.9      What interventions are recommended for children and adolescents with **ADHD**?
   D.    **Educational Issues Involving Adolescents with Disabilities**
         4.10     What is **Public Law 92–142?**
         4.11     What is the **Individuals with Disabilities Act (IDEA)**?
         4.12     What does **least restrictive environment (LRE)** mean?
         4.13     What is meant by **inclusion?**
   E.    **Adolescents Who Are Gifted**
         4.14     What are the criteria for **giftedness**?
         4.15     According to **Winner,** what are the three characteristics of **adolescents who are gifted**?
         4.16     What are some characteristics that characterize **gifted adolescents**?
         4.17     What program options exist for **students who are gifted**?

# EXERCISES

## KEY TERMS COMPLETION EXERCISE

Each key term is presented in the form of an incomplete sentence. Complete each sentence by either defining the term or giving an example. Compare your definitions with those given at the end of the study guide chapter.

1.    A benefit of the **direct instruction approach** is

_____

_____


2.    The **cognitive constructivist approaches** emphasize

_____

_____


3.    **Social constructivist approaches** focus on

_____

_____

4. You typically see evidence of the **top-dog phenomenon** in

_____

_____

5. The benefits of an **authoritative strategy of classroom management** are

_____

_____

6. The benefits of an **authoritarian strategy of classroom management** are

_____

_____

7. A **permissive strategy of classroom management** can lead to

_____

_____

8. I can tell that Jovan is in a **jigsaw classroom** because

_____

_____

9. Having a **learning disability** means

_____

_____

10. Having an **attention deficit/hyperactivity disorder (ADHD)** suggests

_____

_____

11. With the institution of **Public Law 94–142** came

_____

_____

12. The **Individuals with Disabilities Education Act (IDEA)** is

_____

_____

13. Placement in the **least restrictive environment** means

_____

_____

14.    **Inclusion** means

_____

_____

15.    **Adolescents who are gifted** are

_____

_____

## KEY PEOPLE IN THE STUDY OF ADOLESCENCE

Match the person with the concept of adolescent development with which they are associated.

____    1. James Kaufman       A. Believed teachers should help students achieve industry
____    2. Jacqueline Eccles   B. Pioneered research on the jigsaw classroom
____    3. Erik Erikson        C. Studied how developmentally appropriate school environments could
                                  meet students' needs
____    4. Joyce Epstein       D. Has argued that the extremes of *inclusion* or *accommodation* can be
                                  detrimental for kids
____    5. Jonathan Kozol      E. Believes that parents need to be more involved in schools
____    6. John Ogbu           F. Anthropologist who says American schools exploit minority students
____    7. Elliot Aronson      G. Author of *Savage Inequities*
____    8. Ellen Winner        H. Believes that a community team approach is best to educate students
____    9. James Comer         I. Conducted research about gifted children

## "DR. DETAIL'S" MATCHING EXERCISE

Match the person with his/her contribution to the understanding of adolescents.

____    1. Arthur Powell,      A. Searched the nation finding and describing the best middle schools
            Eleanor Farrar, and
            David Cohen
____    2. Roberta Simmons     B. Philanthropist who donated money to start the I Have A Dream Program.
            and Dale Blyth
____    3. Joan Lipsitz        C. Studied self-esteem in students participating in varied numbers of
                                  extracurricular activities
____    4. Margaret Beale      D. Developed the metaphor of the "shopping mall" high school
            Spencer
____    5. Eugene Lang         E. Suggested that "well-meaning" teachers, acting out of misguided
                                  liberalism, fail to challenge students of color to achieve
____    6. Diana Baumrind      F. Described the effective teacher as one secure in his/her own identity and
                                  sexuality
____    7. Jacob Kounin        G. Provided the original idea of an authoritative classroom management
                                  strategy
____    8. Stephanie Feeney    H. Studied classroom management styles to identify effective teachers

# ADOLESCENT MYTH AND FACT

Which of the following statements regarding adolescents are true (T) and which are false (F)?

1.   The creation of middle schools has been influenced by the earlier onset of puberty in recent years.  T or F

2.   Middle school, as opposed to the $7^{th}$ through $9^{th}$ grade junior high schools, serve to reduce the number of times adolescents are "bottom dogs."  T or F

3.   Many high school students are not only poorly prepared for college, they are also poorly prepared for the workforce.  T or F

4.   Over the past decade, there has been an increase in the number of high school dropouts.  T or F

5.   Males are more likely to drop out of school than are females.  T or F

6.   In the U.S., the most likely student to drop out of high school is an African American student.  T or F

7.   Today's college freshman are experiencing more stress and depression than those in the past.  T or F

8.   U.S. colleges teach very specific job-related skills that allow for easy transition from college to the workforce.  T or F

9.   A bigger school is a better school.  T or F

10.  Greater academic gains are noted when class size is 20 or fewer students.  T or F

11.  Researchers recently have found continuing support for the importance of an authorative teaching style in adolescent development.  T or F

12.  Effective teachers and ineffective teachers respond to student misbehaviors the same way.  T or F

13.  ADHD decreases in adolescence.  T or F

14.  Heredity has been determined to be the primary reason children develop ADHD.  T or F

15.  The term *mainstreaming* has now been replaced by the *least restrictive environment*.  T or F

16.  All students with ADHD respond positively to prescription stimulants.  T or F

17.  According to Winner (1996), gifted students are often socially isolated or considered 'nerds.'  T or F


# APPROACHES TO EDUCATING STUDENTS
# SECTION REVIEW

1.   What is the direct instruction approach to student learning?

     _____

     _____


2.   What are cognitive constructivist approaches to student learning?

     _____

     _____

3.	What are social constructivist approaches to student learning?

_____

_____

4.	Match the APA Learner-Centered Psychological Principle with its description.

### Cognitive and Metacognitive Factors

____	1.	nature of the learning process

A.	Successful learners can create a repertoire of thinking and reasoning strategies to achieve complex goals.

____	2.	goals of the learning process

B.	Successful learners can create meaningful, coherent representations of knowledge.

____	3.	construction of knowledge

C.	Higher order strategies for selecting and monitoring mental operations facilitate creative and critical thinking.

____	4.	strategic thinking

D.	The learning of complex subject matter is more effective when it is an intentional process of constructing meaning and experience.

____	5.	thinking about thinking

E.	Successful learners can link new information with existing knowledge in meaningful ways.

____	6.	context of learning

F.	Learning is influenced by environmental factors, including culture, technology, and instructional practices.

### Motivational, Instructional, Developmental, Social, and Individual Difference Factors

____	1.	motivational and emotional influences on learning

A.	The learner's creativity, higher order thinking, and natural curiosity all contribute to motivation to learn.

____	2.	intrinsic motivation to learn

B.	Acquiring complex knowledge and skills requires extended learner effort and guided practice. Without learners' motivation to learn, the willingness to exert this effort is unlikely without coercion.

____	3.	effects of motivation on effort

C.	What and how much is learned is influenced by the learner's motivation, which, in turn, is influenced by the learner's emotional states, beliefs, interests, goals, and habits of thinking.

____	4.	developmental influences on learning

D.	Setting appropriately high and challenging standards and assessing the learner and learning progress are integral aspects of the learning experience.

____	5.	social influences on learning

E.	Learning is influenced by social interactions, interpersonal relations, and communication with others.

____	6.	individual differences in learning

F.	Learners have different strategies, approaches, and capabilities for learning that are a function of prior experience and heredity.

____	7.	learning and diversity

G.	Learning is most effective when differential development within and across physical, cognitive, and socioemotional domains is taken into account.

____	8.	standards and assessment

H.	Learning is most effective when differences in learner's linguistic, cultural, and social backgrounds are considered.

5.      What are some criticisms of the constructivist approaches?

_____

_____

6.      What are some criticisms of the direct instruction approach?

_____

_____

7.      What are some criticisms of No Child Left Behind?

_____

_____

8.      What is meant by 'teaching to the test'?

_____

_____

## TRANSITIONS IN SCHOOLING
## SECTION REVIEW

1.      What is the origin of junior high schools?

_____

_____

2.      What is a 6-3-3 system?

_____

_____

3.      What are some criticisms of junior high and middle schools?

_____

_____

4.      Is the sixth- through eighth-grade middle school transition easier than the transition to junior high?

_____

_____

5. Why is the transition to middle- or junior-high school stressful?

_____

_____

6. What is the top-dog phenomenon?

_____

_____

7. What did the Carnegie Foundation recommend about the redesign of middle schools?

_____

_____

8. Why are today's college freshmen suffering from more depression and stress than in the past?

_____

_____

9. Over the past 40 years, what has accounted for the drop in the numbers of dropouts?

_____

_____

10. What educational deficiencies do students who drop out experience in adulthood?

_____

_____

11. What factors are associated with dropping out of school?

_____

_____

12. What approaches can be used to reduce the rate of dropping out and improve students' experiences?

_____

_____

## THE SOCIAL CONTEXTS OF SCHOOLS
## SECTION REVIEW

1. What is the most desirable classroom/school size?

_____

_____

2.      What are some benefits of a small school?

_____

_____

3.      What are some benefits of a large school?

_____

_____

4.      What are the components of a positive classroom climate?

_____

_____

5.      What is the authoritative strategy of classroom management?

_____

_____

6.      What is the authoritarian strategy of classroom management?

_____

_____

7.      What is the permissive strategy of classroom management?

_____

_____

8.      How does parental involvement with schools change as students get older?

_____

_____

9.      Why do student-teacher relationships often deteriorate after the transition to junior high?

_____

_____

10.     What is Epstein's framework for improving parent involvement in schooling?

_____

_____

11.     List three things teachers can do to improve the likelihood that students will cooperate with them in the classroom.

_____

_____

12.   Is popularity related to academic outcomes?

_____

_____

13.   How significant is the problem of bullying in American schools?

_____

_____

14.   What is the effect of poverty on student learning?

_____

_____

15.   How does ethnicity affect school experiences?

_____

_____

16.   What is a jigsaw classroom?

_____

_____

17.   What are some social policy recommendations for improving schools for adolescents?

_____

_____

## ADOLESCENTS WHO ARE EXCEPTIONAL
## SECTION REVIEW

1.   What are the characteristics of a learning disability?

_____

_____

2.   How are learning disabilities defined?

_____

_____

3.   How is ADHD defined?

_____

_____

4. What is the controversy related to the diagnosis and treatment of ADHD?

_____

_____

5. What interventions are recommended for adolescents with ADHD?

_____

_____

6. What is Public Law 92–142?

_____

_____

7. What is the Individuals with Disabilities Education Act (IDEA)?

_____

_____

8. What does least restrictive environment mean?

_____

_____

9. What is inclusion?

_____

_____

10. According to Winner, what are the three characteristics of adolescents who are gifted?

_____

_____

11. What are some characteristics that characterize gifted adolescents?

_____

_____

12. What program options exist for students who are gifted?

_____

_____

# EXPLORATIONS IN ADOLESCENT DEVELOPMENT

Compare and contrast the following aspects of secondary schools in Australia, Brazil, Germany, Japan, Russia, and the United States: (a) mandatory age; (b) number of levels; (c) role of sports; (d) entrance and exit exams; (e) content and philosophy; and (f) foreign language education.

_____

_____

_____

# COGNITIVE CHALLENGE

1.  In three sections, list the things you liked most about high school, liked least about high school, and would change about schools in general to make them more effective.

    liked most

    _____

    _____

    liked least

    _____

    _____

    would change

    _____

    _____

2.  Think back on your high school classmates that were of diverse ethnic, religious, and socioeconomic background. How well did your school meet the social and educational needs of these students? Knowing what you know now, how would you have responded to the needs of these students if you had been a teacher at the school?

    _____

    _____

    _____

# ADOLESCENCE IN RESEARCH

Examine the UCLA survey conducted by Sax & others (2003), and detail the method and hypotheses (if available) the researchers used and the conclusions they reached.

## ☒ COMPREHENSIVE REVIEW

1.  According to Greene and Forster (2003), there are three important markers for success in college. Which of the following is NOT one of these markers?
    a.  taking basic courses in high school
    b.  scores in the top 40% on high school aptitude tests
    c.  passing a 12<sup>th</sup> grade reading test
    d.  the student graduated on time

2.  If you wish to be an academic success in school, which crowd should you affiliate with?
    a.  the jocks             c.  the druggies
    b.  the nerds             d.  the brains

3.  Which country has the largest college attendance in the world?
    a.  Belgium               c.  Ireland
    b.  United States         d.  Canada

4.  A major current concern among educators regarding middle schools or junior highs is that
    a.  there are not enough of them to accommodate the growing population.
    b.  they are becoming "watered down" versions of high school.
    c.  the curriculum is too basic for the growing needs of children of that age.
    d.  there is a shortage of teachers for these schools.

5.  Which of the following is NOT a mandate brought forward by IDEA (Individuals with Disabilities Education Act?
    a.  evaluation and eligibility determination
    b.  appropriate education
    c.  medical intervention
    d.  a least restrictive environment

6.  According to Winner (1996), which of the following is NOT a characteristic of being gifted?
    a.  precocity
    b.  marching to their own drummer
    c.  I.Q. above 125 on standardized tests
    d.  a passion to master

7.  The top-dog phenomenon refers to
    a.  the superior formal operational reasoning of high school students compared to junior high students.
    b.  the dating advantage that junior high school girls have over junior high school boys.
    c.  the self-perceptions of junior high school students who attend supportive and stable schools.
    d.  the lowered status experienced by students when they move from elementary to junior high school.

8.  Darren has been complaining about not being able to make good grades. He says he used to feel good in school, but now feels like a little fish in a big pond. Darren
    a.  probably has the same school crises as girls of his age.
    b.  is struggling with the transition to junior high school.
    c.  is becoming self-conscious because of the emergence of formal operational thought.
    d.  probably has developed the underdog adjustment disorder associated with junior high entry.

9.  Effective schools for young adolescents have all of the following characteristics EXCEPT
    a.  similar methods of grouping students.
    b.  emphasis on the school context as a community.
    c.  curricula emphasizing self-exploration and definition.
    d.  responsiveness to their community political milieus.

10. What percent of students in the United States receive special education or related services?
    a.    4%          b.    6%          c.    10%          d.    20%

11. Freddy is the oldest boy in his middle school and the best athlete. Which of the following is likely true about Freddy?
    a.  He is probably very unpopular.   c.   He is probably a *top dog*.
    b.  He is probably a poor student.    d.   He is probably truant.

12. Which of the following is NOT a recommendation by the 1989 Carnegie Council on Adolescent Development?
    a.  involving parents and community leaders in the schools
    b.  boosting students' health and fitness with more in-school programs and helping students who need public health care get it
    c.  merging multiple small school districts into larger districts to offer more programs and better utilize resources
    d.  lowering student-to-counselor ratios from several hundred-to-1 to 10-to-1

13. The report from the Carnegie Commission encourages
    a.  disbanding middle schools in favor of a longer stay in elementary school.
    b.  eliminating high schools and moving from junior high directly to college prep schools.
    c.  arranging middle school students in smaller groups.
    d.  eliminating middle schools in favor of junior high schools.

14. _____ students are least likely to complete high school
    a.  African American
    b.  Latino
    c.  Native American
    d.  Non-Latino White American

15. About 50 percent of the dropouts do so for school-related reasons, whereas another 20 percent drop out of high school
    a.  for economic reasons.
    b.  because they are unable to read and write well.
    c.  because they are in trouble with law-enforcement authorities.
    d.  for cultural reasons.

16. Small schools are more likely to
    a. be associated with prosocial behavior than large schools.
    b. provide fewer opportunities for school participation than large schools.
    c. promote better academic achievement than large schools.
    d. promote more antisocial behavior than large schools.

17. The _____ classroom is characterized by teachers who serve as facilitators of student learning rather than teaching in the traditional manner.
    a. open
    b. new wave
    c. multi-dimensional
    d. California

18. Young adolescents appear to respond well to teachers who
    a. let the students set the limits in the classroom.
    b. are pals.
    c. are insensitive to student criticism.
    d. use natural authority.

19. A teacher says to a student, "Thank you for being quiet in class today for a change." With which type of student is this more likely to occur?
    a. a "trouble-maker"
    b. a White-American student
    c. an African-American student
    d. the "best" student in the class

20. Among minority youth who stay in school, poor academic performance is linked to
    a. the refusal of other students to study with them.
    b. the unwillingness to engage in cooperative learning.
    c. the language barriers.
    d. coming from a poor, single-parent family.

21. The Education for All Handicapped Children Act mandated that all states provide _____ for all handicapped children?
    a. free health care
    b. educational programs for their parents
    c. free testing programs
    d. individualized educational programs

22. *Inclusion* refers to
    a. teaching handicapped children in public schools.
    b. assigning handicapped children to regular classrooms.
    c. giving handicapped children a high educational priority.
    d. assuring handicapped children interact with nonhandicapped children whenever possible.

23. Shawna, a second grader, has no trouble with math, science, or art; but she cannot spell, read, or write. It is likely that Shawna has a(n)
    a. visual impairment.
    b. speech handicap.
    c. learning disability.
    d. attention deficit.

24. Timothy is suffering from attention-deficit hyperactivity disorder (ADHD). Which of the following symptoms is he most likely NOT to be experiencing?
    a. short attention span.
    c. below-normal intelligence.

b.     easily distracted.          d.     high levels of physical activity.

25. What type of drug is used to control attention-deficit hyperactivity disorder?
    a.    stimulant          c.    tranquilizer
    b.    depressant        d.    relaxant

26. The I Have a Dream program (IHAD) was created by Eugene Lang to help in
    a.    alleviating the school violence problem in America.
    b.    boosting student literacy rates.
    c.    decreasing the likelihood of a child dropping out of school.
    d.    getting troubled kids off of the streets.

27. What is the best school size?
    a.    500 to 600 or fewer    c.    1,000 to 1,500
    b.    800 to 1,000        d.    2,000 or more

28. _____ is the only country in the world that has high school athletics and sports as an integral part of the educational system.
    a.    South Africa       c.    Italy
    b.    Japan             d.    The United States

29. Duane, a college graduate, will earn approximately _____ more during his lifetime than Brian, a high school graduate.
    a.    $40,000          c.    $60,000
    b.    $400,000        d.    $600,000

30. Boys are identified as learning disabled _____ as often as girls.
    a.    three times       d.    four times
    b.    twice            c.    equally

31. _____ is the most likely reason for dropping out of school?
    a.    Economic reasons
    b.    Having a friend who dropped out
    c.    Being suspended
    d.    Pregnancy

## ADOLESCENCE ON THE SCREEN

- *To Sir, With Love* tells the story of a black engineer who takes a job in a rough London school.

- *The Breakfast Club* portrays how students in a Saturday detention class coalesce as a group.

- *Dangerous Minds* depicts a female teacher struggling to deal with tough inner city teenagers.

- *Dead Poet's Society* stars Robin Williams as an English teacher who tries to change the way students learn literature.

- *Middle School Confessions* (HBO) is a documentary that portrays in shocking detail the crisis in today's middle schools in America.

## ADOLESCENCE IN BOOKS

- *Adolescence in the 1990s,* edited by Ruby Takanishi (Teachers College Press, 1993), features a number of experts on adolescence addressing the risks and opportunities for adolescents in today's world. Many chapters focus on improving the quality of schooling for adolescents.

- *Successful Schools for Young Adolescents*, by Joan Lipsitz (Transaction Books: NJ, 1984), is a classic resource for people involved in middle school education.

- *Endangered Minds*, by Jane M. Healy (Simon and Schuster: NY, 1999), clearly depicts the problems existing in our schools and makes specific suggestions on how to change things.

- *Failure to Connect: How Computers Affect Our Children's Minds, and What We Can Do About It*, by Jane M. Healy (Simon and Schuster: NY, 1999), presents a very strong case "against" the use of computers in modern classrooms.

## ADOLESCENCE IN RESEARCH

Concerning the 1987 study by Simmons and Blyth comparing school systems with a 6–3–3 arrangement and those with an 8–4 arrangement, state the hypothesis, the research methods (if known), the research conclusions, and the implications and applications for adolescent development.

_____

_____

# Answer Key

## KEY TERMS

1. **direct instruction approach** A teacher-centered approach that is characterized by teacher direction and control, mastery of academic skills, high expectations for students' progress, and maximum time spent on learning tasks.

2. **cognitive constructivist approaches** Emphasizes the adolescent's active, cognitive construction of knowledge and understanding; an example of this approach is Piaget's theory.

3. **social constructivist approach** Focus on collaboration with others to produce knowledge and understanding; an example of this approach is Vygotsky's theory.

4. **top-dog phenomenon** The circumstance of moving from the top position (in elementary school, the oldest, biggest, and most powerful students) to the lowest position (in middle or junior high school, the youngest, smallest, and least powerful).

5. **authoritative strategy of classroom management** Encourages students to be independent thinkers and doers but still involves effective monitoring. Authoritative teachers engage students in considerable

verbal give-and-take and show a caring attitude toward them. However, they still declare limits when necessary.

6. **authoritarian strategy of classroom management** Is restrictive and punitive. The focus is mainly on keeping order in the classroom rather than on instruction and learning.

7. **permissive strategy of classroom management** Offers students considerable autonomy but provides them with little support for developing learning skills or managing their behavior.

8. **jigsaw classroom** Students from different cultural backgrounds are placed in a cooperative group in which they have to construct different parts of a project to reach a common goal.

9. **learning disability** Describes individuals who 1) are of normal intelligence or above, 2) have difficulties in a least one academic area and usually several, and 3) their difficulties cannot be attributed to any other diagnosed problem or disorder, such as mental retardation.

10. **attention deficit/hyperactivity disorder (ADHD)** Is a disability in which children and adolescents show one or more of the following characteristics over a period of time: 1) inattention, 2) hyperactivity, and 3) impulsivity.

11. **Public Law 94–142** The Education for All Handicapped Children Act, which requires all students with disabilities to be given a free, appropriate education and provides the funding to help implement this education.

12. **Individuals with Disabilities Education Act (IDEA)** This spells out broad mandates for services to all children and adolescents with disabilities. These include evaluation and eligibility determination, appropriate education and the Individualized Education Program (IEP), and least restrictive environment.

13. **least restrictive environment** A setting that is as similar as possible to the one in which the children, or adolescents without a disability are educated; under the Individuals with Disabilities Education Act, the child or adolescent must be educated in this setting.

14. **inclusion** Educating a child or adolescent with special education needs full-time in a general school program.

15. **adolescents who are gifted** They are characterized by having above average intelligence (usually defined as an IQ of 120 or higher) and/or superior talent in some domain such as art, music, or mathematics.

## KEY PEOPLE IN THE STUDY OF ADOLESCENCE

| | | | | | |
|---|---|---|---|---|---|
| 1. | D | 4. | E | 7. | B |
| 2. | C | 5. | G | 8. | I |
| 3. | A | 6. | F | 9. | H |

## "DR. DETAIL'S" MATCHING EXERCISE

| | | | | | | | |
|---|---|---|---|---|---|---|---|
| 1. | D | 3. | A | 5. | B | 7. | H |
| 2. | C | 4. | E | 6. | G | 8. | F |

## ADOLESCENT MYTH AND FACT

| | | | | | |
|---|---|---|---|---|---|
| 1. | T | 7. | T | 13. | F |
| 2. | F | 8. | F | 14. | F |
| 3. | T | 9. | F | 15. | F |
| 4. | F | 10. | T | 16. | F |
| 5. | T | 11. | T | 17. | T |
| 6. | F | 12. | T | | |

## APPROACHES TO EDUCATING STUDENTS
## SECTION REVIEW

1. A teacher-centered approach that is characterized by teacher direction and control, mastery of skills, high expectations for students' progress, and maximum time spent on learning tasks.

2. These emphasize the adolescent's active, cognitive construction of knowledge, and understanding.

3. These focus on collaboration with others to produce knowledge and understanding.

4. *Cognitive and Metacognitive Factors*

| | | | | | |
|---|---|---|---|---|---|
| **1.** | D | **3.** | E | **5.** | C |
| **2.** | B | **4.** | A | **6.** | F |

*Motivational, Instructional, Developmental, Social, and Individual Difference Factors*

| | | | | | |
|---|---|---|---|---|---|
| **1.** | C | **4.** | G | **7.** | H |
| **2.** | A | **5.** | E | **8.** | D |
| **3.** | B | **6.** | F | | |

5. The direct instruction enthusiasts say that the constructivist approaches do not give enough attention to the content of a discipline, such as history or science.

6. Social constructivist and learner-centered advocates argue that the direct instruction approach turns children into passive learners and does not challenge in areas of creativity and critical thinking.

7. On criticism of NCLB is that stresses that using a single score from a single test as the sole indicator of students' progress and competence represents a vary narrow aspect of students skills.

8. It is drilling students to memorize isolated facts that are likely to show up on tests later.

## TRANSITIONS IN SCHOOLING
## SECTION REVIEW

1. Junior highs were justified based on physical, cognitive, and social changes that characterize early adolescence.

2. It is a common system where students are grouped 1st through 6th grade, 7th through 9th grade, 10th through 12th grade.

3. A major concern is that the middle and junior high schools, over time, has simply become watered down high schools, offering a simplified version of the same curriculum and extra curricular activities.

4. The sixth through eighth transition generally goes well, but can be complicated by the fact that this period encompasses much of puberty for the average child.

5. Because of the onset of puberty.

6. The circumstance of moving from the top, power position to the lowest position, due to changing schools.

7. Develop smaller communities; lower student-to-counselor ratios; involve parents and community leaders; develop curriculum that produces competent students; have teachers team-teach in more flexible curriculum blocks; boosting students' health and fitness.

8. Many report that they feel overwhelmed.

9. Laws requiring more time in school have been passed and there is a consensus that a high school diploma is the basis for finding a good job.

10. They have lower grades, especially in reading.

11. Reasons can be school-related, economic, family-related, peer-related, and personal.

12. Approaches that bridge the gap between school and work, such as the "I Have a Dream" foundation.


## THE SOCIAL CONTEXTS OF SCHOOLS
## SECTION REVIEW

1. Classrooms about 20, schools 500–600.

2. Safe, personalized climate.

3. More course offerings.

4. Teachers who more carefully monitor activities have the better classroom climates.

5. Encourages students to be independent thinkers and doers but still involves effective monitoring. Authoritative teachers involve students in considerable verbal give and take.

6. This is restrictive and punitive to maintain order.

7. This offers students considerable autonomy but provides them with little support for developing learning skills or managing their behavior.

8. Parents are often active in early education, but become less involved when children grow into adolescents.

9. Part of the problem appears to be higher self-confidence and self-efficacy found in teachers of children in lower grades, as opposed to those teaching seventh grade or above.

10. a. Parents need to be knowledgeable about adolescent health and safety issues.
    b. Schools need to communicate with families about school programs and the individual progress of the adolescents.
    c. Parents need to be more involved in schools assisting teachers.
    d. Parents need to be involved in their children's homework.
    e. Parents need to be involved in decision making at school.
    f. Schools need to collaborate with community organizations.

11.     a.     Develop a positive relationship with students.
         b.     Get students to share and assume responsibility.
         c.     Reward appropriate behavior.

12.     Being popular is associated with academic success, whereas being rejected by peers is related to more negative academic outcomes.

13.     Thirty percent of sixth- through tenth-graders say they have been involved in moderate or frequent bullying,

14.     Adolescents from backgrounds of poverty have more difficulties on average.

15.     Ethnicity and poverty tend to go hand-in-hand with fewer educational opportunities and poorer schools for those children from impoverished backgrounds.

16.     Where students from different cultural backgrounds are placed in cooperative groups in which they have to construct different parts of a project to reach a common goal.

17.     Comer recommends (1) a governance and management team that develops a comprehensive school plan, (2) a mental health or school support team, and (3) a parents program.


## ADOLESCENTS WHO ARE EXCEPTIONAL SECTION REVIEW

1.     Normal intelligence versus sub-normal performance.

2.     Adolescents with a learning disability are of normal intelligence and have difficulties in a least one academic area and usually several, and their difficulty cannot be attributed to any other diagnosed problem.

3.     ADHD is a disability in which children and adolescents show one or more of the following characteristics over a period of time: inattention, hyperactivity, and impulsivity.

4.     The controversy is that in many parts of the country it is over-diagnosed and over-medicated.

5.     Many recommend a combination of academic, behavioral, and medical interventions to help students.

6.     The Education for All Handicapped Children Act.

7.     IDEA spells out broad mandates for services to all children and adolescents with disabilities.

8.     A setting that is similar as possible to the one in which the children without a disability are educated.

9.     Inclusion used to be called mainstreaming. It means educating a child or adolescent with special education needs full-time in a general school program.

10.     (a) precocity, (b) marching to their own drummer, and (c) a passion for mastery

11.     Above average intelligence and/or superior talent in some domain, such as art, music or math.

12.     (a) Special classes, (b) acceleration and enrichment in the regular classroom setting, (c) mentor and apprenticeship programs, (d) work/study and community service programs.

# EXPLORATIONS IN ADOLESCENT DEVELOPMENT

1.      Brazil—14; Russia—17; Germany, Japan, Australia, and U.S.—15 to 16.

2.      Most schools have two or more levels (elementary, junior/middle, and high school), but Germany has three ability tracks.

3.      U.S. is the only country in the world that has integrated sports into the public school system. Private schools in other countries may have organized sports.

4.      Japanese secondary schools have entrance exam, but other five countries do not; only Australia and Germany have exit exams.

5.      Russia emphasizes preparation for work, but gifted students attend special schools; Brazil requires that students take four foreign languages, due to the country's international characters; Australian students take courses in sheep husbandry and weaving, activities important to the country's economics and culture; Japanese students take courses in Western languages, literature, physical education, and art.

# COGNITIVE CHALLENGE

1.      No answer provided. Individual activity.

2.      No answer provided. Individual activity.

# ADOLESCENCE IN RESEARCH

Surveys were given to more than 300,000 freshmen at over 500 colleges and universities. This crosssectional study compared results from both 1985 and 2003 to see how stress and depression were impacting students. Their results suggest that today's college freshmen are under more stress and are experiencing more depression than students in 1985.

## ⊠ COMPREHENSIVE REVIEW

| 1. | b | 9. | a | 17. | a | 25. | a |
|----|---|----|---|-----|---|-----|---|
| 2. | d | 10. | c | 18. | d | 26. | c |
| 3. | d | 11. | c | 19. | c | 27. | a |
| 4. | b | 12. | c | 20. | d | 28. | d |
| 5. | c | 13. | c | 21. | d | 29. | d |
| 6. | c | 14. | c | 22. | d | 30. | a |
| 7. | d | 15. | a | 23. | b | 31. | c |
| 8. | b | 16. | a | 24. | c | | |

# ✧ Chapter 12   Achievement, Careers, and Work

**Learning Goals with Key Terms and Key People in Boldface**

**1.0**   **DISCUSS ACHIEVEMENT IN THE LIVES OF ADOLESCENTS**
   **A.**   **The Importance of Adolescence in Achievement**
   1.1   What is the importance of achievement in adolescence?
   1.2   What determines how well adolescents adapt to social and academic pressures?
   **B.**   **Achievement Processes**
   1.3   What is **intrinsic motivation**?
   1.4   What is **extrinsic motivation**?
   1.5   What are the self-determining characteristics of **intrinsic motivation**?
   1.6   What can be done to increase students' internal motivation?
   1.7   What is **Csikszentmihalyi's** concept of **flow**?
   1.8   When is **flow** most likely to occur?
   1.9   What is **mastery orientation**?
   1.10   What is meant by **helpless orientation**?
   1.11   What is **performance orientation**?
   1.12   What is **self-efficacy**?
   1.13   What is **Bandura's** view of **self-efficacy**?
   1.14   What is **Schunk's** view of **self-efficacy**?
   1.15   What are some educational applications for **self-efficacy**?
   1.16   How does goal-setting benefit students' self-efficacy and achievement?
   1.17   How do **Dweck** and **Nicholls** define goals?
   1.18   What are the characteristics of a good planner?
   **C.**   **Time Management**
   1.19   What are Covey's tips for improving time management?
   **D.**   **Mentoring**
   1.20   How can a mentoring program benefit adolescents?
   **E.**   **Some Obstacles to Achievement**
   1.21   Why do individuals procrastinate?
   1.22   What forms can procrastination take?
   1.23   What are some strategies for reducing procrastination?
   1.24   According to Covington, how do people avoid failure and protect their self-worth?
   1.25   What are **self-handicapping strategies**?
   1.26   What can be done to reduce high anxiety levels in adolescents?
   **F.**   **Ethnicity and Culture**
   1.27   What are the respective roles of ethnicity and culture in achievement?
   1.28   Why is it important to consider diversity of achievement within an ethnic group?
   1.29   How do American adolescents size up against their Asian counterparts in terms of achievement?
**2.0**   **DESCRIBE THE ROLE OF WORK IN ADOLESCENCE AND COLLEGE**
   **A.**   **Sociohistorical Context of Work in Adolescence**
   2.1   How likely are adolescents to hold full-time jobs today as opposed to in the 1800s?

2.2      How many adolescents work part-time?

2.3      What kind of jobs are adolescents working today?

2.4      Do male and female adolescents take the same types of jobs, and are they paid equally?

**B.**      **Advantages and Disadvantages of Part-Time Work in Adolescence**

2.5      Does the increase in work have benefits for adolescents?

2.6      What are the advantages of part-time work for adolescents?

2.7      What are the disadvantages of part-time work for adolescents?

**C.**      **Work Profiles of Adolescents Around the World**

2.8      How does work in adolescence vary in different countries around the world?

**D.**      **Working While Going to College**

2.9      What percentage of U.S. undergraduate students work?

2.10      Does work during college increase the likelihood of dropping out?

**F.**      **Work/Career-Based Learning**

2.11      What is work/career-based learning?

2.12      What three types of high schools exemplify a college-and-career approach?

2.13      What are single-theme schools?

2.14      What are schools-within-schools?

2.15      What are majors, clusters, or pathways in the school curriculum?

2.16      What is the value of cooperative education programs?

**3.0**      **CHARACTERIZE CAREER DEVELOPMENT IN ADOLESCENCE**

**A.**      **Theories of Career Development**

3.1      What are the three theories of career development?

3.2      What are the characteristics of **Ginzberg's developmental career choice theory**?

3.3      What are the characteristics of **Super's** vocational **career self-concept theory**?

3.4      What is the nature of **Holland's personality type theory** of career development?

**B.**      **Cognitive Factors**

3.5      Why do adolescents have difficulties making career choices?

3.6      How is career development related to identity development in adolescence?

3.7      According to **Csikszentmihalyi** and **Schneider** (2000), how do U.S. adolescents develop attitudes and acquire skills to achieve their career goals?

**C.**      **Identity Development**

3.8      Does vocational identity development play a leading role in identity development?

**D.**      **Social Contexts**

3.9      What are the most important social contexts that influence career development?

3.10      What roles do socioeconomic status, parents and peers, schools, gender, and ethnicity play in career development?

# Exercises

## KEY TERMS COMPLETION EXERCISE

Each key term is presented in the form of an incomplete sentence. Complete each sentence by either defining the term or giving an example. Compare your definition with those given at the end of the study guide chapter.

1.      **Extrinsic motivation** causes

_____

_____

2. **Intrinsic motivation** is noted when

_____

_____

3. **Flow** describes

_____

_____

4. **Mastery orientation** is a very good approach to

_____

_____

5. A **helpless orientation** can lead to

_____

_____

6. When people have a **performance orientation** they

_____

_____

7. **Self-efficacy** is a belief

_____

_____

8. **Self-handicapping** strategies are used when

_____

_____

9. **Developmental career choice theory** is Ginzberg's theory that

_____

_____

10. **Career self-concept theory** is Super's theory that

_____

_____

11. **Personality type theory** is Holland's belief that

_____

_____

# KEY PEOPLE IN THE STUDY OF ADOLESCENCE

Match the person with the concept of adolescent development with which they are associated.

| | | |
|---|---|---|
| ____ | 1. Mihalyi Csikszentmihalyi | A. Developed strategies for improving motivation of hard-to-teach and low-achieving adolescents |
| ____ | 2. Anna Roe | B. Proponent of the career self-concept theory |
| ____ | 3. Carol Dweck | C. Examined the work experience of California students |
| ____ | 4. Albert Bandura | D. Credited with the development of the personality type theory of career development |
| ____ | 5. Dale Schunk | E. Conceptualized the developmental career choice theory |
| ____ | 6. Sandra Graham | F. Studies cross-cultural comparisons of school performance |
| ____ | 7. Harold Stevenson | G. Believes that self-efficacy influences a student's choice of tasks |
| ____ | 8. Ellen Greenberger and Laurence Steinberg | H. Believes that self-efficacy is a critical factor in student development |
| ____ | 9. Eli Ginzberg | I. Studies ethnic differences in achievement |
| ____ | 10. Donald Super | J. Uses the term "flow" to refer to optimal experiences in life |
| ____ | 11. John Holland | K. Believes that parent-child relationships play an important role in occupation selection |

# "DR. DETAIL'S" THEORY MASTERY EXERCISE

Complete the table by listing the career areas that match each of Holland's personality types.

| Personality Type | Career |
|---|---|
| Realistic | |
| Intellectual | |
| Social | |
| Conventional | |
| Enterprising | |
| Artistic | |

Complete the table by listing the career areas that match each of Ginzberg's career choice stages.

| Career Choice Stage | Careers |
|---|---|
| Fantasy | |
| Tentative | |
| Realistic | |

Complete the table by listing the developmental information that match each of Super's career choice phases.

| Phase | Developmental Information |
|---|---|
| Crystallization | |
| Specification | |
| Implementation | |
| Stabilization | |
| Consolidation | |

## ADOLESCENT MYTH AND FACT

Which of the following statements regarding adolescents are true (T) and which are false (F)?

1.      When adolescents study hard because they want to avoid parental disapproval, this is intrinsic motivation.  T or F

2.      According to Carol Dweck, adolescents show one of two distinct responses to difficult circumstances: a mastery orientation or a helpless orientation.  T or F

3.      Mastery- and helpless-oriented adolescents do NOT differ in general ability.  T or F

4.      Too often parents and teachers attempt to protect adolescents' self-esteem by setting low standards.  T or F

5.      Big Brother/Big Sister programs are not mentoring programs.  T or F

6.      One strategy for avoiding failure is to not try at all.  T or F

7.      Today, 7 of every 10 students receives a high school diploma.  T or F

8.      U.S. adolescents are far more likely to participate in paid labor while in school than European and East Asian adolescents.  T or F

9.      Career development in NOT related to identity development in adolescence.  T or F

10.     Parents do NOT strongly influence the career choices of their adolescents.  T or F

11.     The motivation for work is the same for both males and females.  T or F


## ACHIEVEMENT
## SECTION REVIEW

1.      What determines how well adolescents adapt to social and academic pressures?

_____

_____


2.      Complete the table by filling in the outcomes for each of the combinations of students' perceived level of skill and challenge.

### Students' Perceived Level of Skill

| Perceived Level of Challenge | Low | High |
|---|---|---|
| Low | | |
| High | | |

3.      What are the self-determining characteristics of intrinsic motivation?

_____

_____

4.      What is flow?

_____

_____

5.      When is flow most likely to occur?

_____

_____

6.      Why is it important that parents and teachers NOT set the bar too low for adolescents?

_____

_____

7.      What is mastery orientation?

_____

_____

8.      What is helpless orientation?

_____

_____

9.      What is performance orientation?

_____

_____

10.     What is self-efficacy?

_____

_____

11.     Contrast Bandura's and Schunk's views of self-efficacy.

_____

_____

12.     How do Dweck and Nicholls define goals?

_____

_____

13.     What are Covey's tips for improving time management?

_____

_____

14. Why do individuals procrastinate?

_____

_____

15. What forms can procrastination take?

_____

_____

16. What are some strategies for reducing procrastination?

_____

_____

17. According to Covington, how do people avoid failure and protect their self-worth?

_____

_____

18. What are the respective roles of ethnicity and culture in achievement?

_____

_____

19. How do American adolescents size up against their Asian counterparts in terms of achievement?

_____

_____

20. According to Brophy, what does it take to reach a discouraged student?

_____

_____

21. What is failure syndrome and where does it come from?

_____

_____

22. What are self-handicapping strategies?

_____

_____

23. According to Covington, what strategies can teachers use to protect student self-worth and avoid failure?

_____

_____

# WORK
## SECTION REVIEW

1. How many adolescents work full-time today, as opposed to in the 1800s?

   _____

   _____

2. Do male and female adolescents take the same types of jobs, and are they paid equally?

   _____

   _____

3. What are the advantages of part-time work for adolescents?

   _____

   _____

4. How does work in adolescence vary in different countries around the world?

   _____

   _____

5. Does work during college increase the likelihood of dropping out?

   _____

   _____

6. What can be done to bridge the gap between school and work?

   _____

   _____

7. What are single-theme schools?

   _____

   _____

# CAREER DEVELOPMENT
## SECTION REVIEW

1. What are the three theories of career development?

   _____

   _____

2. How is career development related to identity development in adolescence?

   _____

   _____

3.      What are the most important social contexts that influence career development?

_____

_____

4.      Does vocational identity development play a leading role in identity development?

_____

_____

5.      Why do adolescents have difficulties making career choices?

_____

_____

## COGNITIVE CHALLENGE

1.      What are your career dreams? With your dreams in mind, write down your specific work, job, and career goals for the next 20 years, 10 years, and 5 years. Begin with the long-term goals first so that you can envision how to plan now to reach that "dream" career goal.

_____

_____

2.      What achievement-related challenges did you encounter in middle school and high school? How did you resolve them? Looking back, how might you have coped with these challenges in a more effective way?

_____

_____

3.      How long have you had your current career goals? Since kindergarten? Since elementary school? Since secondary school? Or has it only been recently that you have started to focus on your career?

_____

_____

## ADOLESCENCE IN RESEARCH

Concerning the research of Mihalyi Csikszentmihalyi and Barbara Schneider (2000), state the hypothesis, the research methods (if known), the research conclusions, and the implications and applications for adolescent development.

_____

_____

1. The motive with the greatest impact on the quality of adult life is
   a. sexuality.                       c. affiliation.
   b. fear.                            d. achievement.

2. Aaron studies very hard. He concentrates on the sciences because he wants to become an environmental biologist. Aaron could be described as
   a. motivated.                       c. unrealistic.
   b. intelligent.                     d. a hurried adolescent.

3. Meghan believes that if she practices hard, stays focused, and tries her hardest she can eventually become an outstanding volleyball player. Meghan has which orientation?
   a. mastery                          c. internal
   b. helpless                         d. performance

4. A parent of an adolescent decides to join the community band. His daughter asks why he joined, since he won't make any money and few people attend the concerts. He responds, "I just like playing with the band." He is _____ motivated.
   a. achievement                      c. extrinsically
   b. intrinsically                    d. mastery

5. One key feature of the helpless orientation is
   a. attributing failure to internal causes.
   b. overestimating the role of effort.
   c. underestimating the importance of external incentives.
   d. fear of failure.

6. It is very difficult and dangerous to make sweeping generalizations about achievement motivation in ethnic minority adolescents because
   a. it has never been studied systematically.
   b. there is more variability within groups than among groups.
   c. all American groups score lower than Asian groups.
   d. social class is a more powerful predictor.

7. Japanese children often outperform American children in math and science areas, perhaps because all of the following are true except that
   a. Japanese parents have higher expectations.
   b. Japanese children spend more time in school each week.
   c. Japanese teachers are better trained in math and science.
   d. the Japanese school year is longer.

8. According to your text, the major reason for the "super achiever" image of Asian American adolescents (whose parents immigrated to the United States in the late 1960s to mid-1970s) is that
   a. their families have had more time to adjust to the culture.
   b. they are more intelligent.
   c. the males are encouraged to excel more than the females.
   d. they come from better-educated families.

9. According to Eli Ginzberg, youngsters between the ages of 11 and 17 years progressively evaluate three aspects of career choice. The order of occurrence is:
   a. values, capacities, and interests.
   b. interests, capacities, and values.
   c. interests, values, and capacities.
   d. capacities, values, and interests.

10. When individuals complete their education or training and enter the workforce, Donald Super refers to this as the _____ stage.
    a. crystallization          c. stabilization
    b. implementation           d. specification

11. Your son always had a way with words and got along well with peers and adults. According to John Holland, he would prefer the job of
    a. social worker.           c. construction worker.
    b. bank teller.             d. sales manager.

12. The most important contribution made by John Holland's personality type theory to the career field was its
    a. consideration of the role of motivation on job performance.
    b. introduction of the conventional personality type.
    c. focus on psychological testing as a way of insuring job suitability.
    d. emphasis on linking individuals' personalities to the characteristics of given jobs.

13. In order to benefit from career guidance courses and to show more systematic career planning, students need
    a. accurate knowledge concerning the educational requirements of careers.
    b. self-directed opportunities to engage in career exploration.
    c. courses that are taught by trained guidance counselors.
    d. to be in the implementation stage of vocational choice.

14. When both parents work and seem to enjoy it,
    a. the parents try to live vicariously through their children's occupational choices.
    b. boys and girls learn work values from both parents.
    c. boys and girls aspire to higher status occupations.
    d. schools don't need to motivate students to get a good education.

15. Which kind of job employs the most adolescents in part-time work?
    a. unskilled laborers        c. restaurant work
    b. clerical assistants       d. retail

16. An adolescent female (16 years of age) who takes a part-time job can expect to
    a. make more money than males.
    b. work shorter hours than males.
    c. easily find a job as a newspaper carrier.
    d. easily find a job as a gardener.

17. _____ represents an advantage of working during adolescence?
    a. Extensive on-the-job training
    b. Improved ability to manage money

c. Improved school grades

d. Greater enjoyment of school

18. A number of adolescent problem behaviors are associated with part-time work, such as insufficient sleep and exercise. At what level of work does this begin to be apparent?
a. 1 to 5 hours per week
b. 6 to 10 hours per week
c. 15 to 20 hours per week
d. more than 20 hours per week

19. Which of the following is the best example of a "distal goal"?
a. Seth, who is hoping to see the Star Wars movie this weekend.
b. Ben, who wants to get an "A" on his math quiz on Friday.
c. Peggy, who wants to be a college professor eventually.
d. Mary, who is hoping that Ben asks her to the high school prom.

20. When a recent study compared the top 25 percent of students in different countries, the U.S. students
a. were found to be much stronger than students from other countries.
b. compared favorably to the "select" group from other countries.
c. did not do well in comparison.
d. were stronger in physical education, but weaker in math.

21. Sherry consistently blames her poor performance on tests on high levels of anxiety. This is an example of
a. setting unreachable goals.      c. sham effort.
b. procrastination.                d. the academic wooden leg.

22. Out of every ten students attending school in the U.S. today, _____ will receive a high school diploma.
a. 9                              c. 7
b. 8                              d. 5

## ADOLESCENCE ON THE SCREEN

- *Cider House Rules* depicts an orphan who rejects the medical profession his foster father planned for him—until he chooses it for himself.

- *October Sky* is the true story of Homer Hickman, a West Virginia coal miner's son, who went from setting off rockets in his back yard to joining the NASA space program.

- *Stand and Deliver* is the story of Jaime Escalante's math classrooms in a predominantly Chicano Southern California high school.

## ADOLESCENCE IN BOOKS

- *All Grown Up & No Place to Go: Teenagers in Crisis*, by David Elkind (Addison-Wesley: MA, 1984), argues that teenagers are expected to confront adult challenges too early in their development.

- *Mentors*, by Thomas Evans (Peterson's Guides: NJ, 1992), describes the experiences of motivated individuals, from corporate executives to parents.

- *What Color Is Your Parachute?* by Richard Bolles (Ten Speed Press: CA, 2000), is a popular book on career choice that is updated annually.

## Answer Key

### KEY TERMS

1.  **extrinsic motivation** Response to external incentives such as rewards and punishments.

2.  **intrinsic motivation** Internal motivational factors such as self-determination, curiosity, challenge, and effort.

3.  **flow** Csikszentmihalyi's concept that describes optimal life experiences, which he believes occur most often when people develop a sense of mastery and are absorbed in a state of concentration when they are engaged in a activity.

4.  **mastery orientation** An outlook in which individuals focus on the task rather than on their ability, have positive affect, and generate solution-oriented strategies that improve performance.

5.  **helpless orientation** An outlook in which individuals focus on their personal inadequacies often attribute their difficulty to a lack of ability, and display negative affect (including boredom and anxiety). This orientation undermines performance.

6.  **performance orientation** An outlook in which individuals are concerned with performance outcome rather than performance process. For performance-oriented students, winning is what matters.

7.  **self-efficacy** The belief that one can master a situation and produce positive outcomes.

8.  **self-handicapping** Some adolescents deliberately do not try in school, put off studying until the last minute, and use other self-handicapping strategies so that if their subsequent performance is at a low level, these circumstances, rather than lack of ability, will be seen as the cause.

9.  **developmental career choice theory** Ginzberg's theory that children and adolescents go through three career-choice stages: fantasy, tentative, and realistic.

10. **career self-concept theory** Super's theory that individuals' self-concepts play a central role in their career choices and that in adolescence individuals first construct their career self-concept.

11. **personality type theory** Holland's belief that an effort should be made to match an individual's career choice with his or her personality.

### KEY PEOPLE IN THE STUDY OF ADOLESCENCE

| | | | | | | | |
|---|---|---|---|---|---|---|---|
| 1. | J | 4. | H | 7. | F | 10. | B |
| 2. | K | 5. | G | 8. | C | 11. | D |
| 3. | A | 6. | I | 9. | E | | |

## "DR. DETAIL'S" THEORY MASTERY EXERCISE

Holland's personality type:

| Personality Type | Career |
|---|---|
| Realistic | labor, farming, truck driving, construction |
| Intellectual | math and science careers |
| Social | teaching, social work, counseling |
| Conventional | bank tellers, secretaries, file clerks |
| Enterprising | sales, politics, management |

Ginzberg's career choice stages:

| Career Choice Stage | Careers |
|---|---|
| Fantasy | Doctor, superhero, teacher, movie star, etc. |
| Tentative | Big plans of youth are changed to fit skills and abilities. |
| Realistic | Explore careers and settle upon one within reach that fits their goals and personality |

Super's career choice phases:

| Phase | Developmental Information |
|---|---|
| Crystallization | Age 14 to 18, develop ideas that mesh with existing self-concept |
| Specification | Age 18 to 22, narrow career choices and take steps toward career |
| Implementation | Age 21 to 24, compete education and training |
| Stabilization | Age 25 to 35, enter their career of choice |
| Consolidation | After 35, seek to reach higher status positions |

## ADOLESCENT MYTH AND FACT

| | | | | | | | |
|---|---|---|---|---|---|---|---|
| 1. | F | 4. | T | 7. | F | 10. | F |
| 2. | T | 5. | F | 8. | T | 11. | T |
| 3. | T | 6. | T | 9. | F | | |

## ACHIEVEMENT SECTION REVIEW

1.   Psychological, motivational, and contextual factors.

2.   **Students' Perceived Level of Skill**

| Perceived Level of Challenge | Low | High |
|---|---|---|
| Low | Apathy | Boredom |
| High | Anxiety | Flow |

3. Adolescents want to believe that they are doing something because of their own will.

4. The concept of optimal life experiences, which occur most often when people develop a sense of mastery.

5. More likely to occur when materials are mastered.

6. Parents and teachers sometimes attempt to protect adolescents' self-esteem by setting low standards. However, in reality it is more beneficial to set standards that challenge adolescents and expect high levels of performance. Adolescents who are not challenged become fragile, develop low standards, and end up with poor self-confidence.

7. Focusing on the task rather than on ability and generating solution-oriented strategies to completion.

8. Focusing too much on personal inadequacies and displaying negative affect.

9. Involves being concerned with outcome rather than process.

10. The belief that one can master a situation and produce favorable outcomes.

11. Bandura — believes that self-efficacy is a crucial factor in whether or not adolescents achieve. Schunk — believes that self-efficacy influences a student's choice of activities; therefore it has an important indirect role.

12. They define goals in terms of immediate achievement-related focus and definition of success.

13. Covey gives these tips: Spend time on important non-urgent activities before they become urgent; don't let your life be ruled by urgency; do important activities early – to avoid increasing stress; set priorities for your tasks and complete them in that order.

14. The reasons include poor time management, difficulty concentrating, fear and anxiety, negative beliefs, personal problems, boredom, unrealistic expectations, perfectionism, or fear of failure.

15. —ignoring the task with hopes that it will go away
—underestimating the work involved in the task or overestimating your ability
—spending too much time on the computer or playing games
—substituting a lower priority activity
—believing that delays won't hurt you
—finishing only a part of the task
—becoming paralyzed when presented with two alternatives

16. —Acknowledge that procrastination is a problem
—Identify your values and goals
—Work on your time management
—Divide the task into smaller parts
—Use behavioral strategies
—Use cognitive strategies

17. -nonperformance: i.e., don't even try
-procrastination: postpone doing things
-set unreachable goals: by setting goals too high, you assure failure; therefore you have a ready-made excuse.

18. Ethnicity and culture play and important role in achievement. The orientation of the parents in particular is important. SES is more associated with poor achievement than is ethnicity or culture.

19. There are differences in school, parent attitudes and the likelihood of students doing homework. Taken together, Asian students often out-perform American students.

20.     Convince them that effort and work pay off.

21.     Having low expectations for success. It comes from falling behind and struggling with academics with mostly failure as a result.

22.     Some adolescents deliberately do not try in school; this way they have an excuse if they fail.

23.     (a) Give these adolescents assignments that are interesting and stimulate curiosity. (b) Establish a reward system. (c) Help adolescents set challenging but realistic goals. (d) Strengthen the association between effort and self-worth. (e) Encourage students to have positive beliefs about their abilities. (f) Improve teacher-student relations.

## WORK
## SECTION REVIEW

1.      In the 1800's fewer than 1 in 20 graduated from high school, so most worked. The number working full time has decreased today with 9 of 10 receiving diplomas before entering the workforce full time.

2.      Males work more labor-intensive jobs, work longer hours, and get paid more than females.

3.      Better time management skills, and spending money.

4.      In many developing countries where it is common for adolescents to not attend school on a regular basis, and boys are more likely to earn an income. High school aged kids in the U.S. are more likely to hold a job. Kids in Europe and Asia also often have jobs, more so than most other countries.

5.      As the number of hours worked increases, the likelihood of dropping out of college also increases.

6.      (a) monitored work experiences, (b) community youth-guided services, (c) vocational education should be redirected, (d) incentives need to be introduced, (e) career information and counseling need to be improved, and (f) more school volunteers should be used.

7.      The curriculum is organized around a single theme, such as agriculture.

## CAREER DEVELOPMENT
## SECTION REVIEW

1.      Ginzberg's development theory, Super's self-concept theory, and Holland's personality type theory.

2.      Career decidedness and planning are positively related to identity achievement, whereas career planning and decidedness are negatively related to identity moratorium and identity diffusion statuses.

3.      SES, parents and peers, schools, gender, culture, and ethnicity.

4.      Yes.

5.      It is suggested that most do not spend nearly enough time with career counselors in high school (under 3 hours).

## COGNITIVE CHALLENGE

1.      Individual activity. No answers provided.

2.      Individual activity. No answers provided.

3.      Individual activity. No answers provided.

## ADOLESCENCE IN RESEARCH

Csikszentmihalyi and Schneider studied how U.S. adolescents develop attitudes and acquire skills to achieve their career goals and expectations. They assessed (using questionnaires) the progress of more than 1,000 students from 13 school districts across the United State (cross-sectional). Among the findings: (a) girls anticipated the same lifestyles as boys in terms of education and income; (b) lower-income minority students were more positive about school than more affluent students; (c) students who got the most out of school were those who perceived school as more play like than work like; and (d) clear vocational goals and good work experiences did not guarantee a smooth transition to adult work.

---

## ⊠ COMPREHENSIVE REVIEW

| | | | | | | | |
|---|---|---|---|---|---|---|---|
| 1. | d | 7. | c | 13. | a | 19. | c |
| 2. | a | 8. | d | 14. | b | 20. | c |
| 3. | a | 9. | b | 15. | d | 21. | d |
| 4. | b | 10. | b | 16. | b | 22. | a |
| 5. | a | 11. | a | 17. | b | | |
| 6. | d | 12. | d | 18. | a | | |

# ✧ Chapter 13   Culture

**Learning Goals with Key Terms and Key People in Boldface**

1.0     **DISCUSS THE ROLE OF CULTURE IN ADOLESCENCE DEVELOPMENT**
A.     **What is Culture?**
        1.1     What is **culture**?
        1.2     What is **socioeconomic status**?
        1.3     What is **ethnicity**?
B.     **The Relevance of Culture for the Study of Adolescence**
        1.4     What is the relevance of **culture** for the study of adolescence in the twenty-first century?
        1.5     What is an example of **ethnocentrism**?
        1.6     Are ethnic differences often interpreted as deficits?
C.     **Cross-Cultural Comparisons**
        1.7     What are **cross-cultural studies**?
        1.8     In what context did the study of adolescence emerge in **cross-cultural** comparisons?
        1.9     How do adolescents around the world spend their time?
D.     **Models of Cultural Adaptation**
        1.10    What four models have been used to understand cultural changes within and between cultures?
        1.11    What is **assimilation**?
        1.12    What is **acculturation**?
        1.13    What is **alternation model**?
        1.14    What is the multiculturalism?
        1.15    What is the advantage of using the **multicultural model**?
E.     **Rites of Passage**
        1.16    What is meant by **rites of passage**?
        1.17    How are rites of passage different for American and primitive cultures?

2.0     **DESCRIBE HOW SOCIOECONOMIC STATUS AND POVERTY ARE RELATED TO ADOLESCENT DEVELOPMENT**
A.     **What is Socioeconomic Status**
        2.1     What is meant by socioeconomic status?
        2.2     What is the significance of socioeconomic status for adolescent development?
        2.3     How does socioeconomic status affect the families, neighborhoods, and schools of adolescents?
B.     **Sociometric Variations in Families, Neighborhoods, and Schools**
        2.4     What effect do socioeconomic variables in families, neighborhoods, and schools have on adolescent development?
        2.5     How do low-socioeconomic parents differ from their middle-SES counterparts?
C.     **Poverty**
        2.6     What is poverty?
        2.7     What percentage of U.S. children lives in poverty?
        2.8     Why is poverty among American youth so high?
        2.9     What is the nature of the subculture of the poor?
        2.10    What is meant by the **feminization of poverty**?

2.11    What effects do persistent and long-lasting poverty have on development?

2.12    What was the impact of the Quantum project?

**3.0    SUMMARIZE HOW ETHNICITY IS INVOLVED IN ADOLESCENT DEVELOPMENT**

**A.    Immigration**

3.1    What stressors are experienced by immigrants?

3.2    Is there a relationship between acculturation and adolescent problems in the United States?

**B.    Adolescence: A Special Juncture for Ethnic Minority Individuals**

3.3    Are ethnic minority youth impacted by a lack of role models?

**C.    Ethnic Issues**

3.4    How do history, the economy, and social experiences produce legitimate differences between ethnic minority groups and between ethnic minority groups and the White majority?

3.5    How does failure to recognize diversity lead to stereotyping?

3.6    What is **prejudice**?

3.7    In what ways do ethnic minority adolescents experience prejudice, discrimination, and bias?

3.8    Why is adolescence a critical juncture in the development of ethnic minority individuals?

3.9    What are some of the complicating effects of the "browning" of America?

**D.    Ethnic Minority Adolescents**

3.10    What are some defining characteristics of African-American adolescents?

3.11    Why is low SES a problem among black youth?

3.12    What helps to diminish the impact of single parent families amongst African-American youth?

3.13    Where are national origins of Latino adolescents?

3.14    What is a Chicano?

3.15    What roles do families play in the lives of Latino youth?

3.16    What countries do Asian American adolescents represent?

3.17    What accounts for the strong achievement orientation of Asian American youth?

**E.    The United States and Canada: Nations with Many Cultures**

3.18    What discriminations have Native American adolescents endured?

3.19    How is America a cultural mosaic?

3.20    What are included in Canadian cultures?

3.21    How do adolescents in Canada compare to adolescents in the United States?

3.22    What are the main ethnic ties of Canadian adolescents?

**4.0    CHARACTERIZE THE ROLES OF THE MEDIA AND TECHNOLOGY IN ADOLESCENT DEVELOPMENT**

**A.    Use of Media**

4.1    What are the functions of media?

4.2    How do adolescents use media?

**B.    Television**

4.3    What are the functions of television for adolescents?

4.4    What are the special concerns raised by television today?

4.5    How strongly does televised violence influence a person's behavior?

4.6    What impact is television having on the sexual behaviors of youth?

**C.    The Media and Music**

4.7    How important is music to adolescents?

4.8    How do adolescents' music tastes change during the course of adolescence?

4.9    What adolescent needs does music fulfill?

**D.      Technology, Computers, and the Internet**
    4.10    How is the technological revolution affecting teenagers today?
    4.11    What is the **Internet**?
    4.12    What are some concerns surrounding **Internet** regulation?
    4.13    What is **e-mail**?
    4.14    What is the importance of **e-mail** for adolescents?
    4.15    What are some concerns regarding how adolescents use the **Internet**?
    4.16    What inequities might arise because of the technological revolution?
    4.17    How have computers affected schools?
    4.18    What is the relationship between technology and adolescent learning?
**E.      Social Policy and Media**
    4.19    What social policy recommendations concerning the media would benefit adolescents?

# Exercises

## KEY TERMS COMPLETION EXERCISE

Each key term is presented in the form of an incomplete sentence. Complete each sentence by either defining the term or giving an example. Compare your definitions with those given at the end of the study guide chapter.

1.    **Culture** is the

   _____

   _____

2.    A person's **socioeconomic status (SES)** is

   _____

   _____

3.    Because of Octavio's **ethnicity,** he often

   _____

   _____

4.    **Ethnocentrism** leads to

   _____

   _____

5.    **Cross-cultural studies** are used in order to

   _____

   _____

6.    **Assimilation** is seen when

   _____

   _____

7.    **Acculturation** results from

 

 

8.    The **alternation model** assumes that

 

 

9.    The **multicultural model** promotes

 

 

10.   **Rites of passage** are evidenced in

 

 

11.   An example of **prejudice** is

 

 

12.   The term **Chicano** means

 

 

13.   The **Internet** is the

 

 

14.   **E-mail** is used for

 

 

15.   **Feminization of poverty** refers to

 

 

## KEY PEOPLE IN THE STUDY OF ADOLESCENCE

Match the person with the concept of adolescent development with which they are associated.

____    1.  Richard Brislin        A. Asian American researcher who studies prejudice and discrimination
____    2.  Vonnie McLoyd       B. A cross-cultural psychologist who argues that intimate contact reduces
                                          conflict between individuals from different ethnic backgrounds

___  3.  Stanley Sue              C.  Co-director of the Harvard Immigration Projects
___  4.  Carola Suárez-Orozco     D.  Studied the effect on children of ethnic minority mothers' poverty and
                                       stress

## "DR. DETAIL'S" PUZZLE EXERCISE

### Across
1.    A dimension of culture based on heritage, nationality, race, religion, and language.
2.    Cultural change that occurs with first-hand contact between two cultural groups.
3.    An unjustified negative attitude toward a person due to his/her membership in a group.
4.    The name politically conscious Mexican American adolescents give themselves.
5.    The core of computer-mediated communication.

### Down
1.    The behavior, patterns, and beliefs of a particular group of people.
2.    Absorption of ethnic minority groups into a dominant group.
3.    Stands for electronic mail.

## ADOLESCENT MYTH AND FACT

Which of the following statements regarding adolescents are true (T) and which are false (F)?

1.    It is NOT unusual for people to accept a cultural value at one point in their lives and reject it at another.
      T or F

2.    It is common for most people in all cultures to believe their culture is 'natural' and 'correct.'  T or F

3.    Global interdependence is no longer a matter of belief or choice, it is an inescapable reality.  T or F

4.    According to Reed Larson, U.S. adolescents use their discretionary time on structured tasks.  T or F

5.  Parents in industrialized countries place a higher value on obedience and responsibility than parents in non-industrialized countries.  T or F

6.  Primitive cultures have more clearly delineated rites of passage than adolescents have in the U.S.  T or F

7.  Examples of professions like doctors, lawyers and accountants fall into the upper-SES category.  T or F

8.  In Western culture, lower-SES parents are more likely to use harsh physical punishment in disciplining their children.  T or F

9.  The percent of children living in poverty in the U.S. is lower than those in most industrialized nations.  T of F

10. A single father is less likely to live in poverty than a single mother.  T or F

11. The term *Ethnicity* does NOT refer to the race of an individual.  T or F

12. Because Mexican, Cuban, and Puerto Rican immigrants are Latinos, they share a common ethnic background.  T or F

13. Canada has two official languages, English and Spanish.  T or F

14. Television viewing tends to peak in childhood and decline in adolescence, when more outdoors activities are available to youth.  T or F

15. The amount of violence viewed on television at age 8 is significantly related to the seriousness of criminal acts performed as an adult.  T or F

16. Most children who use the Internet, never access an adult or sex-oriented web site.  T or F

## CULTURE AND ADOLESCENCE
## SECTION REVIEW

1.  Describe Brislin's features of culture (1993).

    a. _____

    _____

    b. _____

    _____

    c. _____

    _____

    d. _____

    _____

    e. _____

    _____

    f. _____

g. _____

_____

2. What is socioeconomic status?

_____

_____

3. What is ethnicity?

_____

_____

4. List five common features of ethnocentrism present in all cultures.

a. _____

_____

b. _____

_____

c. _____

_____

d. _____

_____

e. _____

_____

5. Why are socioeconomic status (SES) and ethnicity important dimensions of culture?

_____

_____

6. What are cross-cultural studies?

_____

_____

7. Do adolescents around the world spend their time in a similar way as U.S. adolescents?

_____

_____

8.      What four models have been used to understand the process of adaptation within and between cultures?

_____

_____

9.      What is the alternation model?

_____

_____

10.     What is multiculturalism?

_____

_____

11.     What is meant by rites of passage?

_____

_____


## SOCIOECONOMIC STATUS AND POVERTY
## SECTION REVIEW

1.      What are four psychological ramifications for adolescents living in poverty.

        a.      _____

        b.      _____

        c.      _____

        d.      _____

2.      What is meant by socioeconomic status (SES)?

_____

_____

3.      What is the most common marker of poverty?

_____

_____

4.      Compare the poverty rate of adolescents in the United States to those living in Canada and Sweden.

_____

_____

5.     Compare the poverty rate of African American and Latino adolescents with the overall adolescent poverty rate in the United States.

_____

_____

6.     Give three explanations for why poverty is so high among American youth.

a.     _____

_____

b.     _____

_____

c.     _____

_____

7.     What is meant by the feminization of poverty?

_____

_____

## ETHNICITY
## SECTION REVIEW

1.     What is ethnicity?

_____

_____

2.     What are some stressors commonly experienced by immigrants?

_____

_____

3.     Are ethnic minority youth impacted by a lack of role models?

_____

_____

4.     Are ethnic differences often interpreted as deficits?

_____

_____

5.     How does failure to recognize diversity lead to stereotyping?

_____

6.    What is prejudice?

_____

_____

7.    What are some defining characteristics of African-American adolescents?

_____

_____

8.    Why is low SES a problem among black youth?

_____

_____

9.    Where are the national origins of Latino adolescents?

_____

_____

10.   What is a Chicano?

_____

_____

11.   What role do families play in the lives of Latino youth?

_____

_____

12.   What accounts for the strong achievement orientation of Asian American youth?

_____

_____

13.   What discriminations have Native American adolescents endured?

_____

_____

## THE MEDIA AND TECHNOLOGY
## SECTION REVIEW

1.    What are the six functions of media for adolescents?

_____

2.  How strongly does television influence a child's negative behavior?

_____

_____

3.  What impact is television having on the sexual behaviors of youth?

_____

_____

4.  How important is music to adolescents?

_____

_____

5.  What is the Internet?

_____

_____

6.  What are some concerns regarding how adolescents use the Internet?

_____

_____

7.  What is the relationship between technology and adolescent learning?

_____

_____

8.  What social policy recommendations were made by the Carnegie Council on Adolescent Development regarding the effects of the media?

_____

_____

## COGNITIVE CHALLENGE

1.  Take a moment to imagine how your life might have been different if you were of another race or ethnic background. Would your friends be the same? Would you live in the same neighborhood? How might your family be different? Would your attitude toward education be different?

_____

_____

## ADOLESCENCE IN RESEARCH

Concerning the evaluation of the Quantum Opportunities Program, comparing mentored students with a nonmentored control group, state the hypothesis, the research methods (if known), the research conclusions, and the implications and applications for adolescent development.

_____

_____

## ☒ COMPREHENSIVE REVIEW

1.  The learning and shared behavioral patterns, beliefs, and values of a group of people that are passed on from one generation to the next are known as
    a.  culture.
    c.  ethnicity.
    b.  minority.
    d.  socioeconomic status.

2.  Family income is a good measure of
    a.  ethnicity.
    c.  culture.
    b.  social class.
    d.  ethnocentrism.

3.  _____ is a tendency to favor one's own group over others.
    a.  Ethnicity
    c.  Culture
    b.  Social class
    d.  Ethnocentrism

4.  _____ has a focused emphasis on the individual, as opposed to a group orientation?
    a.  Japan
    c.  America
    b.  Mexico
    d.  India

5.  In comparison to adolescents from other cultures, American adolescents are often described as more
    a.  passive.
    c.  achievement-oriented.
    b.  rebellious.
    d.  mentally healthy.

6.  Of the different ethnic groups living in America, which is the most achievement oriented?
    a.  African-American
    c.  Latino
    b.  Asian American
    d.  Anglo-American

7.  U.S. adolescents spend about _____% as much time on schoolwork as East Asian adolescents do.
    a.  20%
    c.  60%
    b.  40%
    d.  80%

8.  The melting pot belief in the United States assumes which process of cultural change?
    a.  assimilation
    c.  accommodation
    b.  acculturation
    d.  cultural schema shifting

9.    _____ is NOT an adolescent rite of passage.
a.    Gaining of knowledge or secrets associated with maturity
b.    Participation in athletics
c.    Experimentation with sexuality
d.    Gaining entry into the adult world

10.   Freddy is a typical adolescent boy in the U.S. He is LEAST likely to _____ in his free time?
a.    hang out              c.    read a novel
b.    watch TV              d.    play video games

11.   _____ is NOT a disadvantage experienced by ethnic minority youth in poverty?
a.    Prejudice             c.    Affirmative action
b.    Bias                  d.    Discrimination

12.   _____ is NOT a model of adaptation within and between culture?
a.    Accommodation         c.    Acculturation
b.    Assimilation          d.    Alternation

13.   Children from low-SES backgrounds are at high risk for all of the following EXCEPT
a.    depression.           c.    academic success.
b.    peer conflict.        d.    low self-confidence.

14.   Ben like to "talk things through" with his children, and he does NOT believe in spanking them. Which of the following is most likely true about Ben?
a.    Ben is poorly educated.
b.    Ben is a higher-SES parent.
c.    Ben goes to church regularly.
d.    Ben is a lower-SES parent.

15.   Which of the following is LEAST likely to make use of the extended family unit?
a.    African American
b.    Anglo-American
c.    Latino
d.    Asian American

16.   According to research by Lee, successful African-American students are most likely to have mentioned _____ as having an important influence on their lives.
a.    their father          c.    Jesus Christ
b.    Bill Clinton          d.    Jessie Jackson

17.   Of the following, which is the LEAST likely to be classified as an immigrant?
a.    Armenian              c.    Mexican
b.    African American      d.    Vietnamese

18.   Rituals such as bar mitzvah and confirmation are examples of
a.    rites of passage.
b.    cultural transitions of sexuality.
c.    evidence of ethnocentrism.
d.    family traditions.

19. The most common rite of passage for American adolescents is probably
   a. a religious ceremony.
   b. going off to college.
   c. graduating from high school.
   d. buying the first car.

20. ___ percent of adolescents in the United States live in poverty.
   a. Eleven      c. Seventeen
   b. Thirty-three      d. Twenty

21. The adolescent raised in a single-parent, female-headed household is more likely than not to be
   a. sexually active.      c. in trouble with the law.
   b. promiscuous.      d. poor.

22. When an adolescent has a negative attitude about another individual because that individual belongs to a particular group, the adolescent is exhibiting
   a. values.      c. prejudice.
   b. an opinion.      d. cognitive narrowing.

23. The average child and adolescent (between 8 and 18 years) in the United States devotes _____ to 'leisure-time media' in any given day?
   a. about 2 hours      c. about 4 hours
   b. in excess of 7 hours      d. approximately 5 hours

24. El Puente is a social program for ____ Latinos.
   a. low-income      c. Protestant
   b. female      d. English-speaking

25. Which ethnic minority adolescent group has the highest suicide rate in the United States?
   a. African American      c. Native American
   b. Hispanic      d. Asian

26. Compared to the United States, the ethnic subcultures of Canadian adolescents tend to be organized more along the lines of
   a. economic power.      c. religious participation.
   b. political affiliation.      d. gender differences.

27. Adolescents spend approximately _____ of their waking hours with some form of mass media.
   a. one-eighth      c. one-half
   b. one-third      d. two-thirds

28. Television has been criticized for all of the following EXCEPT
   a. teaching adolescents that problems are easily resolved.
   b. declining national achievement test scores.
   c. increasing the leisure activities of adolescents.
   d. creating passive learners.

29. Which is the most accurate conclusion about the long-term effects of watching television violence?
   a. Watching television violence causes crime.

b.      Watching television violence has no relationship to crime.

c.      Watching television violence may be associated with violence in some young people.

d.      Watching television violence makes young people less afraid of being a victim.

## ADOLESCENCE ON THE SCREEN

- *Of Hopscotch and Little Girls* powerful documentary film explores the plight of girls growing up to be women in different cultures.

- *Daughters of the Dust* explores life and development on a barrier island off the coast of South Carolina. The Gullah subculture, an isolated African-American group, is the focus.

- *Saturday Night Fever* highlights the lives of older adolescents during the disco era of the 1970s.

- *Pulp Fiction* is a parody of drug use, violence, and down-and-out diner bandits.

- *Woodstock* captures the drug and rock culture of the 1960s.

- *Fresh* shows the challenges faced by a 12-year-old trying to grow up in one of America's roughest neighborhoods.

- *Whale Rider* deals with the challenges associated with upholding cultural tradition in a changing world.

## ADOLESCENCE IN BOOKS

- *The Adolescent & Young Adult Fact Book*, by Janet Simons, Belva Finlay, and Alice Yang (Children's Defense Fund, 1991), describes the role of poverty and ethnicity in adolescent development.

- *Children's Journey Through the Information Age*, by Sandra Calvert (McGraw-Hill: IA, 1999), covers topics related to the information age, including television and computers.

- *Understanding Culture's Influence on Behavior*, by Richard Brislin (Harcourt Brace: FL, 1993), details the role of culture in behavior and development.

- *Failure to Connect: How Computers Affect Our Children's Minds, and What We Can Do About It*, by Jane M. Healy (Simon and Schuster: NJ, 1999), presents a very strong case against the use of computers in modern classrooms.

# Answer Key

## KEY TERMS

1.      **culture** The behavior, patterns, beliefs, and all other products of a particular group of people that are passed on from generation to generation.

2.      **socioeconomic status (SES)** A grouping of people with similar occupational, educational, and economic characteristics.

3.      **ethnicity** A dimension of culture based on cultural heritage, nationality, race, religion, and language.

4.      **ethnocentrism** A tendency to favor one's own group over other groups.

5.  **cross-cultural studies** Studies that compare a culture with one or more other cultures. Such studies provide information about the degree to which adolescent development is similar, or universal, across cultures, or about the degree to which it is culture specific.

6.  **assimilation** The absorption of ethnic minority groups into the dominant group, which often means the loss of some or virtually all of the behavior and values of the ethnic minority group.

7.  **acculturation** Cultural change that results from continuous, first-hand contact between two distinctive cultural groups.

8.  **alternation model** This model assumes that it is possible for an individual to know and understand two different cultures. It also assumes that individuals can alter their behavior to fit a particular social context.

9.  **multicultural model** This model promotes a pluralistic approach to understanding two or more cultures. It argues that people can maintain their distinctive identities while working with others from different cultures to meet common national or economic needs.

10. **rites of passage** Ceremonies or rituals that mark an individual's transition from one status to another, especially into adulthood.

11. **prejudice** An unjustified negative attitude toward an individual because of her or his membership in a group.

12. **Chicano** The name politically conscious Mexican American adolescents give themselves, reflecting the combination of their Spanish-Mexican-Indian heritage and Anglo influence.

13. **Internet** The core of computer-mediated communication. The Internet is worldwide and connects thousands of computer networks, providing an incredible array of information adolescents can access.

14. **e-mail** Stands for electronic mail and is a valuable way the Internet can be used. Written messages can be sent to and received by individuals as well as large numbers of people.

15. **feminization of poverty** The fact that far more women than men live in poverty. Likely causes are women's low income, divorce, and the resolution of divorce cases by the judicial system, which leaves women with less money than they and their children need to adequately function.

## KEY PEOPLE IN THE STUDY OF ADOLESCENCE

1.  B
2.  D
3.  A
4.  C

## "DR. DETAIL'S" PUZZLE EXERCISE

| *Across* | | *Down* | |
|---|---|---|---|
| 1. | ethnicity | 1. | culture |
| 2. | acculturation | 2. | assimilation |
| 3. | prejudice | 3. | e-mail |
| 4. | Chicano | | |
| 5. | Internet | | |

# ADOLESCENT MYTH AND FACT

| | | | | | | | |
|---|---|---|---|---|---|---|---|
| 1. | T | 5. | F | 9. | F | 13. | F |
| 2. | T | 6. | T | 10. | T | 14. | F |
| 3. | T | 7. | F | 11. | F | 15. | T |
| 4. | F | 8. | T | 12. | F | 16. | F |

# CULTURE AND ADOLESCENCE
## SECTION REVIEW

1.
   a.   Culture is made up of ideals, values, and assumptions about life that guide people's behaviors.
   b.   Culture is made by people.
   c.   Culture is transmitted from generation to generation.
   d.   Culture's influence is noticed most in well-meaning clashes between people from very different cultural backgrounds.
   e.   Despite compromises, cultural values remain.
   f.   People react emotionally when their cultural values are violated or when their cultural expectations are ignored.
   g.   People accept a cultural value at one point in their life and reject it at another.

2.   SES refers to a grouping of people with similar occupational, educational, and economic characteristics.

3.   Ethnicity is based on cultural heritage, nationality, race, religion, and language.

4.
   a.   People believe that what happens in their culture is natural and correct and that what happens in other cultures is unnatural and incorrect.
   b.   People perceive their cultural customs as universally valid, that is, good for everyone.
   c.   People behave in ways that favor their own cultural group.
   d.   People feel proud of their cultural group.
   e.   People feel hostile toward other cultural groups.

5.   Because both influence levels of power, influence and prestige within a culture.

6.   These involve the comparison of a culture with one or more other cultures, which provides information about the degree to which adolescent development is similar, or universal, across cultures, or the degree to which it is culture-specific.

7.   U.S. adolescents spend more time in paid work and less time doing schoolwork.

8.   (1) assimilation, (2) acculturation, (3) alternation, and (4) multiculturalism.

9.   This model assumes that it is possible for an individual to know and understand two different cultures.

10.   This model promotes a pluralistic approach to understanding two or more cultures.

11.   These are ceremonies or rituals that mark an individual's transition from one status to another, especially into adulthood.

# ETHNICITY
## SECTION REVIEW

1.   Ethnicity is race and cultural background and tradition.

2. Language barriers, dislocations, separation from support networks, changes in SES, and the pressure to retain culture while at the same time acculturating.

3. Within communities there is often a lack of role models. So African-American youth in particular either seek White middle class values, or they are drawn to black role models whose success was gained in atypical ways (e.g., sports).

4. Traditionally, this has been the case, but it depends on the situation.

5. Stereotyping discounts individuality. By lumping someone inextricably to an ethnic group and discounting individuality, one increases the likelihood of both positive and negative stereotyping.

6. Prejudice is an unjustified negative attitude toward an individual because of the individual's membership in a group.

7. The majority stay in school, do not take drugs, do not prematurely get married or become parents, are employed, are not involved in crime, and grow up to be very productive despite disadvantage.

8. Low SES places people in worse neighborhoods and at poorer schools. This leads to many other problems.

9. Most are from Mexico.

10. Chicano is the name politically conscious Mexican American adolescents give themselves to reflect the combination of their Spanish-Mexican-Indian heritage and Anglo influence.

11. Church and family are very important in the lives of Latino youth.

12. There is a general expectation for success that places pressure on these kids to perform at a high level.

13. Native Americans have experienced an inordinate amount of discrimination. Terrible abuse and punishment, among other things.

## SOCIOECONOMIC STATUS AND POVERTY
## SECTION REVIEW

1. 
   a. The poor are often powerless.
   b. The poor are often vulnerable to disease and disaster.
   c. Only a limited number of options (e.g., jobs) are open to them.
   d. Being poor means having less prestige.

2. The grouping of people with similar occupational, educational, and economic characteristics.

3. Its most common marker is the federal poverty threshold.

4. The overall poverty rate for American adolescents is 17 percent. In Canada it is 9 percent, whereas in Sweden it is only 2 percent.

5. The overall poverty rate is 17 percent. The poverty rate for African American and Latino adolescents is 40 percent.

6. 
   a. Economic changes have eliminated many blue-collar jobs that paid reasonably well.
   b. Increase in the percentage of youth living in single-parent families headed by the mother.
   c. Reduction of government benefits during the 1970s and 1980s.

7. This refers to the fact that far more women than men live in poverty.

# THE MEDIA AND TECHNOLOGY
# SECTION REVIEW

1.  a.  Entertainment
    b.  Information
    c.  Sensation
    d.  Coping
    e.  Gender-role modeling
    f.  Youth culture identification

2.  Adolescents spend a third or more of their waking hours with some form of mass-media, most often TV. Research has suggested that the amount of TV watched at age 8 is directly correlated with problem behaviors in adulthood.

3.  Adolescents like to watch TV with much sexual content. It tends to lead them to make errors in judgment with regard to what typical sexual activity is.

4.  Very important. Two-thirds of all records and tapes are purchased by those 10- to 24-years old.

5.  The core of computer mediated communication.

6.  Of the 1,000 most visited sites, 10 percent are adult sex oriented. Forty-four percent of adolescents have viewed an adult Internet site. Twenty-five percent of adolescents have visited an Internet site that promotes hate groups. Twleve percent of adolescents have visited a site where they can obtain information about how to purchase a gun.

7.  The numbers of computers in schools have increased dramatically, but it has not influenced adolescent learning.

8.  (a) Encourage socially responsible programming, (b) support public efforts to make the media more adolescent friendly, (c) encourage media literacy programs as part of school curricula, youth and community organizations, and family life, (d) increase media presentations of health promotions, (e) expand opportunities for adolescents' views to appear in the media.

# COGNITIVE CHALLENGE

1.  No answer provided. Individual activity

# ADOLESCENCE IN RESEARCH

An evaluation of the Quantum project compared the mentored students with a nonmentored control group. The methods were experimental. The hypothesis was that the features of the Quantum project would help overcome the intergenerational transmission of poverty and its negative outcomes. The mentored students were involved in academic-related activities, community service projects, and cultural enrichment and personal development activities. Students also received financial incentives for participating, including bonuses for every 100 hours of education. Sixty-three percent of the mentored students graduated from high school, but only 42 percent of the control group did. Forty-two percent of the mentored group is currently enrolled in college, but only 16 percent of the control group. The control-group students were twice as likely as mentored students to receive food stamps or be on welfare and they had more arrests. The conclusion is that programs like the Quantum project have the potential to help overcome the intergenerational transmission of poverty and its negative outcomes.

COMPREHENSIVE REVIEW

| 1. | a | 9. | b | 17. | b | 25. | c |
|---|---|---|---|---|---|---|---|
| 2. | b | 10. | c | 18. | a | 26. | a |
| 3. | d | 11. | c | 19. | c | 27. | b |
| 4. | c | 12. | a | 20. | c | 28. | c |
| 5. | c | 13. | c | 21. | d | 29. | c |
| 6. | b | 14. | b | 22. | c | | |
| 7. | c | 15. | b | 23. | b | | |
| 8. | a | 16. | c | 24. | a | | |

# ✦ Chapter 14   Adolescent Problems

**Learning Goals with Key Terms and Key People in Boldface**

**1.0**   **DISCUSS TWO MAIN APPROACHES TO UNDERSTANDING ADOLESCENT PROBLEMS AND THE CHARACTERISTICS OF THESE PROBLEMS**

   **A.**   **The Biopsychosocial Approach**
   1.1   What is the **biopsychosocial approach**?
   1.2   What roles do the three factors play in the development of problem behavior?

   **B.**   **The Developmental Psychopathology Approach**
   1.3   What is the focus of **developmental psychopathology**?
   1.4   Compare and contrast **internalizing** and **externalizing problems**.
   1.5   According to **Sroufe,** anxiety problems in adolescence are linked with what?

   **C.**   **Characteristics of Adolescent Problems**
   1.6   What correlation did **Achenbach** find between SES and behavior problems?

   **D.**   **Resilience**
   1.7   Why might the study of resilience be important in understanding problem behavior?

**2.0**   **DESCRIBE SOME MAIN PROBLEMS THAT CHARACTERIZE ADOLESCENTS**

   **A.**   **Drug Use**
   2.1   Why do people use drugs?
   2.2   What is **tolerance**?
   2.3   What is **physical dependence**?
   2.4   What are the characteristics of **psychological dependence**?
   2.5   What was the nature of drug use in the 1960s and 1970s?
   2.6   What has been the trend of drug use in the 1980s and 1990s?
   2.7   How does adolescent drug use in the United States compare to that in other industrialized countries?
   2.8   What type of drug is alcohol?
   2.9   How much is alcohol used by American adolescents?
   2.10   What are some potential negative outcomes of alcohol abuse?
   2.11   What are the risk factors for adolescent alcohol use?
   2.12   Is there a genetic predisposition to alcoholism?
   2.13   Is there a personality profile for someone who is likely to develop an alcohol problem?
   2.14   What are some possible preventative strategies for alcoholism?
   2.15   What drugs other than alcohol are harmful to adolescents?
   2.16   What are the nature and characteristics of **hallucinogens,** LSD, and marijuana?
   2.17   What are the most widely used **stimulants**?
   2.18   How does cigarette smoking play a role in the drug problems of youth?
   2.19   Have school health programs had success in deterring youth from smoking?
   2.20   What is the history of cocaine use?
   2.21   How many adolescents use cocaine?
   2.22   How prevalent is the use of amphetamines among adolescents?
   2.23   What is Ecstasy, and what are some special concerns associated with it?
   2.24   What are **depressants**?

2.25      How has the use of depressants changed over the past 25 years?

2.26      What are the risks of using **anabolic steroids**?

2.27      What role does early drug use play in adolescent development?

2.28      How can parents and peers help prevent adolescent drug abuse?

2.29      What school-based intervention programs can help reduce adolescent drug use?

**B.**      **Juvenile Delinquency**

2.30      What is **juvenile delinquency**?

2.31      What is the difference between **index offenses** and **status offenses**?

2.32      Is it appropriate to try juveniles as adults in court?

2.33      What is **conduct disorder**?

2.34      What percentage of adolescents engage in delinquent behaviors?

2.35      In the Pittsburgh Youth Study, what were noted as the three developmental pathways to delinquency?

2.36      What are the predictors of delinquency?

2.37      What is Erikson's beliefs regarding youth and delinquency?

2.38      Can siblings influence delinquency?

2.39      Why is the high rate of youth violence an increasing concern?

2.40      What percent of public schools experience one or more serious violent incidents each year?

2.41      What factors are often present in at-risk youths and seem to propel them toward violence?

2.42      What strategies have been proposed for reducing youth violence?

**C.**      **Depression and Suicide**

2.43      What is the rate of depression in females as opposed to males?

2.44      How serious a problem is depression in adolescence?

2.45      What is a **major depressive disorder**?

2.46      Will a depressed adolescent be more likely to suffer from depression as an adult?

2.47      What are the treatments for depression?

2.48      What is the rate of adolescent suicide and how has it changed since the 1950s?

2.49      Why do adolescents attempt suicide?

2.50      What proximal and distal factors are involved in suicide?

2.51      What is the psychological profile of the suicidal adolescents like?

**3.0**      **SUMMARIZE THE INTERRELATION OF ADOLESCENT PROBLEMS AND WAYS TO PREVENT OR INTERVENE IN PROBLEMS**

**A.**      **Adolescents with Multiple Problems**

3.1      Which four problems affect adolescents the most?

3.2      Are adolescent problem behaviors interrelated?

**B.**      **Prevention and Intervention**

3.3      What are the common components of successful prevention/intervention programs for adolescent problem behaviors?

# Exercises

## KEY TERMS COMPLETION EXERCISE

Each key term is presented in the form of an incomplete sentence. Complete each sentence by either defining the term or giving an example of it. Compare your definitions with those given at the end of the study guide chapter.

1. The **bio-psycho-social approach** focuses on

   _____

   _____

2. **Developmental psychopathology** focuses on

   _____

   _____

3. **Internalizing problems** appear as

   _____

   _____

4. Examples of **externalizing problems** are

   _____

   _____

5. **Tolerance** of a drug means

   _____

   _____

6. **Physical dependence** on a drug means

   _____

   _____

7. **Psychological dependence** on a substance suggests

   _____

   _____

8. **Hallucinogens** are a grouping of drugs that

   _____

   _____

9. Overuse of **stimulants** can lead to

   _____

   _____

10. The use of **depressants** in recent years has

    _____

    _____

11.    **Anabolic steroids** are used to

_____

_____

12.    Involvement in **juvenile delinquency** leads to

_____

_____

13.    **Index offenses** are crimes that

_____

_____

14.    **Status offenses** are crimes that

_____

_____

15.    Example of a **conduct disorder** is

_____

_____

16.    A **major depressive disorder** is

_____

_____

## KEY PEOPLE IN THE STUDY OF ADOLESCENCE

Match the person with the concept of adolescent development with which they are associated.

| | | |
|---|---|---|
| ____ | 1. Thomas Achenbach and Craig Edelbrock | A. Believe(s) that resilient children triumph over life's adversities |
| ____ | 2. Lloyd Johnston, Patrick O'Malley, and Gerald Bachman | B. Found that adolescents from lower-SES background were more likely to have problems than those from a middle-SES background |
| ____ | 3. Norman Garmezy | C. Monitored the drug use of America's high school students through a project at the University of Michigan |
| ____ | 4. Joy Dryfoos | D. Interviewed young men who were murderers |
| ____ | 5. James Garbarino | E. Interested in the interrelationship between adolescent problem behaviors |

## "DR. DETAIL'S" MATCHING EXERCISE

Match the following contributors to the study of adolescence to their area of contribution.

| | | |
|---|---|---|
| ____ | 1. Alan Sroufe | A. Experimented with therapeutic uses of cocaine |
| ____ | 2. Ann Masten | B. Proposed a developmental model of adolescent drug abuse |
| ____ | 3. Sigmund Freud | C. Studied traits associated with alcoholism |
| ____ | 4. Lloyd Johnson, Patrick O'Malley, and Gerald Bachman | D. Believe(s) that adolescents, whose development has restricted them from acceptable social roles, might choose a negative identity |
| ____ | 5. Robert Cloninger | E. Found that anxiety problems in adolescence are linked with anxious/resistant attachment in infancy |
| ____ | 6. Cheryl Perry | F. Found that good intellectual functioning and parenting served protective roles in keeping adolescent from antisocial behaviors |
| ____ | 7. Judith Brooks | G. Developed the Midwestern Prevention Program |
| ____ | 8. Mary Ann Dentz | H. Taught conflict resolution training in schools |
| ____ | 9. Erik Erikson | I. Have/Has monitored the drug use of American Seniors in public and private schools |
| ____ | 10. David and Roger Johnson | J. Developed an approach to stop smoking by adolescents |

## ADOLESCENT MYTH AND FACT

Which of the following statements regarding adolescents are true (T) and which are false (F)?

1. An example of an internalizing problem in adolescence is juvenile delinquency.  T or F

2. An example of an externalization problem in adolescence is anxiety.  T or F

3. According to Alan Sroufe, avoidant attachment in infancy is related to conduct problems in adolescence. T or F

4. According to Edelbrock (1989), arguing and fighting are behaviors more often seen in older adolescents. T or F

5. The United States has the highest rate of adolescent drug use of any industrialized nation.  T or F

6. The recent downturn in drug use by U.S. adolescents has been particularly attributed to the terrorist attacks of Sept. 11, 2001.  T or F

7. Alcohol is the 'drug' most widely used by U.S. students.  T or F

8. Females are more likely than males to engage in binge drinking.  T or F

9. Almost one half of U.S. college students say they drink heavily.  T or F

10. There is evidence of a genetic predisposition to alcoholism in adolescents.  T or F

11. Drug "trips" on LSD are generally always unpleasant or frightening.  T or F

12. Marijuana use does not greatly affect school performance.  T or F

13. Smoking in the adolescent years causes permanent genetic changes in the lungs.  T or F

14. Stores requiring identification before selling cigarettes has significantly reduced access that youth have to tobacco.  T or F

15. Crack is a purified, inexpensive form of cocaine.  T or F

16. Ecstasy is one of the few drugs that does not carry with it the risk of significant side effects or health risks.  T or F

17. Females have a higher rate of depression than males because they face more discrimination than males do.  T or F

18. Homosexual adolescents may be more vulnerable to suicide, according to some researchers.  T or F


## EXPLORING ADOLESCENT PROBLEMS
## SECTION REVIEW

1. What are the three factors that might be the basis for adolescent problem behavior?

   _____

   _____

2. What are two social factors that influence the development of adolescent problems?

   _____

   _____

3. What is the focus of developmental psychopathology?

   _____

   _____

4. Compare and contrast internalizing and externalizing problems?

   _____

   _____

5. According to Sroufe, anxiety problems in adolescence are linked with what?

   _____

   _____

6. What correlations did Achenbach find between SES and behavior problems?

   _____

   _____

7. Why might the study of resilience be important in understanding problem behavior?

   _____

   _____

# PROBLEMS AND DISORDERS
## SECTION REVIEW

1. Identify the class of drugs by placing a "D" for depressants, "S" for stimulants, and "H" for hallucinogens.

   _____ 1.  Marijuana          _____ 5.  Tranquilizers
   _____ 2.  Alcohol            _____ 6.  Cocaine
   _____ 3.  Barbiturates       _____ 7.  Narcotics
   _____ 4.  Amphetamines       _____ 8.  LSD


2. What is tolerance?

   _____

   _____


3. What is physical dependence?

   _____

   _____


4. What is the attraction that humans have to drugs?

   _____

   _____


5. What type of drug is alcohol?

   _____

   _____


6. What are the risk factors for adolescent alcohol use?

   _____

   _____


7. What are some possible preventative strategies for alcoholism?

   _____

   _____


8. Have school health programs had success in deterring youth from smoking?

   _____

   _____


9. How many adolescents use cocaine?

   _____

   _____

10. What are depressants?

_____

_____

11. How has the use of depressants changed over the past 25 years?

_____

_____

12. What seven criteria have been generally accepted as necessary for effective school-based drug abuse prevention programs?

a. _____

_____

b. _____

_____

c. _____

_____

d. _____

_____

e. _____

_____

f. _____

_____

g. _____

_____

13. Complete the table for listing the association with delinquency that matches each antecedent of delinquency.

| Antecedent | Association with Delinquency |
|---|---|
| Identity | |
| Self-control | |
| Age | |
| Sex | |

| | |
|---|---|
| Expectations for education and school grades | |
| Parental influences | |
| Peer influences | |
| Socioeconomic status | |
| Neighborhood quality | |

14. What is the nature of juvenile delinquency?

_____

_____

15. In the Pittsburgh Youth Study, what were noted as the three developmental pathways to delinquency?

_____

_____

16. What is Erikson's beliefs regarding youth and delinquency?

_____

_____

17. What are the four factors often present in at-risk youth that seem to propel them toward acts of violence?

a. _____

b. _____

c. _____

d. _____

18. What four recommendations for reducing youth violence were suggested by The Oregon Social Learning Center?

a. _____

b. _____

c. _____

d. _____

19. What is a major depressive disorder?

_____

_____

20. What is the cadre approach to reducing violence?

_____

_____

21. What proximal and distal factors are involved in suicide?

_____

_____

## INTERRELATION OF ADOLESCENT PROBLEMS AND PREVENTION / INTERVENTION SECTION REVIEW

1. What four problems affect the most adolescents?

_____

_____

2. Are adolescent problem behaviors interrelated?

_____

_____

3. What are the common components of successful prevention/intervention programs for adolescent problem behaviors?

_____

_____

## COGNITIVE CHALLENGE

1. Imagine that you have just been appointed the head of the President's Commission on Adolescent Drug Abuse. What would be the first program you would try to put into place? What would be its main components? Would it be school-focused? What role, if any, would the media play in promoting the program?

_____

_____

2. Why are the consequences of risky behavior more serious today than they have ever been?

_____

_____

3.   What role might David Elkind's conceptualizations of the Personal Fable and Imaginary Audience have played in the atrocities at Columbine and Thurston High Schools?

_____

_____

## ADOLESCENCE IN RESEARCH

The Search Institute in Minneapolis conducted research that led to the prescription of 40 developmental assets that adolescents need to achieve positive outcomes. State the hypothesis, methods used, and conclusions of the Search Institute research project.

_____

_____

## ⊠ COMPREHENSIVE REVIEW

1.   Scientists who adopt a biological approach usually focus on all of the following EXCEPT
     a.   the brain as a cause of problems.
     b.   drug therapy treatments.
     c.   distorted thoughts as causes of problems.
     d.   genetic factors as causes of problems.

2.   _____ are NOT emphasized by the 'bio-psych-social' approach?
     a.   Biological factors          c.   Cognitive factors
     b.   Psychological factors       d.   Social factors

3.   The condition where a greater amount of a drug is needed to produce the same effect is referred to as
     a.   tolerance.                  c.   psychological dependence.
     b.   physical dependence.        d.   emotional dependence.

4.   Physical need for a drug that is accompanied by unpleasant withdrawal symptoms when the drug is withdrawn is referred to as
     a.   tolerance.                  c.   psychological dependence.
     b.   physical dependence.        d.   emotional dependence.

5.   Strong desire and craving to repeat the use of a drug for various emotional reasons is referred to as
     a.   tolerance.                  c.   psychological dependence.
     b.   physical dependence.        d.   emotional dependence.

6.   Robin has been told he has an internalizing disorder. Which of the following is NOT something that Robin might have?
     a.   shyness
     b.   attention deficit/hyperactivity disorder
     c.   anxiety
     d.   depression

7.   Predictors of adolescent problems are called
     a.   risk factors.                              c.   behavior checklists.
     b.   performance assessments.                   d.   guided probes.

8.   _____ is NOT one of the behavioral problems most likely to cause adolescents to be referred to
     a clinic for mental health problems?
     a.   Sadness                                    c.   Anger
     b.   Poor school performance                    d.   Unhappiness

9.   This behavior has been called "suicide in slow motion" by experts.
     a.   drinking                                   c.   smoking
     b.   using cocaine                              d.   sexual promiscuity

10.  _____ experimented with therapeutic uses of cocaine?
     a.   Jean Piaget                                c.   Sigmund Freud
     b.   Erik Erikson                               d.   Lawrence Kohlberg

11.  In _____, cigarette smoking by eighth graders in the U.S. reached its peak
     a.   1973                                       c.   2001
     b.   1996                                       d.   2002

12.  Most developmentalists accept an interactionist approach to the study of abnormal behavior because
     a.   the evidence shows that all disorders have both psychological and sociocultural causes.
     b.   neither the biological nor psychological and sociocultural viewpoints can account for the
          complexity of problems.
     c.   it's the only way to keep peace in the profession.
     d.   adolescents tell us that the interactionist approach is best.

13.  Which nation has the highest rate of adolescent drug use?
     a.   Thailand                                   c.   United States
     b.   Germany                                    d.   France

14.  Which of the following is NOT a risk factor for abuse of alcohol?
     a.   heredity                                   c.   alcohol tolerance
     b.   peer relations                             d.   family influences

15.  About ____ percent of U.S. college students refer to themselves as heavy drinkers?
     a.   10                                         c.   25
     b.   50                                         d.   66

16.  _____ and _____ behavioral problems are the most common causes for adolescent mental health
     referrals.
     a.   Conflict with parents; substance abuse
     b.   Poor schoolwork; depression
     c.   Suicide attempt; depression
     d.   Substance abuse; poor schoolwork

17.  Randi is a college student. Randi is NOT a binge drinker. Which of the following is most likely true
     regarding Randi?
     a.   Randi is a traditional-age student living away from home.

b.        Randi lives in a sorority.

c.        Randi lives at home.

d.        Randi lives in a fraternity.

18.    Your textbook indicates that adolescents use drugs
   a.        because Sigmund Freud used cocaine.
   b.        as adaptations to changing environments.
   c.        as aids to sexual gratification.
   d.        because their parents use drugs at home.

19.    Drugs that modify an individual's perceptual experiences and produce hallucinations are known as
   a.    stimulants.              c.    hallucinogens.
   b.    depressants.            d.    anabolic steroids.

20.    Smoking is most likely to start in which grades?
   a.    $5^{th}$ through $7^{th}$        c.    $9^{th}$ through $11^{th}$
   b.    $7^{th}$ through $9^{th}$        d.    $11^{th}$ through graduation

21.    Andrew is a 17-year-old adolescent who has been drinking white wine for about three years. Andrew has noticed that over this period, it takes more and more wine to get "looped." This indicates
   a.        the wine producers have decreased the alcoholic content.
   b.        tolerance.
   c.        the disorganized thinking associated with ingesting alcohol at a young age.
   d.        his psychological dependence.

22.    The most widely used illicit drug is
   a.    marijuana.            c.    barbiturates.
   b.    cocaine.               d.    alcohol.

23.    Which of the following is NOT a primary explanation for the significant decline in smoking rates for children and adolescents since 1996?
   a.        increased fear of lung cancer
   b.        increased tobacco prices
   c.        less tobacco advertising targeting youth
   d.        more antismoking advertising

24.    _____ is NOT a risk factor for alcohol abuse?
   a.        Secure attachment to parents
   b.        Having friends who abuse alcohol
   c.        Coming from an unhappy home
   d.        Susceptibility to peer pressure

25.    The parents of an 11-year-old boy have been advised by a psychologist to provide more structure in the home, more caring support, and a more stimulating environment. According to Robert Cloninger, what are they trying to prevent in their son?
   a.        eventually acquiring a sexually transmitted disease
   b.        attempting suicide
   c.        alcoholism as an adult
   d.        the youngster from eventually abusing his parents

26. Which of the following is NOT a form of amphetamine?
   a. diet pills               c. pep pills
   b. Xanax                    d. uppers

27. Nembutal and Seconal are
   a. stimulants.              c. opiates.
   b. hallucinogens.           d. depressants.

28. Of the new school-based drug prevention programs, _____ appear(s) to be the most promising?
   a. counselor-led programs
   b. the use of testimonials from ex-drug users
   c. social skills training
   d. attendance at juvenile court when drug cases are heard

29. In the United States, theft, rape, and assault are _____ offenses.
   a. status                   c. matrix
   b. index                    d. conduct

30. Between February and September, Harry, a 14-year-old, ran away from home twice and got involved in a series of break-and-enter offenses. The parents say he is "out of control." According to your text, the court psychiatrist will likely diagnose him as
   a. being a delinquent.      c. a problem child.
   b. having a conduct disorder. d. having poor parents.

31. _____ would say that delinquency is a manifestation of the search for "Who am I?"
   a. Gilbert Botvin           c. John Bowlby
   b. Peter Blos               d. Erik Erikson

32. _____ is NOT associated with juvenile delinquency?
   a. Negative identity        c. Failed self-control
   b. Learned helplessness     d. Lower-class culture

33. A recent review of all the approaches to prevention of delinquency by Dryfoos has revealed that _____ seems to be effective.
   a. a multiple components approach
   b. work experience
   c. preventative casework
   d. security guards in school

34. How common is suicide in adolescence?
   a. It is the most common cause of death in adolescents.
   b. It is the second most common cause of death in adolescents.
   c. It is the third most common cause of death in adolescents.
   d. It is the fourth most common cause of death in adolescents.

35. _____ is a characteristic of successful programs for reducing adolescent problems.
   a. Removing adolescents from the situation that seems to be causing their problems
   b. Making sure that each adolescent gets personal attention from a responsible adult
   c. Coordinating the activities of different agencies and institutions
   d. Beginning intervention programs early in adolescent's lives

36.    Which of the following is NOT one of the four problems that affects the most adolescents?
   a.    drug abuse          c.    shyness
   b.    juvenile delinquency  d.    school-related problems

## ADOLESCENCE ON THE SCREEN

- *Ordinary People* Shows a young man struggling with depression and thoughts of suicide as a result of surviving an accident that took his younger brother's life.

- *Trainspotting* portrays the grim reality of lives ruined by heroin addiction.

- *The Killer at Thurston High* (Frontline) tells the events that led up to Kip Kinkel's assault on his parents and the school at Thurston. The content is shocking, but gives much insight.

- *The River's Edge* A group of high school friends must come to terms with the fact that one of them killed another.

## ADOLESCENCE IN BOOKS

- *Developmental Psychopathology*, edited by Suniya Luthar, Jacob Burack, Dante Cicchetti, and John Weisz (Cambridge University Press: MA, 1999), explores the many aspects of developmental psychopathology.

- *Lost Boys*, by James Garbarino (The Free Press: NY, 1999), examines why young men grow up to be murderers.

# Answer Key

## KEY TERMS

1.    **bio-psycho-social approach** Emphasizes that problems develop through an interaction of biological, psychological, and social factors.

2.    **developmental psychopathology** Focuses on describing and exploring the developmental pathways of problems and disorders.

3.    **internalizing problems** Occur when individuals turn problems inward. Anxiety and depression.

4.    **externalizing problems** Occur when individuals turn problems outward. Such as juvenile delinquency.

5.    **tolerance** A greater amount of a drug is needed to produce the same effect.

6.    **physical dependence** The physical need for a drug that is accompanied by unpleasant withdrawal symptoms when the drug is discontinued.

7.    **psychological dependence** The strong desire and craving to repeat the use of a drug for various emotional reasons, such as a feeling of well-being and reduction of distress.

8.    **hallucinogens** Drugs that alter an individual's perceptual experiences and produce hallucinations—also called psychedelic or mind-altering drugs.

9.   **stimulants**  Drugs that increase the activity of the central nervous system.

10.  **depressants**  Drugs that slow the central nervous system, bodily functions, and behavior.

11.  **anabolic steroids**  Drugs derived from the male sex hormone, testosterone. They promote muscle growth and lean body mass.

12.  **juvenile delinquency**  A broad range of child and adolescent behaviors, including socially unacceptable behavior, status offenses, and criminal acts.

13.  **index offenses**  Whether they are committed by juveniles or adults, these are criminal acts, such as robbery, rape, and homicide.

14.  **status offenses**  Performed by youths under a specified age, these are juvenile offenses that are not as serious as index offenses. These offenses may include such acts as drinking under age, truancy, and sexual promiscuity.

15.  **conduct disorder**  The psychiatric diagnostic category for the occurrence of multiple delinquent activities over a 6-month period. These behaviors include truancy, running away, fire setting, and cruelty to animals, breaking and entering, and excessive fighting.

16.  **major depressive disorder**  The diagnosis when an individual experiences a major depressive episode and depressed characteristics, such as lethargy and depression, for two weeks or longer and daily functioning becomes impaired.

## KEY PEOPLE IN THE STUDY OF ADOLESCENCE

| | | | | |
|---|---|---|---|---|
| **1.** | B | | **4.** | E |
| **2.** | C | | **5.** | D |
| **3.** | A | | | |

## "DR. DETAIL'S" MATCHING EXERCISE

| | | | | |
|---|---|---|---|---|
| **1.** | E | | **6.** | J |
| **2.** | F | | **7.** | B |
| **3.** | A | | **8.** | G |
| **4.** | I | | **9.** | D |
| **5.** | C | | **10.** | H |

## ADOLENCENT MYTH AND FACT

| | | | | | | | |
|---|---|---|---|---|---|---|---|
| 1. | F | | 7. | T | | 13 | T |
| 2. | F | | 8. | F | | 14. | F |
| 3. | T | | 9. | T | | 15. | T |
| 4. | F | | 10. | T | | 16. | F |
| 5. | T | | 11. | F | | 17. | T |
| 6. | T | | 12. | F | | 18. | T |

## EXPLORING ADOLESCENT PROBLEMS
## SECTION REVIEW

1.    Psychological, sociocultural, and biopsychosocial.

2.    Socioeconomic status and neighborhood quality.

3.    Focuses on describing and exploring the developmental pathways of problems.

4.    Internalizing problems occur when individuals turn their problems inward. Externalizing problems occur when problems are turned outward.

5.    They are linked with anxious/resistant attachment in infancy.

6.    Adolescents from a lower SES background were more likely to have problems than those from a higher SES background.

7.    It may give important insight into why some children, against all odds, succeed.

## PROBLEMS AND DISORDERS
## SECTION REVIEW

1.

| | | | | |
|---|---|---|---|---|
| **1.** | H | | **5.** | D |
| **2.** | D | | **6.** | S |
| **3.** | D | | **7.** | D |
| **4.** | S | | **8.** | H |

2.    A greater amount of a drug is needed to produce the same effect.

3.    Physical need for a drug that is accompanied by unpleasant withdrawal symptoms when the drug is discontinued.

4.    Since the beginning of recorded history humans have searched for substances that would sustain and protect them as well as provide them with pleasurable sensations. Individuals are attracted to drugs because they help them adapt to an ever-changing environment.

5.    It is a widely used and powerful drug.

6.    Heredity, family influences, peer relations, personality characteristics, and the college transition.

7.    A strong family support system is a very important preventative strategy.

8.    No. While informative, their impact has been minimal.

9.    In 1999 it had dropped to 2.6 percent.

10.   Drugs that slow down the central nervous system, bodily functions, and behavior.

11.   The use of depressants has dropped dramatically over the past 25 years.

12.   a.    Early intervention in schools is believed to be more effective than later intervention.
      b.    School-based drug-abuse prevention requires a kindergarten through grade 12 approach.
      c.    Teacher training is important.
      d.    Social skills training is a most-promising new approach to prevention.
      e.    Peer-led programs are often more effective than those led by teachers or counselors.
      f.    More programs aimed at high-risk kids are needed.
      g.    The most effective programs are often part of community-wide programs.

13.

| Antecedent | Association with Delinquency |
|---|---|
| Identity | Negative identity |
| Self-control | Low degree |
| Age | Early initiation |
| Sex | Males |
| Expectations for education and school grades | Low expectations and low grades |
| Parental influences | Low monitoring, low support, ineffective discipline |
| Peer influences | Heavy influence, low resistance |
| Socioeconomic status | Low |
| Neighborhood quality | Urban, high crime, high mobility |

14. It refers to a broad range of behaviors, from socially unacceptable, to status offenses to criminal acts.

15. (a) authority conflict, (b) covert conflict, and (c) overt conflict.

16. He believes that adolescents whose development has restricted them from acceptable social roles might choose a negative identity.

17.
   a. Early involvement with drugs and alcohol.
   b. Easy access to weapons.
   c. Association with a deviant peer group.
   d. Pervasive exposure to violence in the media.

18.
   a. Recommit to raising children safely and effectively.
   b. Make prevention a reality.
   c. Give more support to schools.
   d. Forge effective partnerships among families.

19. An individual experiences a major depressive episode and depressed characteristics, such as lethargy and hopelessness, for at least two weeks or longer and daily functioning becomes impaired.

20. In the cadre approach, a small number of students are trained to serve as peer mediators for the entire school.

21. Drugs may present a proximal risk for suicide. Distal risks tend to be things that grow out of the family history or environment.

## INTERRELATION OF ADOLESCENT PROBLEMS AND PREVENTION/INTERVENTION SECTION REVIEW

1. Drug abuse; juvenile delinquency; sexual problems; school-related problems.

2. Adolescents tend to have more than one problem, and researchers tend to suggest that these are interrelated.

3. (a) Intensive individualized attention, (b) Community-wide multiagency collaborative approaches, and (c) Early identification and intervention.

# COGNITIVE CHALLENGE

1.      Individual activity. No answer provided.

2.      Individual activity. No answer provided.

3.      Individual activity. No answer provided.

# ADOLESCENCE IN RESEARCH

The research method was survey with descriptive statistics. The hypothesis was that a set of external and internal assets could be used to predict success in life. External assets included things such as support, empowerment, boundaries and expectations, and effective time use. Internal assets included things like commitment to learning, positive values, social competencies, and positive identity. The fewer the assets reported by the 12,000 ninth- to twelfth-graders, the more likely was alcohol use and other problem behaviors.

## ⊠ COMPREHENSIVE REVIEW

| | | | | | |
|---|---|---|---|---|---|
| 1. | c | 14. | c | 27. | d |
| 2. | c | 15. | b | 28. | b |
| 3. | a | 16. | b | 29. | b |
| 4. | b | 17. | c | 30. | b |
| 5. | c | 18. | b | 31. | d |
| 6. | b | 19. | c | 32. | b |
| 7. | a | 20. | b | 33. | a |
| 8. | c | 21. | b | 34. | c |
| 9. | c | 22. | d | 35. | a |
| 10. | c | 23. | a | 36. | c |
| 11. | b | 24. | a | | |
| 12. | b | 25. | c | | |
| 13. | c | 26. | b | | |

# ✦ Chapter 15   Health, Stress, and Coping

Learning Goals with Key Terms and Key People in Boldface

**1.0   DESCRIBE THE ROLE OF ADOLESCENCE IN HEALTH**
- **A.   Adolescence: A Critical Juncture in Health**
  - 1.1   Why are health related behaviors of adolescents so important?
  - 1.2   In a health-conscious nation, why do so many adolescents participate in unhealthy activities and behaviors?
- **B.   Risk-taking Behavior**
  - 1.3   To what extent do adolescents engage in risk-taking?
- **C.   Health Services**
  - 1.4   What are some reasons that adolescents might not be receiving adequate health care?
- **D.   Leading Causes of Death**
  - 1.5   What are the three leading causes of death in adolescence?

**2.0   SUMMARIZE THE EATING PATTERNS AND EATING DISORDERS OF ADOLESCENCE**
- **A.   Nutrition**
  - 2.1   Define **basal metabolism rate**?
  - 2.2   Why is the consumption of "fast food" a concern for today's adolescents?
  - 2.3   Why are eating patterns formed in childhood of special interest to medical professionals?
  - 2.4   Why is the amount of fat in our diets in American Culture a special concern?
- **B.   Eating Disorders**
  - 2.5   What are some of the findings about which adolescent girls are more likely to develop an eating disorder?
  - 2.5   What type of interventions have shown success in reducing adolescent obesity?
  - 2.6   Compare and contrast **anorexia nervosa** and **bulimia nervosa**.

**3.0   EVALUATE THE NATURE OF EXERCISE AND SPORTS IN ADOLESCENTS' LIVES**
- **A.   Exercise**
  - 3.1   Do American youth get adequate exercise?
  - 3.2   How does the activity and eating patterns of U.S. adolescents compare to their counterparts in other countries?
  - 3.3   How are schools responsible for the poor condition of adolescents today?
  - 3.4   Does pushing children or adolescents to exercise make a difference?
  - 3.5   Can physical exercise reduce adolescent stress?
- **B.   Sports**
  - 3.6   How does participation in sports impact upon adolescents?
  - 3.7   What are some positive side benefits of adolescents' involvement in sports?
  - 3.8   What are some potential negative outcomes of youth participation in sports?
  - 3.9   What is the **female athlete triad**?

**4.0   CHARACTERIZE THE SLEEP PATTERNS OF ADOLESCENTS**
  - 4.1   Why have adolescents' sleep patterns become a recent focus of interest?
  - 4.2   How important are stable sleep patterns in adolescence?
  - 4.3   What can be the results of disrupted sleep in adolescence?

**5.0    DISCUSS STRESS AND COPING IN ADOLESCENCE**

    **A.    Stress**

        5.1      Contrast acute and chronic stressors.

        5.2      What are some criticisms of the daily-hassles approach to evaluating **stress**?

        5.3      What is **general adaptation syndrome**?

        5.4      What is meant when it is stated that females are more likely to "tend and befriend"?

        5.5      Explain **acculturative stress**.

    **B.    Coping**

        5.6      Define **coping**.

        5.7      Contrast **problem-focused coping** with **emotion-focused coping**.

# Exercises

## KEY TERMS COMPLETION EXERCISE

Each key term is presented in the form of an incomplete sentence. Complete each sentence by either defining the term or giving an example of it. Compare your definitions with those given at the end of the study guide chapter.

1.    **Basal metabolism rate (BMR)** gradually declines

 

 

2.    **Anorexia nervosa** is characterized by

 

 

3.    **Bulimia nervosa** is characterized by

 

 

4.    **Stress** can cause

 

 

5.    According to Selye, the **General adaptation syndrome (GAS)** is

 

 

6.    **Acculturative stress** is defined as

 

 

7.   Mary demonstrates **coping** by

_____

_____

8.   **Problem-focused coping** is

_____

_____

9.   An example of **emotion-focused coping** is

_____

_____

## KEY PEOPLE IN THE STUDY OF ADOLESCENCE

Match the person with the event or concept in adolescent development with which they are associated.

|     |     |                    |     |     |
|-----|-----|--------------------|-----|-----|
| ___ | 1.  | Laurence Steinberg | A.  | developed the terms for the general adaptation syndrome (GAS). |
| ___ | 2.  | Mary Carskadon     | B.  | proposed that females are less likely to show a fight-or-flight response to stress than are males. |
| ___ | 3.  | Hans Selye         | C.  | called poverty the single most important social problem facing young people in the United States. |
| ___ | 4.  | Shelley Taylor     | D.  | classified coping strategies as problem-focused and emotion-focused. |
| ___ | 5.  | Bruce Compas       | E.  | noted author focused primarily on issues related to adolescent health and development. |
| ___ | 6.  | Richard Lazarus    | F.  | conducted a number of research studies on adolescent sleep patterns. |

## ADOLESCENT MYTH AND FACT

Which of the following statements regarding adolescents are true (T) and which are false (F)?

1.   It is common for health-care providers to receive special training in working with adolescents.  T or F

2.   African American male adolescents are three times more likely to be killed by guns than by natural causes?  T or F

3.   Females have higher nutritional energy needs than males.  T or F

4.   African American girls and Latino boys are at high risk of being overweight during adolescence.  T or F

5.   Eating patterns established in childhood are NOT associated with obesity in adulthood.  T or F

6.   Some individuals inherit a tendency to be overweight.  T or F

7.   Identical twins, even when they are reared apart, have similar weights.  T or F

8.   The fact that the obesity rate has doubled in the U.S. since 1900 provides strong evidence of the role of genetics in the disorder.  T or F

9.   Anorexia nervosa typically begins in the early to middle teenage years.  T or F

10.  When anorexia nervosa occurs in males, the symptoms are very different from those of females.  T or F

11. Most bulimics cannot control or restrict their eating.  T or F

12. Many women who develop bulimia were somewhat overweight before the onset of the disorder.  T or F

13. High school aged females are far more likely to exercise than their male counterparts.  T or F

14. The more television an adolescent watches, the more likely he/she is to be overweight.  T or F

15. Coaches of adolescent athletes who focus on winning are more successful in winning games than coaches who focus adolescents on developing their skills.  T or F

16. When allowed to start high school classes later in the day, adolescents appear to perform better in school.  T or F.

17. Consistent exposure to stress can negatively affect an adolescents' immune system.  T or F

18. The death of one's spouse does not significantly increase the health risk to the surviving spouse.  T or F

19. Living in poverty is a significant source of stress, according to the Social Readjustment Rating Scale.  T or F

20. Studies suggest that adolescent cope more effectively with stress if they have a close relationship with their father.  T or F

## EXPLORING ADOLESCENT HEALTH
## SECTION REVIEW

1. In a health-conscious nation, why do so many adolescents participate in unhealthy activities and behaviors?

   _____

   _____

2. What are some reasons that adolescents might not be receiving adequate health care?

   _____

   _____

3. What are the three leading causes of death in adolescence?

   _____

   _____

## NUTRITION
## SECTION REVIEW

1. Define basal metabolism rate.

   _____

   _____

2. Why is the amount of fat in our diets in American culture a special concern?

   _____

   _____

3.     What types of interventions have shown success in reducing adolescent obesity?

_____

_____

4.     Compare and contrast **anorexia nervosa** and **bulimia nervosa**.

_____

_____

## EXERCISE AND SPORTS
## SECTION REVIEW

1.     Do American youth get adequate exercise?

_____

_____

2.     How does the activity and eating patterns of U.S. adolescents compare to their counterparts in other countries?

_____

_____

3.     How are schools responsible for the poor condition of adolescents today?

_____

_____

4.     Does pushing children or adolescents to exercise make a difference?

_____

_____

5.     Can physical exercise reduce adolescent stress?

_____

_____

6.     How does participation in sports impact on adolescents?

_____

_____

## SLEEP
## SECTION REVIEW

1.     How important are stable sleep patterns in adolescence?

_____

_____

2.    How did Mary Carskadon propose to improve the performance of adolescents in high school?

_____

_____


## STRESS AND COPING
## SECTION REVIEW


1.    Contrast acute and chronic stressors.

_____

_____


2.    What are some criticisms of the daily-hassles approach to evaluating stress?

_____

_____


3.    What is meant when it is stated that females are more likely to "tend and befriend."

_____

_____


4    Explain acculturative stress.

_____

_____


5.    Define coping.

_____

_____


6.    Contrast problem-focused coping and / with emotion-focused coping.

_____

_____


## EXPLORATIONS IN ADOLESCENCE

Do you practice a healthy lifestyle? Take an introspective look at your diet, your patterns of exercise, and the methods you use for coping with stress.

_____

_____

_____

_____

## COGNITIVE CHALLENGE

If you could trade places with the U.S. Surgeon General and could make adolescent health and welfare your number one priority, what approaches would you take to get adolescents to lose weight, take fewer risks, and get more exercise? Explain.

_____

_____

_____

_____

## ADOLESCENCE IN RESEARCH

Review the research conducted by Pate and others (2000) investigating sports participation by adolescents, state the hypothesis, the research methods (if known), the research conclusions, and the implications and applications for adolescent development.

_____

_____

_____

_____

## ⊠ COMPREHENSIVE REVIEW

1.  Which of the following is NOT one of the three leading causes of death in adolescence?
    a.  accidents                 c.  homicide
    b.  AIDS                      d.  suicide

2.  Which is the leading cause of death in adolescence?
    a.  accidents                 c.  homicide
    b.  AIDS                      d.  suicide

3.  Of the adolescent deaths between the age of 15 and 24, _____% are due to accidents.
    a.  20%                       c.  70%
    b.  50%                       d.  90%

4.  What percent of motor vehicle fatalities involving adolescents involve a blood alcohol level over 0.10 percent?
    a.  20%                       c.  70%
    b.  50%                       d.  90%

5.  Since the 1950's, the adolescent suicide rate has
    a.  tripled                   c.  doubled
    b.  stayed the same           d.  increased by five times

6. The typical food choice for adolescents is
   a. fresh vegetables
   b. foods high in protein and energy value
   c. fruits
   d. whole-grain products

7. Who, of the following, is LEAST likely to have a disordered pattern of eating?
   a. Meghan, whose parents are health and exercise enthusiasts
   b. Sara, who has a very negative relationship with her parents
   c. Cindy, who is sexually active with her boyfriend
   d. Sharron, whose main goal in life is to look like Jessica Simpson

8. Which of the following is least likely to be overweight?
   a. Adam, who is a 3-sport athlete
   b. Jasmine, who watches 6 hours of TV each day
   c. Julie, whose mother is severely overweight
   d. Bernie, whose father is severely overweight

9. This eating disorder involves the relentless pursuit of thinness through starvation.
   a. pica                         c. obesity
   b. bulimia nervosa              d. anorexia nervosa

10. Which of the following is NOT a "main" characteristic of anorexia nervosa?
    a. a distorted body image
    b. self-induced vomiting
    c. an intense fear of gaining weight
    d. weighing less than 85 percent of one's normal weight.

11. The incidence of anorexia in U.S. adolescent girls is about
    a. 5%                          c. 10%
    b. 1%                          d. 20%

12. Which of the following is NOT a common characteristic of an American girl who is anorexic?
    a. She is White                c. She is high achieving
    b. She is from a poor family   d. She is competitive

13. This eating disorder typically follows a binge-and-purge eating pattern.
    a. pica                        c. anorexia
    b. obesity                     d. bulimia nervosa

14. Which of the following is NOT a characteristic of Bulimia?
    a. they self-induce vomiting at least twice a week
    b. episodes of purging must last for at least 3 months
    c. their weight drops to 85% of what is considered normal for them
    d. they use a laxative to purge food from their system

15. ____% of bulimia cases are women.
    a. 100%                        c. 90%
    b. 70%                         d. 50%

16. By age 18, nearly ___% of African American girls report that they do not engage in any regular activity.
    a. 10%                                c. 40%
    b. 70%                                d. 100%

17. ____% of bulimia cases are men.
    a. 1%                                 c. 4%
    b. 10%                                d. 30%

18. When compared with youth from other countries, U.S. youth are MOST likely to
    a. exercise                           c. eat fried foods
    b. eat fruits                         d. eat vegetables

19. Meghan improved her performance on her volleyball team dramatically during the course of the season. Which of the following is MOST likely true?
    a. Meghan thrives on the applause she hears when she makes a good shot
    b. Meghan wants to win at all costs
    c. Meghan enjoys being the best on her team
    d. Meghan has a mastery focus

20. Which of the following is NOT one of Selye's General Adaptation Syndrome (GAS) stages?
    a. reaction                           c. alarm
    b. resistance                         d. exhaustion

21. During this stage of the General Adaptation Syndrome, the body adapts to the continued presence of the stressor.
    a. reaction                           c. alarm
    b. resistance                         d. exhaustion

22. According to Kanner and others (1981), what are the most common hassles of college students?
    a. bad roommates, washing clothes, and preparing food
    b. birth control and sexually transmitted infections
    c. money shortages and bad instructors
    d. wasting time, being lonely, and meeting high standards

23. He calls poverty "the single most important social problem facing young people in the United States."
    a. Daniel Arnoux                      c. Richard Rahe
    b. Bruce Compas                       d. Thomas Holmes

24. Cindy is having difficulty in her Psychology class. She asks her professor after class if he can recommend new strategies for studying to her so she might do a better job of preparing for class. Cindy's behavior is an example of
    a. emotion-focused coping
    b. academic-focused coping
    c. problem-focused coping
    d. thinking positively

## ADOLESCENCE ON THE SCREEN

- *Killing Us Softly* addresses the manner in which the media puts an inordinate amount of stress on young women to be thin and attractive.

- *Trainspotting* depicts the decadent lifestyle of Scottish teenagers bent on self-destruction through heroin addiction.

- *The Body Beautiful* is a generative example of how our various bodily and social identities are built and given meaning concurrently.

## ADOLESCENCE IN BOOKS

- *The Teen Health Book: A Parents' Guide to Adolescent Health and Well-Being* by Ralph I. Lopez (Newmarket, 2003), is written for the benefit of parents.

- *Promoting the Health of Adolescents: New Directions for the Twenty-First Century*, by Susan Millstein, Anne Petersen, and Elena Nightingale (Oxford University Press, 1994), is written as a guide for parents, teachers, and practitioners.

# Answer Key

## KEY TERMS

1. **basal metabolism rate (BMR)** Is the minimum amount of energy an individual uses in a resting state. It declines with age.

2. **anorexia nervosa** An eating disorder that involves the pursuit of thinness through starvation.

3. **bulimia nervosa** An eating disorder in which an individual follows a binge-and-purge eating pattern.

4. **stress** The response of individuals to stressors, which threaten to tax their coping abilities.

5. **general adaptation syndrome (GAS)** Selye's term for the common effects on the body when stressor are present. There are three stages: alarm, resistance, and exhaustion.

6. **acculturative stress** The negative consequences that result from contact between two distinctive cultural groups.

7. **coping** By managing demanding circumstances in her life, and seeking to reduce stress.

8. **problem-focused coping** The strategy of squarely facing one's troubles and trying to solve them.

9. **emotion-focused coping** Term for responding to stress in an emotional manner, perhaps even making things worse. An example might be *denying* that a problem exists.

## KEY PEOPLE IN THE STUDY OF ADOLESCENCE

1. E        3. A        5. C
2. F        4. B        6. D

## ADOLESCENT MYTH AND FACT

1. F        6. T        11. T       16. T
2. T        7. T        12. T       17. T
3. F        8. F        13. F       18. F
4. T        9. T        14. T       19. F
5. F        10. F       15. F       20. F

# EXPLORING ADOLESCENT HEALTH
## SECTION REVIEW

1.  There is no specific right answer here, but rather a large amount of information that might fuel your response. Peer pressure or the Personal Fable both seem likely to play some part. But is there more?

2.  Few health care providers receive any training in working with adolescents. Many feel unprepared to give contraceptive counseling or deal with difficult topics with a teen's parents.

3.  Accidents, homicides and suicides.


# NUTRITION
## SECTION REVIEW

1.  It is the minimum amount of energy an individual uses in a resting state.

2.  Fast food, in particular, is where a lot of consumed fats come from. It is suspected that this will negatively affect the health of this generation.

3.  A recent review indicated that clinical approaches that focus on the individual adolescent and include a combination of caloric restriction, exercise, reduction of sedentary behavior, and behavior therapy have been moderately effective.

4.  Anorexia nervosa involves starving oneself in the pursuit of being thin. A most prominent feature of this disorder is a distorted body image. Bulimia nervosa is characterized by a pattern of binge eating and purging. The individual does not necessarily get thin.


# EXERCISE AND SPORTS
## SECTION REVIEW

1.  Three recent national studies clearly showed that adolescents are not getting enough exercise.

2.  A recent comparison of adolescents in 28 countries found that U.S. adolescents exercised less and ate more junk food than adolescents in most of the other countries.

3.  Some schools a cutting back physical education offerings, and those that persist are scaled down and really don't offer much active exercise.

4.  It does appear that modest improvements are the result of pushing girls into organized exercise situations.

5.  The four studies noted in the text show improvement across a variety of areas, including reduced stress, as a result of exercise.

6.  Kids who are very involved in sports are physically more healthy, motivated to excel, and are less likely to get involved in drugs and delinquency. The one drawback can be arrogance and a win at all costs attitude.


# SLEEP
## SECTION REVIEW

1.  Very important. It appears that many adolescents, in an effort to stay up later at night, deprive themselves of sleep – which in turn damages their performance in many daily tasks.

2.	Carskadon suggested that early school starting times might be problematic for teens. She has suggested starting school later in the day for older adolescents. Early reports from schools following this suggestion have appeared quite positive.

## STRESS AND COPING
## SECTION REVIEW

1.	Acute stressors are sudden events or stimuli like being unexpectedly injured. Chronic stressors are often illness related.

2.	Critics of the daily-hassles approach argue that it suffers from some of the same weaknesses as life-events scales. Knowing about a person's irritations and problems tell us nothing about his/her perception of stressors.

3.	Women are more likely to negotiate in an effort to protect themselves and their young from harm.

4.	Acculturative stress refers to the negative consequences that result from contact between two distinctive cultural groups.

5.	Coping involves managing taxing circumstances, expending effort to solve problems, and seeking to master or reduce stress.

6.	Problem-focused coping is the strategy of squarely facing one's troubles and trying to solve them. Emotion-focused coping is responding to stress in an emotional manner, especially by using defensive mechanisms (e.g., repression or denial).

## EXPLORATIONS IN ADOLESCENCE

No answers provided—individual reflection and response.

## COGNITIVE CHALLENGE

No answers provided—individual reflection and response.

## ADOLESCENCE IN RESEARCH

Sports participation and health-related behaviors in more than 14,000 U.S. high school students was studied. Approximately 70 percent of the males and 53 percent of the females said they had participated in one or more sports in school and non-school settings. Male athletes reported eating better while avoiding smoking and drug use. Female athletes ate better (fruits, vegetables, etc.) and were less likely to be sexually active.

## ⊠ COMPREHENSIVE REVIEW

| | | | |
|---|---|---|---|
| 1. b | 7. a | 13. d | 19. d |
| 2. a | 8. a | 14. c | 20. a |
| 3. b | 9. d | 15. c | 21. b |
| 4. b | 10. b | 16. b | 22. d |
| 5. a | 11. b | 17. b | 23. b |
| 6. b | 12. b | 18. c | 24. c |